T0305202

Divorce and Domestic Relations Litigation

Divorce and Domestic Relations Litigation

Financial Adviser's Guide

Thomas F. Burrage
Sandra Morgan Little

WILEY

John Wiley & Sons, Inc.

Copyright © 2003 by John Wiley & Sons, Inc., All rights reserved.

Published by John Wiley & Sons, Inc., Hoboken, New Jersey
Published simultaneously in Canada.

For general information on our other products and services, or technical support, please
contact our Customer Care Department within the United States at 800-762-2974, outside
the United States at 317-572-3993 or fax 317-572-4002.

Wiley also publishes its books in a variety of electronic formats. Some content that
appears in print may not be available in electronic books.

For more information about Wiley products, visit our web site at *www.wiley.com*.

Library of Congress Cataloging-in-Publication Data:

Burrage, Thomas F.
    Divorce and domestic relations litigation : financial adviser's guide
/ Thomas F. Burrage, Sandra Morgan Little.
        p. cm.
Includes index.
        ISBN 0-471-22525-8 (cloth : acid-free paper)
    1. Divorce—Law and legislation—United States. 2. Matrimonial
actions—United States. 3. Divorce—Economic aspects—United States.
I. Little, Sandra Morgan. II. Title.
    KF535 .B88 2003
    346.7301'66—dc21

                                                    2002155495

10 9 8 7 6 5 4 3 2 1

About the Authors

THOMAS F. BURRAGE, CPA/ABV, CVA, DABFA, joined Meyners & Company in February 1998 and has been a practicing CPA in Albuquerque since 1973. He is principal-in-charge of the firm's nine-person Litigation and Valuation Services Department. His fields of expertise include litigation support, business valuation, taxation, and management advisory services. He has been qualified as a witness in insurance claims of lost earnings, fraud and malpractice, minority shareholder suits, insider trading cases, damages, business valuation, and domestic relations cases. Tom has testified in district and federal courts throughout New Mexico, been appointed Special Master, settlement facilitator, and in many instances has served as the court's Rule 11-706 witness. He has participated in numerous reported cases.

Tom holds the Accredited in Business Valuation (ABV) designation from the American Institute of Certified Public Accountants and is also a Certified Valuation Analyst. He is a member of the National Association of Certified Valuation Analysts and serves on the NACVA's Mentor Support Group and on its Speakers Bureau. He specializes in work that includes the determination of fair market value of privately held business entities for purposes of retirement benefit programs, estate planning and estate valuations, mergers, acquisitions, sales, marital dissolutions, and buy-sell agreements; expert court testimony; and determination of the value of specific shares of stock, debt instruments, and streams of future payments. He is a contributing editor to the *Guide to Divorce Taxation and the Guide to Tax Planning for High Income Individuals,* both published by Practitioners Publishing Company. Tom was recently named an Editorial Adviser to the *Journal of Accountancy.*

A member of the American Institute of Certified Public Accountants, Tom serves in the organization's Tax and Management Advisory Divisions and sits on its Family Law Task Force. He is also a member of the New Mexico Society of CPAs. Tom is Past

President, Treasurer, and board member of the New Mexico Arts & Crafts Fair, an advisory board member to People Living Through Cancer and the Pastel Society of New Mexico, and a member of the UNM Lobo Club. He also served as Treasurer of New Vision, Inc.

Tom holds a Bachelor of Business Administration degree from the University of New Mexico.

Sandra Morgan Little, JD, is a Shareholder in the Albuquerque, New Mexico, law firm of Little, Gilman-Tepper & Velasquez, P.A. She is Past Chair of the American Bar Association Family Law Section and is a New Mexico Board Certified Family Law Specialist.

Sandra is a Fellow of the American Academy of Matrimonial Lawyers and a Diplomate of the American College of Family Trial Lawyers. She has been listed in *Best Lawyers in America* for over 10 years. She is a frequent lecturer and author in the area of family law.

Contents

Preface

Almost 25 years ago, I was exposed to my first divorce litigation. It involved a partner in our accounting firm and had the issues of spousal support, separate, and community property. Because I was the partner in the firm that dealt with administrative matters, I became a witness by default. The next thing I knew, my partner's attorney was asking my opinion about how my partner's wife's expert was computing my partner's separate interest in our accounting practice. I opined that I thought the expert's methodology was flawed. I became an expert. The trial lasted almost a week and despite a churning stomach, I spent the better part of a day on the witness stand.

The result of the trial was ultimately appealed to the New Mexico Supreme Court and in an unpublished opinion the Court upheld the trial court's view that our side had prevailed. About six months later, my partner's wife's attorney called me to consult on financial matters in another case. From these modest beginnings, a career in litigation and valuation services was born.

Since that time, my partner's attorney has stopped doing domestic relations cases, his wife's attorney has become a domestic relations judge, and I have consulted and testified in hundreds of cases. Well over half of my personal time is now devoted to providing advice and services to the courts, attorneys, and divorcing parties. I head a nine-person department devoted solely to providing litigation and valuation services at Meyners & Company, LLC, an Albuquerque, New Mexico, certified public accounting and consulting firm.

Sandra Morgan-Little was one of the first attorneys to regularly use me in domestic relations cases. In our first few cases, she was still very young and at the beginning of her career. Over the years, we have worked on numerous cases, and taught and written together. In addition to many other professional distinctions earned over the years, she recently completed serving as the President of the American Bar Association Family Law Section. Ms. Morgan-Little is regularly quoted in national publications on all types of matters related to domestic relations.

Almost half of all marriages now end in divorce. Although the concepts of dividing property and providing support appear simple, they are very complex in application. To further complicate matters, each state has different systems that are used in divorces. Despite the fact that each case is unique and different, friends always tell individuals going through a divorce exactly what should occur. It is no wonder that divorcing couples are confused. Much of this confusion can be overcome with the services of an informed financial adviser.

Despite the fact that financial experts are uniquely qualified to assist attorneys and individuals in domestic relations litigation, there has been little organized and consolidated information to help those going through the divorce or their financial advisers to understand the financial impact of the litigation. With the increased emphasis on niches, many practitioners are specializing in litigation and many of those limit their practices to domestic relations. There has been no tool available with which to train financial advisers to become more proficient in rendering services to divorcing couples. The information that is available has been limited to discussions of a specific subject, such as taxation; texts and training limited to the legal profession; or data so jurisdiction- and issue-specific to be useful only in limited geographical areas. Accountants, financial advisors, attorneys, and the general public should find this book useful.

This text was written to help begin to build a body of knowledge that will provide advisers, attorneys, and litigants with the information needed to understand divorce litigation and the underlying theories used to divide property and establish support. It explains how state law, federal law, and the Internal Revenue Code impact each of these theories. It is intended to provide accountants, financial planners, and investment advisers the framework within which to link their skills with the needs of their clients. It describes procedural matters in litigation that impact the practitioner and litigant, such as discovery requests, depositions, and responses to subpoenas. It covers the practitioners' management of cases, including conflicts of interest, engagement letters, client acceptance, and fee arrangements. This book provides the financial professional, as well as the astute divorcing participant, with a single source of information regarding the financial impact, practical course, and underlying theories that impact the financial aspects of divorce litigation. There is no other single source for this information in the marketplace.

In several instances, the text includes cases reported from various state's appellate courts. These cases are not intended to represent the appropriate law from those jurisdictions or any jurisdiction. Rather, the cases are included to provide the reader with examples to help understand many of the issues that exist in divorce litigation and to illustrate types of financial theories argued in court. The cases were chosen to cover both common law and community property jurisdictions. They are intended to demonstrate the commonality of arguments from diverse jurisdictions.

I would like to acknowledge several individuals and groups whose assistance has been instrumental in assembling the knowledge, information, and ultimately the manuscript that has become this book. First and foremost are my friends and associates in the New Mexico legal and accounting community. Without their direction, guidance, and training, this book would have never been conceived. I also want to thank my friends and partners at Meyners & Company, LLC, for their patience while this manuscript was being completed. On a personal level, I want to thank Martha Holt for her cheerfulness and editorial assistance and Judith A. Wagner, CPA/ABV, CVA, and Stephen P. Comeau, JD, CBA, for their intellectual discussions and contributions to these materials. Finally, I want to thank Judy Howarth as my editor and John DeRemigis as my executive editor, both of John Wiley and Sons, Inc. Despite some adversity during this text's production, their continued encouragement insured its completion.

CHAPTER 1

The Financial Adviser's Impact on Divorce Litigation

NATURE AND ADMINISTRATION OF THE PRACTICE

Many times the parties' (also referred to jointly as clients and couples and singularly as individual or client) personal financial adviser is one of the first people individuals with domestic problems consult. Other times an attorney handling the matter for one of the parties may refer the adviser. He may be jointly retained by both parties or even be appointed by the court to provide advice. Generally the asset division between the parties is as simple as identifying, valuing, and dividing the property. Support obligations are normally at least partially determined based on the respective income of the parties. The clients are often concerned about the amounts and nature of income they may have, the amounts and nature of their various assets, and how those items will be divided after the divorce is final. The adviser may be the parties' accountant, stockbroker, certified financial planner, or other trusted person with independent knowledge of the couples' financial affairs.

It is important for the adviser to make a determination of who the client is. This can be a source of confusion when both parties approach the adviser at the same time. The client can be several different entities. It can be the attorney, one of the litigants (individually), both of the litigants (jointly), or the court. In some circumstances, it may be one of the administrative arms of the court. It is imperative to make this determination before performing any services; not doing so may place the adviser in a conflicted position.

While professionals have their own differing sets of ethical considerations, there are a number of factors to consider when a financial adviser is engaged to assist one or more parties in a domestic relations matter. Advisers must consider whether they are individually competent, whether they have the appropriate staffing to complete the engagement, and whether they are able to deal with the inflexible scheduling that occurs in litigation. There must be an examination of whether there are conflicts of interest that may exist with one or more of the parties and/or the attorneys involved in the case. The engagement must be planned, the role documented, and preliminary data gathered.

In circumstances where the adviser has worked for the couple previously, the adviser must exercise caution because of the inherent conflict of interest that exists when one has advised both individuals. In many circumstances, advice rendered with intimate knowledge on behalf of one of the parties can have an adverse impact on the other. Not only could that individual claim damages from the adviser, the adviser can be made to look foolish in a courtroom.

Advisers have numerous skills that can benefit parties in a domestic dispute. In most instances, what has been one household is becoming two. Not only does that mean doubling the expense of the home itself, it means doubling the furniture, appliances, utilities, and many other costs associated with the house. This places budgetary pressure on the couple. They need help minimizing their expenditures while maximizing their cash inflow. Help is needed with budgeting, investment advice, income tax minimization, career choices, and many other areas that have a financial impact on the couple and the children that they may have between them.

Once the adviser's role is determined, it is appropriate to document that role. The role can be documented with an engagement letter, a letter of understanding, a letter from the attorney detailing duties, or a court order. The document should define who the client is, the duties to be performed, limitations on results, the responsibilities of the parties, and the financial arrangements that exist. It is always important for the adviser to take a retainer to bill against because the individuals involved in a divorce are seldom satisfied with the results of litigation. This makes the collection of fees more than problematic. In addition, clients going through this process do not think clearly and may have unrealistic expectations of the potential results of work performed.

It is important to plan the engagement. If the anticipated result is a trial, the attorney or attorneys involved must be an integral part of the adviser's planning process. In all instances, the attorney will be looking to the adviser's testimony and work to prove certain facts at trial. State law and the individual attorney's strategy in the case determine what must be proved and will, therefore, determine the nature and scope of the adviser's work. Even when being called to the witness stand at trial is not anticipated, the adviser must plan and develop work programs. By going through these processes, expectations detailed in the engagement letter or letter of understanding can be met and clearly communicated to the client.

There are engagements that an individual can perform easily without assistance from others. There are, however, engagements that require extensive staffing to perform. In addition, litigation can be very time demanding, with little flexibility in scheduling. It is wise to keep a calendar detailing the cases that are being worked, the attorneys involved, the court where the matter is pending, and the many due dates that are associated with the cases. There are typically deadlines for discovery, reports, depositions, and trial. As multiple cases are worked, the calendar becomes indispensable. It is also necessary to keep a record of all the cases that have historically been worked. One of the first items to check when a new case is brought into the office is whether there are any conflicts of interest that may exist between the parties, their attorneys, and the adviser. Without ongoing record keeping, the adviser will have a difficult time remembering all of the required data. In addition, many courts require an individual preparing to testify as an expert to disclose to the opposing attorney the captions of any cases testified in for the prior four to five years, the attorney for whom the expert worked, and the nature of the testimony given. Because all testimony is typically public record, the opposing attorney has the ability to review that testimony to look for any insights or inconsistencies that may exist.

There are engagements that require budgeting skills, economics training, knowledge of returns on investments, income taxation, earnings available in a given career, valuation skills, and many other areas of specialized knowledge. These factors all must be considered before accepting any engagement. It is not unusual for experts with different training to come to different opinions and conclusions on matters even though they are utilizing the same facts. It is helpful to develop an understanding of the methods used in disciplines outside the adviser's own skill set. One useful method is to begin keeping files of reports rendered by other experts. The adviser should also assume that others are keeping similar files containing the adviser's work, depositions, and reports.

STATE OF THE LAW

One of the most important things the adviser can do is to become familiar with the local court system, the rules that exist within the system, and the normal flow of cases through the system. The attorneys for clients are invaluable sources for this type of information. In addition, the rules that are formalized within the system are available from the courts themselves or the local bar association. Many courts have pro se divisions that can provide information on how, and in what time frame, cases flow through the system. Some courts appoint special masters to hear specific matters. The special masters have the ability to rule on the matters they hear and to issue judgments. The results of these rulings can be appealed after the fact to the court itself. There are administrative divisions of the court that may foster alternative dispute resolution. These agencies may appoint individuals to facilitate the settlement of cases. In most circumstances, these individuals have no power other than that imputed to them as the result of their appointment.

Throughout the United States and its related jurisdictions, the law related to domestic relations cases varies. A discussion of the differences between common law and community property states appears in Chapter 3. While the law may differ from jurisdiction to jurisdiction, the theories applied to cases within those jurisdictions are amazingly similar. This text discusses those theories while notifying the reader when to be alert to each state's different laws. The American Academy of Matrimonial Attorneys is a resource that can be used to determine the status of the law in individual states.

INITIAL MEETINGS WITH COUNSEL OR THE CLIENT

There are a number of tasks that are required at, or prior to, the first meeting to discuss the financial aspects of an engagement. First and foremost, the practitioner should determine whether the practitioner or his firm has any conflicts of interest with any of the parties or attorneys to the case. Exhibit 1.1 is a sample new client

---

EXHIBIT 1.1 Sample New Client Checklist

LITIGATION SUPPORT/BUSINESS VALUATION
NEW CLIENT CHECKLIST

Client Name _____

_____ Client Intake Data Sheet (signed by partner)
_____ Tickler Setup Sheet (if doing tax work)
_____ Add to Pending Lit Support Engagement Status Report

      • Priority   _____
      • Partner   _____
      • Name   _____
      • Type of case   _____
      • Attorneys involved _____
      • Status   _____
      • Status date   _____

_____ Set up Red Pocket, Billing File, Correspondence File
_____ Document Request Form
    ___ Partner's review
    ___ Finalize—send to client or attorney
_____ Engagement Letter
_____ Representation Letter (for Business Valuations)

---

checklist. The second preliminary matter that must be completed is obtaining signatures on an engagement letter. Exhibit 1.2 is a sample engagement letter. The adviser needs to gain an understanding of the issues of the divorce from the attorney, including whether there are child support, spousal support, or property issues. This process will confirm the validity of the services described in the engagement letter. There are a number of dates that must be obtained at the first meeting. They include the date of the marriage, the separation, the filing of the complaint, the children's dates of birth, and the anticipated date of divorce. You will also want to obtain the attorney's name and address, co-counsel's name and address, the name of the opposing party, and the opposing counsel's name and address. All of this information will assist in the conflicts check process.

EXHIBIT 1.2   Sample Engagement Letter

September 9, 2002

_____, Esq.

_____

Albuquerque, New Mexico 871_____

Re: _____

Dear _____:

      This letter will confirm our discussions and the engagement of our firm on behalf of _____, hereafter referred to as the "client", to _____. We have been retained by your firm, to which all reports, communications, and work product will be submitted. We understand that it may be necessary for you to share with us your theories of the case, strategy considerations, mental impressions, conclusions, and other thought processes that relate to your preparation of this matter for trial. It may also be necessary for you to relate to us communications between you and your client. Consequently, we understand that the work performed by us will be confidential, constituting a portion of your work product, and is to be regarded by us as being covered by the attorney-client and attorney work-product privileges.

      We understand that your firm may also wish to engage us to assist you by identifying, and by providing expert witness services concerning, business methods or trade practices, accounting, or financial issues in this matter. In such cases, we understand that any work performed in an expert witness engagement, as well as any other information disclosed to us, may be subject to the rules of discovery as appropriate for expert witnesses. The terms of our subsequent engagement as expert witnesses will also be governed by this letter.

      All workpapers or other documents used by us during the course of this engagement will be maintained in segregated files. At the completion of our engagement, the originals and all copies thereof will be returned to you, upon your written request.

      Our fees in this matter are based on an hourly rate, plus administrative costs, including but not limited to copies, postage, long distance telephone calls, computer expense, courier charges or specially purchased office supplies. Our fees are not contingent upon the outcome of the case. We will bill you at standard rates for all tasks performed by professional or administrative personnel. These rates currently range from $50 to $225 per hour depending on the personnel assigned, plus applicable New Mexico gross receipts tax. We reserve the right to defer rendering further services until payment on past due invoices is received. If we should be requested to testify, we require that we be paid in full for all work performed to date prior to our testimony.

EXHIBIT 1.2 (*Continued*)

We are certain that you recognize that it is difficult to estimate the amount of time that this engagement may require. The fees depend upon the time involved and upon the extent and nature of available information. Fees also depend upon the developments occurring as work progresses. It is our intention to work closely with you to structure our work so that appropriate levels of personnel from our staff are assigned to the various tasks in order to keep fees at a minimum. Any liability of ours will be limited to fees paid and in no event will our firm be liable for incidental or consequential damages.

Select one of the following two paragraphs as applicable

Your firm has agreed to assure payment of all fees incurred in this matter. As a result, no retainer fee has been requested in this matter, although it is the usual practice of this firm to request a retainer to be applied to future billings. We will submit monthly invoices showing amounts billed to the date shown on the invoice. All invoices not paid within 30 days will be subject to a one and one-half percent per month late charge. Appropriate credit will be given to your account for any funds that are paid to the financial adviser from any third-party source allowed by any court, although you will be responsible for the payment of all fees regardless of any court orders which may be entered against any other party regarding the payment of our fees.

The obligations for payment of our fees are not the direct responsibility of your law firm. As a result, a retainer fee of $_____ has been requested in this matter. Monthly invoices will show amounts billed to the date shown on the invoice and the remaining balance of the retainer fee, if any. Any balance remaining due after the application of the credit for the retainer fee is payable when the invoice is received. A service charge of 1.5% per month will be charged against any amounts not paid within thirty days from the date of the invoice. Appropriate credit will be given to the clients' account for any funds that are paid to the financial adviser from any third-party source allowed by any court, although the clients will be responsible for the payment of all fees regardless of any court orders which may be entered against any other party regarding the payment of our fees.

We have performed an internal search for any potential client conflicts based upon the names of the parties and their counsel that you provided. We have not found any client conflicts with respect to any of the parties. To minimize the risk of potential problems, we suggest that you disclose our retention to the other side as soon as possible, but in a manner consistent with your case strategy. Should any possible conflict come to our attention, we will advise you immediately.

(*continues*)

EXHIBIT 1.2 *(Continued)*

The value of our firm's service to you and your client is founded, in part, upon our reputation for professionalism and integrity. Our firm has been engaged from time to time by a significant number of law firms, and it may be that we are or have been engaged by firms representing clients adverse to your client in this matter. Your engagement of our firm is expressly conditioned on your agreement not to use the fact of our current or previous engagement by opposing counsel in other matters as a means of enhancing or diminishing our credibility before a trier of fact.

Any controversy, claim, or counterclaim arising out of or relating to this contract, the breach thereof, or the services performed by the financial adviser shall be settled by binding arbitration before a single arbitrator in accordance with the rules of the American Arbitration Association (AAA), and judgment on the award rendered by the arbitrator may be entered in any court having jurisdiction thereof. The arbitration shall be conducted at a location within Bernalillo County, New Mexico, as determined by the arbitrator. In the event an arbitration or litigation (including but not limited to any proceeding to compel arbitration) is initiated to resolve or settle any dispute or claim between the parties, the prevailing party shall be entitled to recover from the non-prevailing party or parties its reasonable costs, including but not limited to reasonable attorney's fees.

You or the court itself will advise us, with sufficient notice, of the work to be performed by us, the requirement for appearance in court, and the need for any court order approving our employment and/or compensation for services rendered and expenses incurred. You will aid us in obtaining any court orders or approval in these regards. Should information become known that would make our continued involvement in this engagement inappropriate, or should the attorneys or parties involved in this litigation change, we reserve the right to withdraw from this engagement.

Please alter following paragraphs as appropriate depending upon whether the client signs or not

By acknowledging acceptance of the terms of this engagement, you, on behalf of the client, represent and warrant that you have read and agree with the terms of this engagement as set forth in this letter and have advised the client of the terms and conditions set forth herein, including but not limited to the provisions above with respect to arbitration of disputes and claims.

If this is in accordance with your understanding and meets with your approval, please sign and date one copy of this letter in the space provided. We request that your clients also sign an acknowledgment copy of this letter. We are delivering the original and two signed copies of this letter to you so that

---

EXHIBIT 1.2   *(Continued)*

---

each party will have a signed copy and so that you can coordinate getting the client's signature. Please return one fully executed copy to me.

Very truly yours,

The financial adviser

Principal

___/spc

Enclosures

Accepted:

by _____   _____
                                                                                     Date

Acknowledged:

The above letter confirms our understanding of services to be performed by The financial adviser in this matter and our fee arrangement. Any professional responsibility of the financial adviser to communicate information to us as a client will be discharged by communicating such information to our counsel. Also, we agree to accept ultimate responsibility for payment of our fees, and to the arbitration provision, as described above.

by _____   _____
                                                                                     Date

---

Alimony Determination

The adviser can assist in the details or the overall development of an alimony plan. There are typically a number of factors a court must consider in making an award. The relative earnings and earnings capacities of the parties are considered. The nature, value, and earnings of property received are considered. The ages, health, duration of the marriage, and the standard of living of the couple during the marriage are considered. The needs of the individuals are always a factor. In the various states, other factors are detailed. In most jurisdictions, the court determines the equity and amount of the award. Evidence may be submitted to the court detailing the postdivorce cash flow of each party. This analysis may include the appropriate wage each may earn, what investment income exists, the nature and amount of assets that may be available for investment, what taxes the individual will incur, and the short-term and long-term expenses the party may expect. The adviser can assist divorcing couples with any or all of these factors.

Income Determination

The income a party has, or will receive, becomes an issue in many divorces. Income for divorce purposes may be defined in local law. The financial adviser must understand that this definition will differ from the definition of income for income tax purposes, or for the purposes of generally accepted accounting principles.

The income considered by the court will typically include wages, investment income, income from businesses, rentals, royalties, and other sources. Common sources for this information will be income tax returns, books and records of the individuals and businesses, the bank statements, and brokerage statements of the parties. There may be other collateral evidence that should be considered in determining income.

The appropriate wage an individual can expect to receive can be determined in a number of ways. Certainly the wage a person currently collects is a factor. But what if the person is qualified for a position that could create greater income, or what if the person is not working to full capacity? Both circumstances could cause an argument that the individual's current wages are not the earnings the court should consider in its award. If the individual is underemployed, how should the appropriate level of income be determined? Should it be based on local or national statistics? What is the appropriate source for those statistics? How can it be determined if the positions proposed are even available in the local marketplace? Other arguments are based on funding the costs to improve an individual's earnings capacity. This may include a short-term plan for an individual to undertake some specialized training, update skills, or pursue a college degree. In these circumstances, the person may not have short-term earnings capacity, but may develop significant future earnings capacity that may eliminate the need for support in the future. In addition, there are arguments that other factors, such as young children at home, prevent individuals from earning up to their capacity.

Similar disagreements occur over the correct nature and amount of investment income that should be considered by the court. Could the allocation of the assets be modified to increase the income available? Are there nonproductive assets that should be sold and the proceeds reinvested to generate additional income? What is the appropriate rate of return that the assets can earn? Should assets be liquidated to fund living or educational expense? All of these questions create disagreements the courts are called upon to resolve.

It is also not unusual for there to be concerns over unreported or concealed income. In these cases, the financial adviser may want to review several years of check registers, bank statements, brokerage statements, and other documents to determine whether the cost of the lifestyle of the couple may, in fact, exceed the reported income. The steps to competently complete this type of engagement have to be determined on a case-by-case basis.

Taxation of Income

Once the level of income is determined, the income tax costs of collecting that income must be considered. The amount of tax, on an annual basis, changes as a result of tax law changes, property sales, changes in circumstances such as a child leaving for college, and even changes in income levels. Determinations and/or assumptions must be made as to whether the amounts of support received would be taxable or tax-free. These amounts must all be determined and applied to the cash flow analysis for each year considered.

Appropriate Levels of Expenses/Standard of Living

In many states, the parties' standard of living during the marriage is a factor considered by the courts in awarding spousal support, alimony, or child support. In these circumstances, it is necessary for the financial adviser to document the historical expenditure levels of the couple, as this may most closely portray to the court a picture of the historical standard of living. Once this information is obtained, changes that will occur postlitigation must be anticipated. This data will be based on research performed and include information, for example, of projected insurance premiums, rental payments, and other expenditures that will change after the litigation is concluded. The financial adviser will often be requested to prepare an exhibit that details the historical and projected expenditures of the couple.

The level of expense a party should incur when being supported by the other can become a factual, as well as an emotional, issue for the parties and can be difficult for the financial adviser to determine. In some circumstances, the adviser will merely compile the information developed by the individual or the attorney. In other circumstances, the adviser may be asked to determine predivorce lifestyle based on the parties' spending patterns. The law may only allow a subsistence level of support. If that is the case, the adviser may rely on local or national economic statistics to determine expense levels.

Once all of the components have been determined, many advisers will project into the future what changes could be expected in the parties' incomes, expenses, and assets over their respective life expectancies. Comparison of the results over the parties' life expectancies can provide powerful information detailing the amount of support necessary, as well as the amount of support that may be equitable. Many courts will establish higher levels of support if the work shows one party's assets being depleted in the future while the other's continue to grow. In other jurisdictions, the courts are required to consider only the current status of the divorcing couple and will maintain jurisdiction in the future to modify support based on changes in circumstances. There are also jurisdictions that impose a maximum dollar limitation on support.

CHILD SUPPORT

Child support is determined based on guidelines developed on a local basis. Most child support is based on the earnings capacity of the parties. The guidelines may also consider the time-sharing of the children between the parties as well as extraordinary expenses incurred on behalf of the children. These might include expenditures such as private schooling, medical expense, or childcare. The arguments related to this income are, in many respects, similar to the arguments related to alimony or spousal support. There are, however, additional areas of disagreement that occur in the child support arena. Issues can arise if the guidelines provide for support that one of the parties believes is excessive or too little. In some jurisdictions, there can be deviations from the guidelines. As in the case of a writer or actor, the income of one of the individuals may be inconsistent. In other cases, the income may be for a limited duration, such as with a professional athlete. With these types of income fluctuations, there are arguments made regarding the timing of support payments and the establishment of trusts for children. The financial adviser can assist in these matters.

PROPERTY ISSUES

Property issues make up a significant portion of the issues in divorces in which a financial adviser is engaged. Assets must be identified, inventoried, then valued, and finally divided. Financial advisers are involved in each of these processes. Many times the financial adviser will be asked to prepare a statement detailing the fair market value of the assets, liabilities, and the net worth of the divorcing couple. These statements may be then divided into subcategories detailing premarital property, marital or community property, postseparation property, separate property, and commingled or transmuted property.

Identification of Assets

If one or both of the parties to a divorce are not candid, identification of assets can be problematic. In these instances, it may be necessary to use investigators and financial advisers familiar with asset identification techniques. These techniques can be as simple as identifying income on the parties' income tax return and tracing that income to an underlying asset. Or, asset identification can become more complex and require investigative techniques such as chattel searches and title searches in various locales. There will always be the need to review the detailed registers of the couples' various cash and security accounts to look for undisclosed sources of income or expense. These investigations can be expensive to conduct. The adviser would do well to work only on retainer and to insist on the retainer being restored when it is depleted. Unfortunately, most individuals' budgets do not allow for the level of search that would be required to locate every asset and, in some circumstances, every asset will never be found. A coffee can full of cash buried in a garden will defy even the most advanced techniques. The practitioner should also be aware that individuals who are not being honest with each other might not be honest with the adviser. Great care must be exercised with these individuals.

Inventory of Assets

Once the assets have been located, they must be inventoried. Many of these issues may not require the financial adviser's participation, but many will. It is not unusual for individuals to have collectibles or assets in multiple locations. In many circumstances, an individual will be hired to identify and list the individual items of property, the condition of the property, where the property may be located, and, in some cases, the advisability of hiring an expert to appraise the property. In other situations, the process of creating the inventory will provide the parties and their counsel all the information needed to proceed. An example would be the instance of stocks and bonds. In other situations, creation of the list may only be the beginning of a long and complex valuation and division process. For example, this could occur with a large coin or stamp collection.

Valuation of Assets

Valuations can be performed for many different purposes. They can be for estate, sale, purchases, buy-sell, personal financial statements, litigation, and other purposes. It is important that the financial adviser understand that the purpose of the valuation can dictate the procedures and methodology that must be utilized.

Valuation of the assets making up the parties' estate is one of the most hotly disputed issues in a domestic relations case. While there are many areas of potential dispute, the first may be the date on which the asset will be valued. Each state will have differing statutes and case law related to this issue. Financially sophisticated clients may wish to use the timing of separating, filing a divorce petition, or other triggering event to lock in a valuation date that may be to their advantage.

Once the valuation date is established, the next challenge is to determine what valuation method is appropriate. Many may assume that the traditional definition of fair market value would be appropriate. This is not necessarily the case. In many states, the method or methods may be defined by statute. In other states, the methods may be defined by case law. In some states, there may be no definition on which to rely. Valuations can differ depending on the standard of value used. They can differ depending on the time assumed that the asset will be exposed to the marketplace. An item put to auction, without reserve, will normally bring a significantly lower price than an asset exposed to the market for a reasonable period of time. The marketplace assumed in the valuation process can also impact the value determined. A rare stamp for sale in the world market will bring a different price than the same stamp exposed for sale in a small, unsophisticated community.

Within each type of specialized asset that may need to be valued are individual issues that must be addressed. Specialized assets certainly include businesses, real estate, retirement plans, art works, personal property, and other financial assets. Each of these types of property has their own valuation law, and they differ in each state.

Business Valuations

When there is a business that is a marital asset, it typically is the most valuable asset the couple owns. Because closely held businesses are not bought and sold with regularity, the valuation of the business is hotly contested. Examples in business valuation can include whether a buy-sell agreement would be an appropriate measure of value in a closely held corporation, or would the fair market value of the business be more appropriate? Other tough issues include how to value a closely held business when some or all of the value is the individual's personal goodwill, or the individual's professional license to practice. Should the potential value of a covenant not to compete be considered to be marital or community property when the compensation is for not competing postmarriage? Each of these matters is dealt with differently in differing jurisdictions.

When a common expert is to be chosen to value assets, the individual is often disputed and, in some circumstances, the matter is litigated. Experts may become known for values favoring the business owner or the owner's spouse. Each party's attorney will posture to have the most favorable valuation for their client. In most areas of the country, the parties will hire their own specialized appraiser for each specialized asset. The experts will then duel in deposition and trial, with the judge or jury adopting one position, the other position, or, in many cases, picking a value in the middle. There are other areas of the country that try to avoid the dueling experts by having the court appoint, or the parties agree to, a single expert for the valuation work. In either case, there are financial advisers specializing in the valuation of real estate, personal property, collectibles, and businesses. The appraisers have their own standards and ethical considerations with which they must comply. But, the financial adviser should insure that the appraiser is aware of how local law impacts the appraisal and of any significant factors that may impact the appraisal of the property.

Discounts for Marketability and Minority Interest

The Internal Revenue Service and tax courts have recognized for years that interests in closely held (not publicly traded) businesses, especially those subject to restrictions on transfer, are illiquid when compared to other investment alternatives. Therefore, the value of these interests should be discounted. Typical restrictions on transfer of interests in closely held businesses may include a total prohibition of transfer, the requirement of transfer of the asset only to family members, the requirement of transfer at a set (typically low) price. It may also include the necessity of first offering the interest back to the company or to other equity owners before transferring to a third party. When offering the interest back to the company or the other equity owners, the time for which the interim offer must remain open is typically long. These restrictions are many times imposed to discourage third parties from making fair market value offers or purchases of equity interests in the business. In some circumstances, the restrictions may be so effective as to make an equity interest not marketable. This conforms to the interest of the grantors to keep the assets in the entity and entity "in the family."

The rationales for *marketability* discounts are several, beginning with recognition of the fact that, at the very least, a greater amount of time and money will be necessary to bring such interests to market or to locate a market for them, should the investor wish to sell. Additionally, these discounts are justified by the higher levels of risk of loss associated with the possible inability to turn such investments into cash in the immediate future.

When the business interest in question is a noncontrolling or *minority* interest (such as that of a limited partner), authorities have long recognized that another discount, a discount for lack of control, or *minority* discount, should be applied to determine the fair market value of such interests. These discounts are justified in order to compensate the hypothetical passive investor for the additional risk inherent in having to trust an unrelated third party to properly manage the business. It also compensates for the lack of opportunity to control the *books* and to enjoy the *perks* of controlling ownership.

The divorce courts in the various jurisdictions recognize these discounts in varying ways. Should the fact that the business may not be salable be a factor? Some states have ruled salability not to be a factor for valuations in property division. There are issues associated with whether marketability or minority discounts are appropriate for valuations associated with a domestic relations matter. The various states' laws include allowing the discounts, allowing one of the discounts, not allowing any discount, or being silent on the issue.

Valuation of Retirement Plans

There are two general types of retirement plans that require valuation in divorce cases. There are those plans that accumulate funds through the period of their existence. The ultimate benefit received by the beneficiary is the balance in the account at retirement. These plans are sometimes referred to as defined contribution plans, or as money purchase plans. These plans are easy to value as the amount of assets in the plan, at any given point, can be determined, and the levels of vesting can be applied to those values. Some states recognize vesting in differing manners than others. Financial advisers should make themselves aware of the impact of local law on these valuations.

The second type of plan promises a benefit of a computed amount at a fixed date in the future. These plans may provide for a benefit amount based on a percentage of the participant's highest level of salary for a number of years, to be paid in the future for the then-remaining life expectancy of the participant. These plans are referred to as defined benefit plans. The valuation of these plans is more complex. Many courts require that life expectancy, probability of continued employment, probability of death or disability, and reasonable rates of return be considered in the current valuation of the ultimate benefits to be received. These valuations require actuarial assumptions and the use of probability in the valuation. The value of the future benefits in these cases will always differ from the amounts funded in the plans at the time of the dissolution of the marriage.

Some courts will insist retirement plans be valued for property division purposes, and others will impose an in-kind division when the benefits become payable to the beneficiary. Courts that value and divide face the probable challenge of the retirement plan being the most valuable asset in the couple's estate. In those cases, there may not be sufficient other assets to equalize the marital estate. When that occurs, courts will sometimes divide the benefits when they are received. Computations for benefit division include a time division, based on the time the couple was married over the total time the employee was in the plan at retirement. Benefit division may involve a valuation division, where the benefit earned through the date of property division is divided and benefits earned afterwards are not. Each type of division will produce a differing result for the divorcing parties.

Taxation of the Appreciation in Value

The amount and timing of the taxation of the increase in value an asset has realized since its purchase or creation fosters disputes. In determining the amount the individual taking the asset should be charged with in the division, should the potential taxes that would be paid if the asset were sold at the gross value included in the property division be deducted?

There can be no question that some assets will be taxed in the future. Pension plans will be taxed as income to the ultimate recipients of the funds. However, these individuals may or may not be the litigants. The ultimate recipients may be their designated beneficiaries on their death. With other assets, the ultimate tax may or may not be paid. Under our current system of taxation, assets passing through an individual's estate receive a step-up in basis to the fair market value as of the decedent's date of death. In this case, the decedent will never pay the tax, and the beneficiary may also escape the tax. Even if taxes are going to be incurred by the party to the domestic proceeding, the amount can vary based on changes in federal and state tax law. In addition to the varying amount, the timing of the payment can become an issue. In some circumstances, it is impossible to know when the asset may be sold. In the case of an installment sale, the gain on the sale may be deferred or payable over several years. Because of this uncertainty as to the amount and timing of payment of tax, there is inconsistent law that occurs in different jurisdictions. Some jurisdictions will consider the tax issues if they are immediate and determinable with some level of certainty; other jurisdictions will ignore tax consequences as being speculative. Even if the courts do not consider the tax impact on the valuation of marital assets, the financial adviser in settlement negotiations must advise the client of the differences in net values that may be received if the assets are liquidated.

TRACING OF ASSETS

In many cases, assets are part marital or community property and part separate property. In these circumstances, tracings must be performed to determine the respective value of each party's share of the asset. Some states require the specific identification of the funds utilized to acquire the asset, some have systems that apportion the value, and others have systems of reimbursement. Each of these is state specific.

Separate property is traditionally property acquired premarriage, by gift, by inheritance, or traceable to those sources of funds. Marital or community property is traditionally property acquired by other funds or labor during the marriage. Financial advisers are frequently required to trace the source of funds to acquire a particular piece of property. The procedures to perform tracings vary from jurisdiction to jurisdiction.

DIVISION OF PROPERTY

Once the property has been identified, inventoried, and valued, the next challenge is its distribution. Property that is determined to be separate property will be awarded to the party proving its separateness. Property that is marital or community will be divided between the parties based on the discretion of the court. Whether the courts consider certain attributes of property in the division between the parties will dictate to the financial adviser whether to recognize discounts or premiums to the valuations performed for domestic relations legal purposes. For example, the adviser would consider one hundred dollars in cash to be worth more than one hundred dollars that will ultimately be taxed in a qualified retirement plan. This difference may not be considered in the property division by the court. As a result, one of the valuable services the financial adviser can perform is to determine, on the basis of the local law valuations, which assets would be most advantageous for a party to keep, and which would be most appropriate to give up.

OTHER ISSUES

If there is the ability to control the ultimate order rendered in the domestic relations case, there are issues related to other financial matters, and tax attributes that the financial adviser can assist in negotiating. Ongoing issues arise related to Internal Revenue Service audits of returns while the parties were married. Many of these issues are associated with the parties' children. They include which parent may take the exemption for the children, who should pay childcare expenses, and how the parties will fund the children's secondary education. There are issues related to security for alimony or spousal support payment, child support payments, and payments to be made over time to pay off property divisions. Who should carry life insurance on their lives, and who should be the beneficiary of the policy? Most of the issues related to settling or implementing a court's order finalizing a couple's marriage involve some related financial issue. The exception is typically the parenting issues, and even those are not always exempt.

The financial advisers, in whatever role they play, are integral to the process the parties must endure to terminate their relationship. There are many and diverse skills of a financial nature that can benefit an individual going through a divorce. With proper knowledge and understanding, advisers can bring significant value to the process and make a fair fee for their efforts.

CHAPTER 2

The Financial Adviser's Role in Divorce Litigation

THE FINANCIAL ADVISER'S ROLE

The financial adviser can perform many roles in domestic relations and divorce litigation. The adviser needs to understand the various forums and the various roles that the individual can fill. Advocacy proceedings can include trial and arbitration. The adviser can also be involved in other nonbinding proceedings such as mediation and settlement facilitation.

The expert testifies under rules established by the court with jurisdiction over the divorce. Most of the testimony financial advisers can bring to court includes opinions of the adviser. Generally, opinions are not admissible in court, except by individuals qualified as experts. This involves the potential expert testifying as to the qualifications, experience, and special knowledge the expert may possess to render the opinions that the expert may offer. In this qualification process, the court determines whether the individual is qualified as an expert, and whether the testimony to be rendered by the adviser would be helpful to the judge. Unlike others in the trial, the expert can rely on information from third parties. Under normal court rules, this information would be considered hearsay evidence and not be admissible. This gives the adviser a significant advantage in presenting his opinion testimony at trial.

At the beginning of the case, it is important to consider whether the attorney or the client is going to employ the expert. If the attorney engages the expert, there is a presumption that the attorney client privilege will apply to the expert's work. This means the opposing party will not be able to discover the analysis the expert may have performed or any conclusions that may have been reached. This privilege may be important if there is concern over what the expert may discover in the work performed. Once the expert is disclosed as a witness or employed by the client, everything done by the expert is available to the opposing party.

The expert in a trial is expected to be detached from the parties and their issues. Independence and objectivity are invaluable and give the expert credibility with the court. Many in the legal community refer to expert witnesses as *hired guns*. The term is used negatively, typically stereotyping an individual whose opinions are flexible and designed to fit the occasion. Such expert witnesses express these opinions in court and, in return, are paid. The hired gun transaction is complete.

Financial advisers must diligently strive to achieve a different reputation. Litigation services clients must be assured that they are purchasing knowledge, experience, and time, and that the opinions and conclusions are not affected by the payment or amount of the fees. The adviser's proper role is never as an advocate of the client's position, but rather as an individual who evaluates, quantifies, presents supportable options and alternatives, and renders and advocates only his own opinions.

Professional integrity, honesty, and an impeccable reputation for these qualities lead to credibility. Credibility is the distinguishing characteristic of the successful expert witness. Opinions must be formed with foresight, careful thought, and appropriate technical authority.

The client's interest must never be placed above the opinions of the adviser. Objectivity and integrity must be maintained. An understanding must be established with the client concerning the nature, scope, and limitations of the services to be performed. The client must be informed of real or potential conflicts of interest, reservations concerning the scope or benefits of the work, and the significant findings or events associated with the work.

The adviser needs to maintain an objective and independent state of mind in performing litigation services work. This will prevent the unsubstantiated adherence to an attorney's or client's theory as the underlying basis for an opinion. It is important to note that this does not prevent the assumption of hypothetical facts provided by client's counsel. However, it does preclude the formation of an opinion that is not based upon accepted theory, valid assumptions, and facts as supported by the evidence.

The expected consequences of any analysis must be communicated to the client. If the results of an analysis do not coincide with the legal position of a client, the adviser does not have the option to abandon his conclusions.

Litigation services veterans know that the vast majority of cases in which they participate will settle. Providing accurate information and well-reasoned conclusions are keys to successful dispute resolution. This is especially true when such information and conclusions come from an individual with a reputation for integrity and honesty. While preparations must be made for the unusual circumstance of a formal trial, dispute resolution must be the desired goal.

The environment in which the work is performed also prevents experts from becoming *hired guns*. Much of the work is typically referred from lawyers and judges. Without those referrals, advisers performing litigation services would not be able to continue in their specialty. When testifying in local jurisdictions, professionals speak to a small audience. Judges and attorneys express opinions among themselves about the experts who testify before them. Attorneys build files of depositions, reports, and notes of opinions rendered. These files may contain details of the work performed in numerous cases. If there are inconsistencies or unsupportable positions, the opposing lawyer will brutally bare those weaknesses on cross-examination.

Adherence to these principles will also certainly lead to more, and a better quality of, engagements for the adviser, many times from neutral sources. Judges teach whom to believe. If there are appointments of neutral experts to be made in their court, the appointments will go to the credible witnesses. The appointment to a neutral role in a lawsuit is the ultimate affirmation of an expert's credibility. Those who receive referrals of litigation engagements on a regular basis can be proud of the fact that they have withstood the tests of time, attorneys, clients, and judges. Those who make fools of themselves in a jurisdiction seldom get a second chance. When an attorney or the client is *burned* with outlandish testimony, much of the local bar will soon know. Referrals will stop. Bad news travels quickly. However, when credibility is maintained, judges will have respect, attorneys will come for critical analysis, and calendars will be full.

There are few other forums in which advisers' work is subjected to such rigorous and exhaustive review. Highly qualified independent experts review the adviser's reports, depositions, opinions, and testimony. They advise and assist attorneys in cross-examinations. If there is a flaw in logic, a gap in documentation, a lack of objectivity, a conflict of interest, or a question of integrity in the approach, the sins will be bared in all the blazing glory cross-examination can bring.

In addition to any of the adviser's professional standards, the rules of evidence and procedure, as well as underlying case law establish the criteria upon which work is judged. In the federal courts, Rule 26 of the Federal Rules of Evidence provides for a written report laying out the entirety of the testimony to be given. The information must include the documents reviewed, the procedures performed, and the opinions reached. This is provided to all parties months in advance of the trial. In addition, the Daubert case and its successors have established federal standards for the courtroom admissibility of evidence. Many states have adopted similar rules. An individual can get the referral, perform the work, issue the report, and get to the courtroom, but have the ultimate gatekeeper bar the testimony. The system works. Incompetence and lack of adherence to professional standards and methodologies do not survive in the specialty of litigation.

Many financial advisers debate whether they should continue to practice in their traditional roles while working part-time in litigation services. It is the contention of some that litigation practitioners must keep their hand in their area of financial expertise in order to maintain their core competencies. There are others who would say that an individual could not maintain competence while practicing in multiple specialties. Both factions argue that their position increases their integrity and credibility in the courtroom.

This debate will continue into the future. However, when lawyers are asked what they want in a witness, they answer uniformly. They want experience in the area of the subject litigation, and they want experience in the courtroom. The more times the expert has testified the better. They are thrilled if the expert has experience working in the subject area of the litigation. They desire a presence in the courtroom. A passion for the opinion position is a plus, but a passion for the lawsuit is a negative.

The qualities attorneys demand are the qualities of objectivity, integrity, openness regarding potential conflicts of interest, the ability to identify weaknesses in the case, and most importantly, honest communication with the attorney and client. All bring more litigation services business to the adviser's door.

THE DIVORCE PROCESS

In many jurisdictions, there are waiting periods, or periods of required residence, before a divorce case can be filed. These vary from locale to locale and are determined on a jurisdiction basis. Generally, the courts require at least one of the parties to be a resident of the jurisdiction in which the case is filed. With persons living in different states and with differences in each state's laws, there are often disputes over which court may have jurisdiction over a specific divorce. In extreme cases, different matters in the divorce may be tried in different states.

Waiting Period and Complaint

When the waiting period or the residency requirement has been met, a complaint can be filed. The complaint lays out certain factual allegations and details the grounds under which the divorce is filed. States are divided into fault states and no fault states. In states that require fault to be found, there are specific acts or commissions that must be proved before the state can grant a divorce. No-fault states generally allow divorce to occur because the parties are incompatible. These differences cause the trials in fault states to dwell on what the parties may have done, which does not matter in no-fault states. When the complaint is filed, the opposing party is served with notice of the suit. If the parties are communicating, many times the opposing party's attorney can accept service for the potential respondent and avoid the embarrassment of that individual being hunted down by a process server.

Once the complaint is filed, a series of deadlines begins to run. There are a limited number of days within which to file an Answer to the Complaint. The Answer affirms, denies, or disavows knowledge of the allegations in the Complaint. The answer is typically the first document filed in response to the complaint.

At this point there may be a hearing. Whether there is or is not, it is not unusual for protective orders and interim orders to be issued by the court. This is the first opportunity for the financial adviser to participate in the system. These orders will typically prohibit the parties from unilaterally changing anything of importance and from buying or selling property; they will also provide for some transfer of funds between the parties and determine where each party and their children will live. Many times, these orders are kept in place until the court concludes the matter. The orders and their terms and transfer of funds are also typically subject to the review of the court on final hearing.

Discovery

Next begins the discovery process. It can take a number of forms. There is informal discovery where the parties share documents and information. While this is efficient, it is not the most relied upon method. There are Requests for Production of Documents, Interrogatories, and Depositions. Requests for Production of Documents require the opposing party to supply the requested documents and to state under oath that they are true and correct, or if the documents are not supplied, that they do not exist. Interrogatories are a series of questions developed by the attorney that must be answered under oath and in writing. Many times the responses to Interrogatories will include documents that may support the answers. Depositions are formal interviews taken under oath in front of a certified court reporter in which the opposing attorney questions the witness about matters related to the divorce. Attorneys prefer these methods because they are under the control and enforcement of the court and because they are under the oath of truthfulness. If individuals are not truthful in responses, they may be found guilty of perjury. In addition, there are court-imposed deadlines for providing the information requested.

It is during this process that the financial expert will find the second opportunity to assist in the divorce case. There are documents that are needed to form opinions, confirm facts, and provide the information needed to testify. Often, the attorney will ask for the expert's assistance in preparing these requests and in formulating questions to be asked in depositions. It is through this process that the expert may receive the documents that are needed to perform the work and render the opinions required.

There are a number of paths to information that can be utilized. The individual the financial adviser is representing may need to be interviewed. The client's advisers must be contacted. The opposing party, their accountant, legal counsel, and other advisers may need to be interviewed or deposed. Certainly personal and business books and records, financial statements, and tax returns will be reviewed. Exhibit 2.1 shows a document request list that may assist the adviser in listing documents that may be helpful.

EXHIBIT 2.1 Document Request List

It is normal for the adviser to request voluminous information regarding the party's financial affairs. For a hypothetical engagement involving a business, the expert could need the following types of documents:

1. Financial statements (5 years).
   a. Business.
   b. Personal.
2. Tax returns (5 years).
   a. Business.
   b. Personal.
   c. Estate.
   d. Gift.
3. Payroll records.
   a. Business.
   b. Personal.
4. Retirement plan records.
   a. Pension plan.
   b. Profit sharing.
   c. Other plans.
5. Fringe benefits.
   a. Deferred compensation.
   b. Insurance (group/individual, health, etc.).
   c. Medical reimbursement plans.
   d. Cafeteria plan.
   e. Vacation policy.
   f. Sick pay policy.
   g. Legal reimbursement plans.
   h. Child care plans.

(continues)

EXHIBIT 2.1 *(Continued)*

---

    i. Bonus computations.
    j. Commission structure.
    k. Education/tuition reimbursement plans.
  6. Fire/casualty insurance policies (policy limits).
  7. Bank statements/canceled checks.
  8. Corporate minute book.
  9. Buy/sell agreements.
10. Employment contracts.
11. Travel and entertainment policy.
12. Corporate autos provided.
13. Partnership agreements.
14. Major customer contracts.
15. Lease agreements.
16. Notes/contracts payable.
17. Appraisals.
18. Pending litigation.
19. Personal assets used in business.
20. Depreciation schedules.
21. Customer lists.
22. Accounts receivable with aging.
23. Inventory.
24. Accountants' work papers.
25. Schedule of investments.
26. Notes/contracts receivable.
27. List of shareholders.
28. Shares owned by each and total.
29. Shares outstanding.
30. Forecasts.
31. Franchise agreements.
32. Licenses, permits.
33. Patents, trademarks, copyrights.
34. Union contracts.
35. Offers to buy/sell.

Assembling Information and Developing an Opinion

Once the discovery has been completed, the clients interviewed, and the attorneys have provided their legal theory of the case, the expert must develop a position in the case that results in an opinion. This is the most critical time for the expert. The opinion developed must conform to the expert's ethical and professional standards. It must comply with the local case law and must be personally defensible by the expert.

At this time, the expert must be careful not to become an advocate for the client or the attorney. If the expert fails in this charge, he will be easily exposed on cross-examination. Prior to finalizing the opinion, the expert must carefully consider the cross-examination questions that may be asked and what responses the expert will be able to make. The opinion must, at a minimum, be supported by exhibits and may under local rules be required to be supported by a written report. If a full report is required, there are jurisdictions in which the entire opinion, as well as the basis for the opinion, including documents reviewed, testimony considered, and opinions formed must be detailed in the document. If this information is not disclosed in the report, there are jurisdictions in which testimony will not be admissible in the courtroom.

Financial Adviser's Deposition

It is also at this time that the expert may receive a subpoena to appear before a court reporter with all documents and files related to the case to give deposition testimony. Anything and everything that is in the expert's possession is subject to discovery. The adviser must, throughout the engagement, insure that, at all times, the documents in the file are appropriate to be shared with the opposing side. The subpoenas received will require production of the file. It is also imperative the expert understand the case to be presented by the attorney and client for whom work is being performed. This may require extensive time spent with the attorney. There are two different theories attorneys espouse related to expert testimony in deposition. One is for the expert to fully and completely disclose through the deposition testimony the strengths of the case, with hopes that the strengths will cause the case to settle. There is another stream of thought that requires the expert to only answer the questions asked and to not volunteer information. Both theories are widely held, and it is important for the expert to understand which theory the employing attorney wishes to use before entering the deposition. The expert must understand that when in the deposition, the expert is under the total scheduling control of the deposing attorney. While there is politeness, there is no question depositions are conducted in an air of adversity. In most cases, the opposing spouse and the opposing expert will attend the deposition. The expert should always state, when allowed, that his opinion may change when additional information or testimony is provided. The expert should also state that he will respond to the opposing expert's opinions if asked.

Opposing Expert's Deposition

In some jurisdictions, the opposing expert's opinion may be fully disclosed in a written report. In other jurisdictions, no disclosure is required. In either circumstance, the expert may be requested to provide the attorney with questions and strategy for the opposing expert's deposition. In many cases, the expert will attend the deposition to provide the attorney with questions and strategy as the deposition progresses. In every circumstance, the expert will want to read or hear the opposing expert's deposition prior to finalizing his opinions.

Settlement

The next step in the process is to make attempts to settle the case. Prior to the completion of discovery, attorneys are reluctant to make settlement offers. They believe it would be misinformed to make an offer without knowing the quality of the case they can present. This requires the financial adviser to substantially complete the work required, prior to settlement negotiations taking place. The financial adviser will find this frustrating, but a fact that must be accepted. If there has been candid disclosure in the discovery process, and there are few or no significant issues of law, there is a high probability of settlement. Statistics show that as many as 90 percent of the cases settle before trial. Settlement offers are never accepted based on a first offer. It is impossible for one of the parties to know what the other's expectations and priorities may be. Without knowing the opposing party's expectations and priorities, a counteroffer is required. The initial offer and the counteroffer lead to an ongoing negotiation process that can last months or years. Many times, the financial adviser will be involved in this process to help the client understand the long-term financial impact of various proposals. Settlement negotiations are intense and demanding. The negotiations may be the client's best chance of achieving a settlement that is in their best interest. Having the courts make decisions about any matter based on the law, as opposed to the individuals' needs, does not produce a favorable result.

The divorce can be finalized as a result of settlement, or as a result of trial. The final document produced in a divorce is sometimes called a marital settlement agreement or a final order. These documents, along with the decree of divorce, are the documents that end the marriage, provide for support, and divide the property.

TRIALS

There are different roles an adviser can perform related to domestic relations litigation. One is the role of the expert witness. Most advisers filling the expert witness role do not have an existing professional relationship with the client prior to the divorce. More often than not, the expert in the divorce is retained directly by the attorney rather than the client. This process allows the expert to work initially in a consulting role with the attorney. This is valuable because the work the expert performs with this definition of roles may be covered by the attorney-client privilege. This means neither the opposing party nor the opposing attorney can have access to the work of the expert, the files and documents the expert has accumulated, or the expert himself. Many attorneys prefer this relationship until they know and understand the results of the adviser's work. If the expert forms an opinion that is detrimental to the client, the attorney is not required to reveal the expert's existence, or the opinion the expert may have formed.

Once the expert's opinion is formed and the work complete, the attorney may then decide to disclose the existence of the expert to the opposing party. When the disclosure is made, the expert must understand everything in his possession related to the case is subject to discovery by the other side. This includes, but is not limited to, notes, files, workpapers, electronic media, and e-mails. At deposition or informally, the expert may also be required to explain in great detail what was considered, what documents were reviewed, and what opinions were reached. The expert also needs to be cognizant that conversations that may have been held between the attorney, the client, and the expert are subject to the discovery process and must be disclosed to the other side.

The attorney normally provides to the expert documents which are received through the discovery process. These documents that the expert may have requested, along with testimony provided, interviews conducted, and the analysis performed, will provide the basis for any opinions the expert may render at trial.

Testimony

Prior to testimony, the expert may be required to produce exhibits or reports that detail the documents and information considered, the analysis performed, and the opinions reached. Local rules and the attorney representing the client of the financial adviser determine the depth and nature of these reports and exhibits that may be provided to the opposing party. These reports are typically provided to the opposing attorney prior to the adviser's testimony.

Testimony for the financial adviser takes two forms. The first form of testimony the expert will encounter is the deposition. This testimony is used by the opposing party to discover what the expert will say at trial. In this context the expert is on the defensive, trying to improve his client's position in the litigation. When testifying at deposition, the expert must honestly and completely answer the questions posed by the opposing attorney. If the subpoena received by the expert is *duces tecum,* the expert must produce all documents covered by the request. It is important that the adviser understand that the contents of his file will be revealed to the opposing attorney.

The second form of testimony the expert will encounter is at trial. This is where the expert is on the offensive. The initial phase of the expert's testimony at trial is the *qualification* to be considered an expert for purposes of the rules. As explained previously, this is extremely important as it allows the individual to express opinions and to rely on hearsay from third parties to form those opinions.

It is imperative that financial advisers who wish to become testifying experts begin developing a resume early in their career. Many times, the expert's resume is the first exhibit offered during testimony. This document should detail professional qualifications and certifications. Memberships in professional organizations, as well as service on relevant committees within those organizations, need to be disclosed. Significant educational training, as well as speaking engagements, articles written, and publications written, need to be listed. The combination of these items on the resume, as well as the experts' testimony relating their qualifications to the opinions to be rendered in trial, will lead to qualification as an expert witness at trial.

It is not unusual for an expert's qualifications to be challenged. One method of challenge will be for the opposing attorney to request to *voir dire* the expert. This process allows the attorney to question the expert out of the normal order of testimony about the specific qualifications that the expert may possess. If the judge finds the expert is not qualified, or that the testimony will not be helpful to the court, the individual will not be allowed to testify.

Challenges to Testimony

There is another type of challenge that can confront experts. It is based on a case titled *Daubert*. In that case, expert testimony was challenged as not being based on accepted scientific methodologies and procedures. The court was treated as the gatekeeper to prevent testimony without scientific basis from being presented in the courtroom. Testimony was only allowed when there existed a methodology that was established and peer-reviewed that supported the opinions rendered. In some jurisdictions, there have been successful applications of this theory to financial testimony. In others, the theory has been discarded in financial testimony. Advisers must understand the status of this concept prior to serving in their jurisdiction. Financial advisers also need to be aware if there have been successful *Daubert* challenges of financial testimony in the local jurisdiction and, if so, be prepared to prevent that challenge from affecting their testimony.

Direct Examination

Direct examination occurs after the qualification of the adviser as an expert. The attorney representing the client will lead the adviser through a series of questions. It is not unusual for the expert to first be asked to detail what opinions have been formed and what the results of those opinions may be. The second series of questions will lay the foundation for the opinion testimony given. This will include detailing the documents reviewed, the procedures per-formed, and the calculations made. This testimony is helped by the preparation of demonstrative exhibits that support the opinions rendered. To the extent the exhibits can be graphical in nature, the better they are received and understood by the courts. The use of charts and graphs is widely accepted and many times is the most understandable manner in which the expert's opinion can be demonstrated.

Cross-Examination

After direct examination, the expert is subjected to cross-examina-tion. The most important thought the expert must maintain through this process is that he knows more regarding his testimo-ny than the attorney cross-examining him. The opposing attorney performs cross-examination to expose weaknesses in the expert's logic, methodology, and procedures. Responding to cross-exami-nation is a talent that is difficult to train. Questions are framed to require yes or no (sometimes called leading questions) answers and are arranged to lead the expert down logical paths that can impeach the opinions rendered. Upon completion of cross-exami-nation, the expert is typically released from further jurisdiction of the court.

The second role a financial adviser may play at trial is that of a factual witness. It is normal for attorneys to request information and documents from the parties' financial advisers. In these cir-cumstances, the adviser needs to be careful to fully comply with individual ethical requirements regarding the release of informa-tion. There is no question the information will be disclosed, but the professional should be careful to insure compliance with profes-sional and ethical disclosure requirements. Attorneys are sensitive to these requirements and are normally cooperative in assisting the professional achieve an appropriate comfort level.

It is possible the financial adviser may be called as a factual witness at trial. This is the most common role for advisers who have clients getting divorced. If that occurs, subpoenas may be issued and documents required to be produced. In these circumstances, it is important for the adviser to be open and candid in the testimony and document production. To do otherwise can subject the adviser to claims of damage.

NEUTRAL ROLES

There are several neutral roles the financial adviser can perform. The roles of mediator, arbitrator, special master, court-appointed witness, and settlement facilitator are all available.

Mediations are conducted by a mediator who typically has training that facilitates work with the parties to have them craft their own agreement based on their individual needs and not based on legally-imposed requirements. Mediations are conducted in a number of styles that vary from extremely directive to very supportive of the parties' needs. In all cases, mediations are nonbinding. The process is much quicker than the litigation process and promotes a faster resolution of the parties' dispute. There are jurisdictions that require every case to go through the mediation process before it can be tried. If the parties have complete disclosure, mediations are highly successful in allowing parties to settle their affairs in an orderly manner, consider their individual needs, and to proceed with their lives.

In some circumstances, the parties may request arbitration. Arbitration is normally binding and is conducted by one or more trained attorneys or specialists. Arbitration does not have formal discovery and is conducted much more quickly than a trial. Some attorneys do not recommend the arbitration process, as many times, the results are not subject to appeal.

Special masters are appointed by courts to deal with specific issues such as child support, property identification, accounting, or other financial matters. Special masters have powers to require parties to produce documents and information and have power to render judgements. In this process, the findings of the special master can always be appealed to the judge appointing the special master.

Court-appointed witnesses were first conceived under Rule 11-706 of the Federal Rules of Civil Procedure. Conceptually, the witness has a duty and obligation to the judge and not to the litigants. The court provides for the witness to be paid and receive information. The court also details procedures for dealing with the attorneys and the parties. Many judges prefer witnesses appointed by the court, as the witness does not have an allegiance to any party to the litigation.

Settlement facilitation is a process that develops within a limited time frame. Settlement facilitation will last somewhere between four hours to a full day. They are conducted in a directive manner to inform the litigants of weaknesses in their cases, the costs of continued litigation, and the uncertainty of outcomes in the courtroom. Attorneys and judges use this process in various ways. In some jurisdictions, judges assign cases to paid facilitators. In other jurisdictions, opposing attorneys will agree to submit a case to a respected third party for a strong-arm resolution. In no case is settlement facilitation binding unless an agreement is reached, but, in many cases, it provides an efficient resolution to the dispute.

CHAPTER 3

The Determination and Taxation of Divorce Property Divisions

PROPERTY THEORY AND ISSUES

There are generally two unique property ownership or division theories applied in the United States. These theories determine property ownership in marital relationships for purposes of gifting, bequeathing, and dissolution of marriages. First, there is the common law system, sometimes called equitable distribution for divorces, and second, there is the community property system. In most cases, the ownership of property acquired is determined at the time of its acquisition and by the source of the funds used to acquire the property. If property is acquired with marital or community funds, the property is treated as being marital or community property. If property is acquired with separate funds, the property is treated as separate property. When individuals carefully manage their financial affairs, it is possible to keep marital/community property apart from separate property. The courts look to financial advisers to provide documentary evidence of sources of funds used to acquire property. In many circumstances, because the individuals are not careful, or for other reasons, the ownership of property becomes mixed. When the ownership is mixed, disputes arise, and financial advisers are engaged to perform work and render opinions that allow the courts to divide that property.

Common Law or Marital Property

Common law is based on the English legal system where property ownership and division in a divorce are governed by established case precedents. Because it relies on decisions rendered in prior cases, this law varies from state to state. Under common law, property generally falls into one of two categories. Property is either marital property that was acquired during the parties' marriage or it is separate property not subject to division. Marital property is divided by the courts between the parties based on what the court determines is equitable, and based on what the individual state's case law would determine. Separate property is property acquired prior to the parties' marriage, property gifted to the individual, or property inherited by the individual. It also includes property acquired during the marriage using separate funds. Separate property remains the property of its owner, can be willed or gifted by the owner, and is not divided on the dissolution of the marriage. The Florida District Court of Appeal illustrates this well in the *Farrior* opinion. The entire text of the appeal is included as Exhibit 3.1.

EXHIBIT 3.1   *Farrior* Opinion, Florida District Court of Appeal

---

IN THE DISTRICT COURT OF APPEAL OF FLORIDA
SECOND DISTRICT
Case No. 96–01493

MARY LEE FARRIOR,
Appellant,
v.
J. REX FARRIOR, JR.,
Appellee.

Opinion filed June 12, 1998.

   Appeal from the Circuit Court for Hillsborough County; Debra K. Behnke, Judge.

   David A. Maney and Lorena L. Kiely of Maney, Damsker, Harris & Jones, P.A., Tampa; and Stuart C. Markman of Kynes, Markman & Felman, P.A., Tampa, for Appellant.

   A.J. Barranco, Jr. of A.J. Barranco & Associates, P.A., Miami; Robert F. Kohlman of Law Offices of Robert F. Kohlman, Miami; John R. Beranek of Ausley & McMullen, Tallahassee; and Robert W. Fields of Garcia & Fields, P.A., Tampa, for Appellee.

   PER CURIAM.

EXHIBIT 3.1 (Continued)

Mary Lee Farrior, the wife, appeals the final dissolution of marriage and contends the trial court erred in determining that stock inherited by her and remaining in her separate name until the date of dissolution was marital property. The Wife also argues the trial court erred when it failed to award her special equity in marital properties acquired on the strength of her substantial stock holdings. We affirm the trial court's finding that the Wife is not entitled to a special equity. We conclude, however, that the stock inherited by the Wife and titled solely in her name is nonmarital property and, accordingly, reverse and remand for the trial court's reconsideration of the equitable distribution of the marital assets in light of this opinion.

This was a long-term marriage. The parties were married in 1958, when the Wife was twenty-one years old and the husband, J. Rex Farrior, Jr., was thirty-one years old and a practicing attorney in Tampa. At the time of the dissolution in 1996, the total assets for consideration by the trial court were nearly $48 million, three-quarters of that amount being stock in the Wife's name which she inherited from her family. The Husband contends that all of these assets were marital assets as the result of an oral agreement entered between the parties early in the marriage when they agreed "there is no yours or mine, it's all ours."

In its order, the trial court specifically found that the stock in question was initially a nonmarital asset of the Wife. This finding constitutes a rejection of the Husband's argument that the oral agreement, allegedly entered into prior to the acquisition of the stock, converted all assets to marital assets. Although rejecting the oral contract theory, the trial court found that the Wife's separately-owned stock became a marital asset through commingling or intermingling. This finding was based upon three separate factors: first, the parties' equal access to the stock; second, use of the stock by the parties to provide luxuries and enrich their standard of living; and third, use of the stock as collateral for joint marital debts.

We reject the Husband's argument on appeal urging the oral contract as an alternative basis for affirming the equitable distribution scheme. We are persuaded by the parties' actions during their marriage rather than by reports and explanations of their early conversations. In so holding, we agree with the view expressed by one court that concluded, "To allow general conversation between husband and wife to constitute an 'agreement' between the parties, without more, is to turn the institution of marriage into an ongoing contract, the terms of which are mandated by each word spoken between the spouses." *Stainback v. Stainback,* 396 S.E.2d 686, 691 (Va. App. 1990). Accordingly, we turn our review to the factors relied upon by the trial court.

First, in finding that equal access to the funds constituted an intermingling which resulted in the Wife's separate property becoming marital prop-

(continues)

EXHIBIT 3.1   (*Continued*)

erty, the trial court cited four cases. *See Woodard v. Woodard,* 634 So. 2d 782 (Fla. 5th DCA 1994); *Amato v. Amato,* 596 So. 2d 1243 (Fla. 4th DCA 1992); *Crews v. Crews,* 536 So. 2d 353 (Fla. 1st DCA 1988); and *Walser v. Walser,* 473 So. 2d 306 (Fla. 2d DCA 1985). Each of these cases is factually distinguishable because they involved cash deposited into joint accounts to which each of the parties had access. As explained by *Amato,* "funds so intermingled lose their separate identity and become untraceable." 596 So. 2d at 1244 (citations omitted). In this case, the assets were stock certificates that were titled in the Wife's name alone. The stock certificates always maintained a separate identity and never became untraceable.

Additionally, the Husband's access to the stock was not equal to the access enjoyed by the Wife. While the Wife allowed the Husband to make decisions about whether the stock should be sold or traded, and even allowed the Husband to vote the stock, the stock remained titled in the Wife's name alone and was never placed in an account to which the Husband had equal access. Clearly the Wife deferred to the Husband's judgment on financial decisions related to the stock; however, the Husband's management was always dependent upon the Wife's signing of stock certificates. We can find no case, nor were the parties able to provide us with any law, that converts this arrangement into a presumption of gift as occurs when monies are deposited into a joint account and are thereby equally available to either party. Because the evidence does not support a finding that the Husband had equal access to the Wife's stock, we conclude the stock in the Wife's name did not become a marital asset by intermingling.

As a second factor, the trial court relied upon use of the stock to provide luxuries and enrichment to the parties during the marriage. *Claughton v. Claughton,* 483 So. 2d 447 (Fla. 3d DCA 1986), cited by the trial court, held that assets may be converted from nonmarital to marital assets when they are intermingled and "used to provide luxuries for the family and enrich the standard of living." 483 So. 2d at 449. Based on this holding, the Third District remanded for the trial court to determine if the husband's salary and other acquired assets became marital assets through intermingling. *See* 483 So. 2d at 450. We conclude that *Claughton* does not stand for the proposition that providing luxuries and enriching the standard of living is an indication of intermingling. Rather, *Claughton* holds that nonmarital assets *which are intermingled* to provide luxuries and an enriched standard of living should be treated as marital assets.

Although we reject the trial court's interpretation of *Claughton* as applied to the stock itself, we hold that the trial court correctly applied *Claughton* to the acquisitions purchased with income from the stock. In rejecting the Wife's claim of special equity, the trial court correctly found that the many acquisitions of the parties resulted from the Wife's interspousal gift of the income from her nonmarital assets and thus became marital assets.

EXHIBIT 3.1 (Continued)

Third, the trial court concluded that the pledge of the Wife's individually-titled stock as collateral for marital loans resulted in the stock becoming a marital asset. In reaching this conclusion, the trial court relied upon *Adams v. Adams,* 604 So. 2d 494 (Fla. 3d DCA 1992). Even if we were to agree with *Adams,* the trial court found that less than fifty percent of the Wife's separately-held stock was ever used as collateral and thus would not convert all of the Wife's stock into a marital asset. We find no other cases, however, that follow the rule advocated by the Husband. And we conclude there is no equitable basis for a rule that punishes a spouse who uses nonmarital property to finance the acquisition of marital property by then converting the nonmarital collateral to marital property. It is completely illogical to say that the pledge of $10 million in stock to secure a $100,000 debt would convert the $10 million in stock to a marital asset. To the extent our decision conflicts with *Adams,* we certify the conflict.

In reversing this case, we stop to applaud the trial judge's effort to reach a fair resolution in this bitter and hotly-contested dissolution action. Although we may agree that the trial court's decision appears to be fair in light of the long-term marriage, we conclude that it is not legally sustainable under the law of equitable distribution. Section 61.075, Florida Statutes (1995), sets forth the rules for equitable distribution, including definitions of marital and nonmarital property. Section 61.075(5)(b)2 specifically defines nonmarital assets as "[a]ssets acquired separately by either party by noninterspousal gift, bequest, devise, or descent, and assets acquired in exchange for such assets." We conclude the status of the inherited stock did not change during the marriage and thus continued to be a nonmarital asset at the time of the dissolution.

Having determined that the trial court erred in equally dividing all of the separately-owned stock of the Wife, we reverse the equitable distribution. Upon remand, the trial court may make certain adjustments in the equitable distribution that were not considered when it ordered the equal division of all assets. The trial court found that the Wife's stock, although it appreciated passively to a great extent, was also enhanced by the Husband's efforts. To the extent the trial court can find that this stock was enhanced through the efforts of the Husband, the enhancement would become marital property and thus subject to division. We also note that, as part of the equitable distribution, the Husband's inheritance receivable was included as an asset to be divided between the parties. Unless the Husband agreed to the inclusion of this asset to be divided with the marital assets, it appears it would be a separate asset that should be awarded to the Husband.

Accordingly, we reverse. On remand, the trial court shall redetermine the equitable distribution in conformance with this opinion.

Reversed and remanded.

PARKER, C.J., and BLUE and WHATLEY, JJ., Concur.

Each state has its individual laws that determine when the marital estate terminates. In some instances, the estate terminates on the separation of the parties and in others, it terminates upon divorce.

Community Property

There are ten states that follow the community property system of property division: Alaska, California, Arizona, New Mexico, Texas, Louisiana, Wisconsin, Idaho, Nevada, and Washington. All other states are common law states. Of the ten states that follow the community property system, some generally follow the Spanish legal system, Louisiana follows the French legal system, and Wisconsin and California follow a legislated system. General community property theory provides that all property acquired during the marriage is community in nature, is jointly owned by the parties, and is subject to division upon divorce. The community is considered to own the value of any labor produced during the marriage, whether that labor is compensated by a third party or goes to the improvement of property owned by the parties. In a landmark case, the Supreme Court of California illustrates a method with which to divide invested labor from a separate property business in its *Pereira* decision. That decision is included as Exhibit 3.2.

EXHIBIT 3.2 *Pereira* Decision, The Supreme Court of California

---

Pereira v. Pereira

SUPREME COURT of CALIFORNIA
S. F. No. 4882.
156 C 1, 103 P 488, CFLP §G.72

June 30, 1909

ANNA AGNES PEREIRA, Respondent, v. FRANK PEREIRA, Appellant.

APPEAL from an interlocutory judgment of the Superior Court of Alameda County in an action of divorce. William H. Waste, Judge.
Arthur J. Dannenbaum, and Meyer Jacobs, for Appellant.
Snook & Church, Charles S. Wheeler, and J. F. Bowie, for Respondent.
Opinion by Shaw, J.; Angellotti, J., Sloss, J., Henshaw, J., Lorigan, J., and Melvin, J., concurred.

EXHIBIT 3.2 (*Continued*)

DIVORCE—AGREEMENT FOR DIVISION OF PROPERTY IN EVENT OF FUTURE DELINQUENCY OF HUSBAND—CONTRACT AGAINST PUBLIC POLICY.

An agreement between a husband and wife, executed pending an action for divorce instituted by her, whereby she waived the pending cause of action and agreed to dismiss it, and he agreed that in the event he should thereafter so conduct himself as to give her a new cause of action for divorce, and she should establish the same in a subsequent action, he would pay her a specified sum of money, which she agreed to accept in full satisfaction of her property rights, is against public policy and void.

ID.—COMMUNITY PROPERTY—PROFITS OF SEPARATE ESTATE INVESTED IN BUSINESS—INTEREST ON CAPITAL.

Where at the time of his marriage a husband has a definite amount of his separate property invested as capital in his business, which he afterwards continues to carry on at great profit, in determining what portion of such profit is community property, it must be presumed, in the absence of evidence to the contrary, that some of the profits were justly due to the capital invested and would constitute his separate property, and that the amount thereof would be equivalent to at least the usual interest on a long investment well secured.

ID.—APPEAL BY HUSBAND FROM DIVORCE JUDGMENT—INCREASE OF PROPERTY AWARD TO WIFE.

Upon an appeal by the husband from a judgment of divorce, which determined that the community property was of a specified value and awarded the wife a three-fifths part thereof, the court cannot change the judgment by increasing the share of the community property given to her.

ID.—MODIFICATION OF JUDGEMENT ON APPEAL—DEDUCTION OF SEPARATE PROPERTY—LEGAL INTEREST ON CAPITAL OF BUSINESS.

Where the trial court erred in including in such community property any portion of the profits of the business conducted by the husband properly to be credited to his separate property invested therein, and there was no evidence to show that such capital was entitled to a greater return than legal interest, this court may, on an appeal by the husband, upon the wife's application therefor, direct the judgment to be modified, so as to allow the husband, as part of his separate estate, interest at the rate of seven per cent on the amount of such capital.

ID.—INTERLOCUTORY JUDGMENT—PROPERTY RIGHTS MAY BE DETERMINED—CUSTODY OF CHILDREN.

Under the amendment of 1903 to sections 131 and 132 of the Civil Code, the trial court has the power, at the time of rendering the interlocutory

(*continues*)

EXHIBIT 3.2   (*Continued*)

judgment of divorce, to try and determine the issues between the parties to the action with respect to property and the custody of children. While this may, and generally should be done, the court has the power, under such amendment, as it always has had the power under previous laws, to postpone the trial and decision of such issues to any reasonable time after the rendition of the judgment of divorce, whether interlocutory or final.

ID.—POSTPONEMENT OF FINALITY OF INTERLOCUTORY JUDGMENT—PROPER PRACTICE.

The practice is to be commended of the trial court, in an action of divorce, determining all the issues in one trial and rendering an interlocutory judgment declaring the rights of the parties upon all the issues, and providing that the same should in all respects become final only at the time when the decree of divorce became final, in the mean time allowing temporary alimony.

The facts are stated in the opinion of the court.

The plaintiff obtained an interlocutory judgment of divorce on the ground of extreme cruelty. This judgment also declared that the plaintiff should have three-fifths of the community property when the divorce became final, that she should thereafter have custody of her minor child by the marriage, and it provided for temporary alimony to her and for the custody of the child during the time that would elapse between the interlocutory judgment and the final judgment. The defendant appealed from this interlocutory judgment within sixty days after the rendition thereof. This appeal is presented upon the judgment-roll and upon a bill of exceptions containing the evidence.

It is conceded that the evidence was sufficient to justify the divorce and the award of the custody of the child to plaintiff. The claim of the appellant is that the court erred in the finding as to the amount of the community property and in excluding evidence relating thereto.

1. The first point to be noticed is the ruling of the court declaring void a contract between the parties relating to their property and the division thereof, and in refusing to enforce or consider it in that connection. We are of the opinion that the court properly refused to consider this contract on the ground that it was plainly against public policy. The present action was begun on January 21, 1905. A previous action of divorce on the ground of extreme cruelty consisting in large part of the same acts assigned in the present complaint was commenced by the plaintiff against the defendant on September 23, 1904. After that action was begun the parties became reconciled, resumed marital relations, and on November 1, 1904, the plaintiff dismissed the action. On November 4, 1904, in pursuance of negotiations begun before the dismissal but after the reconciliation, the contract in question was exe-

EXHIBIT 3.2 (Continued)

cuted. It was dated November 1st and it recites that the previous action was then pending. Therein the plaintiff expressly waived the cause for divorce alleged in said complaint and agreed to dismiss the action. The contract further provided that none of the relatives of either party should settle in, be invited to, or visit the home without the consent of both parties; that if the husband should thereafter so conduct himself as to give the wife a new cause of action for divorce, and she should establish the same in a subsequent action against him for divorce or maintenance, the husband should thereupon pay to the wife ten thousand dollars, which should be a full satisfaction, settlement, and discharge of all claims of the wife in such action "for alimony, costs, counsel fees, support, maintenance of herself, homestead, homestead right, property and benefit of every kind and character." It also declared that "in the event of the institution of such subsequent action all claims and demands by her or on her part in or to any moneys, property rights, or property, community or otherwise, now or hereafter owned or acquired by" the defendant, other than said ten thousand dollars "are hereby forever settled, liquidated, relinquished, released, waived and abandoned, and no claim, demand, or monetary or property benefit or relief shall ever be claimed, asserted or sought in, by or by reason of said subsequent action, should it be instituted, except only to the extent aforesaid."

The Civil Code provides that the husband and wife may enter into any engagement with the other respecting property which they might enter into if not married, subject to the law as to fiduciary relations in general (sec. 158); and that they may agree, in writing, to an immediate separation and may make provision for the support of either of them and of their children during such separation, but that they cannot by contract, otherwise alter their legal relations, except as to property. (Sec. 159.) There was in this contract no agreement for separation, and, hence, the agreement to pay ten thousand dollars cannot be upheld as a provision for the support of the wife on a separation, as provided in section 159. The real effect of the contract to pay the ten thousand dollars, so far as the husband is concerned, would be to provide against liability for a contemplated wrong to be subsequently inflicted by him upon his wife, and to liquidate such liability in advance of the commission of the wrong. The evidence and findings show that the defendant was then possessed of property worth about seventy-seven thousand dollars, was engaged in a very lucrative business, and was receiving an income of about eleven thousand dollars a year which he had every reason to believe would continue. By this contract, if valid, he was left free to inflict upon his wife the most grievous marital wrongs, such as would compel her to obtain a divorce, secure in the protection of his contract that ten thousand dollars would satisfy all her claims against him of a pecuniary nature or in relation to the com-

(continues)

EXHIBIT 3.2   *(Continued)*

munity property. If he should, after its execution, be moved by evil impulse to commit anew the offenses against his wife which first gave her cause for divorce, or other acts having the same legal effect, the existence of a valid contract of this sort could not but encourage him to yield to his baser inclinations, and inflict the injury. As it was obviously adapted to produce this result, it is to be presumed that this was one of the inducements which made him desire its execution. The law does not countenance such agreements. "Any contract between the parties having for its object the dissolution of the marriage contract, or facilitating that result, . . . is void as contra bonos mores." (*Loveren v. Loveren,* 106 Cal. 512, [39 Pac. 802], quoting *Phillip v. Thorp,* 10 Or. 494; *Beard v. Beard,* 65 Cal. 354, [4 Pac. 229]; *Newman v. Freitas,* 129 Cal. 289, [61 Pac. 907].) In *Seeley's Appeal,* 56 Conn. 206, [14 Atl. 291], the court says: "Inasmuch as the state rests upon the family and is vitally interested in the permanency of a marriage relation once established, it, for the promotion of public welfare, and of private morals as well, makes itself a party to every marriage contract entered into within its jurisdiction, in this sense, that it will not permit the dissolution thereof by the other party thereto. Its consent in the form of a decree of its court passed after hearing in due process of law, is a prerequisite for a divorce. . . . Courts will not enforce any contract which is the price of consent by one party to the marriage relation, to the procurement of a divorce by the other." And, in reference to a similar agreement to that in the case at bar, the court in the case just cited said: "Presumably each party saw in that agreement an individual advantage; to him, in that he possibly paid her less thereby than the judgment of the court upon hearing would compel; to her, in that he refrained therefor from answering the allegations of her petition by proof, and thus possibly permitted a divorce which he could have prevented."

Before the contract was made, or its terms agreed to, the parties had made up their former differences and had become reconciled. It shows by its terms that it is not an agreement to settle property rights accruing by reason of a marital offense already perpetrated and complete as a cause for divorce. There is therefore no force in the claim, as applied to this case, that it is competent evidence, or valid as a settlement of such rights, even if it were conceded that such an agreement might under some circumstances be permitted to stand. The court also found that this contract was procured by the husband through undue influence and by fraud. Our conclusions upon the point that it was against public policy makes it unnecessary to consider the sufficiency of the evidence to sustain these findings.

2. The court found that the community property of the parties was of the value of $57,664.77. It is claimed that this is not sustained by the evidence.

EXHIBIT 3.2 *(Continued)*

There is practically no conflict on the subject, there being no witness to that point except the defendant. The findings state that this property consisted of the real estate on which the defendant carried on business, which was of the value of forty-five thousand dollars, and certain money on hand, making up the remainder. The evidence shows that the plaintiff and defendant intermarried on April 19, 1900. At that time the defendant was, and he ever since has been, carrying on a saloon and cigar business, then producing a net income of about five thousand dollars annually. He owned the cigar and saloon stock and fixtures, worth in all about fifteen thousand five hundred dollars, and had, besides, some six thousand dollars in cash. Soon after the marriage he bought the home wherein the parties afterwards lived, paying twenty-seven hundred dollars therefor, and he afterwards expended thereon twenty-three hundred dollars in improving it. This home is adjudged to be his separate property and plaintiff is given no interest in it. A year and a half after his marriage he bought the property in which he was carrying on business at the price of forty thousand dollars. He paid in cash therefor five thousand dollars and afterwards, out of his income, he paid the balance of the price and accumulated the cash on hand at the time of the trial, in addition, amounting to over twelve thousand dollars. His net income at the time of the trial was about eleven thousand dollars a year. From the time of his marriage to the time of trial he allowed his wife seventy-five dollars a month to run the house and she made her own clothes. There is an unexplained discrepancy between the total amount of his income less the household expenses, and his total gains. He must have received more than he was willing to disclose, if his net income over household expenses amounted to as much as the money which he admits he has received, not allowing anything for his personal expenses.

The court may have believed that he had other property which he had succeeded in concealing. There was some justification for this inference, for he was caught in the act of attempting to conceal $7,761 of the cash on hand by means of a New York draft which he had carried in his pocket for the four months preceding the trial. It appears, however, that the decision of the court was made upon the theory that all of his gains received after marriage, from whatever sources, were to be classed as community property, and that no allowance was made in favor of his separate estate on account of interest or profit on the fifteen thousand five hundred dollars invested in the business at the time of the marriage. This capital was undoubtedly his separate estate. The fund remained in the business after marriage and was used by him in carrying it on. The separate property should have been credited with some amount as profit on this capital. It was not a losing business but a very profitable one. It is true that it is very clearly shown that the principal part of the

(continues)

EXHIBIT 3.2   *(Continued)*

large income was due to the personal character, energy, ability, and capacity of the husband. This share of the earnings was, of course, community property. But without capital he could not have carried on the business. In the absence of circumstances showing a different result, it is to be presumed that some of the profits were justly due to the capital invested. There is nothing to show that all of it was due to defendant's efforts alone. The probable contribution of the capital to the income should have been determined from all the circumstances of the case, and as the business was profitable it would amount at least to the usual interest on a long investment well secured. (*Boggess v. Richards,* 39 W. Va. 576, [45 Am. St. Rep. 938, 20 S. E. 599]; *Trapnell v. Conkling,* 37 W. Va. 252, [38 Am. St. Rep. 30, 16 S. E. 570]; *Penn v. Whitehead,* 17 Gratt. 573, [94 Am. Dec. 478]; *Glidden v. Taylor,* 16 Ohio St. 509, [91 Am. Dec. 98].) We think the court erred in refusing to increase the proportion of separate property and decrease the community property to the extent of the reasonable gain to the separate estate from the earnings properly allowable on account of the capital invested.

It is true that the disposition of the community property by the superior court, in all particulars, including matters committed to its discretion, is subject to revision in this court on appeal. (Civ. Code, sec. 148; *Eslinger v. Eslinger,* 47 Cal. 64; *Brown v. Brown,* 60 Cal. 580; *Strozynski v. Strozynski,* 97 Cal. 192, [31 Pac. 1130].) In each of these cases the supreme court increased the wife's share of the community property from one half, as given by the trial court, to three fourths. But the wife has not appealed and we cannot, upon the husband's appeal, change the judgment by increasing the share of community property given to the wife. The only error, in respect to community property, which we can consider upon this appeal by the husband, is the error in classing as community property that part of the gains which was derived from the "issues and profits" of his separate property (Civ. Code, sec. 163), the amount of which we cannot determine. It will be necessary to remand the case for a retrial of this issue. The court below will be free, upon such new trial, to apportion a larger share of the community property to the plaintiff, or to divide it between the parties in such shares as it shall deem just, under all the circumstances. The present division seems fair in point of fact.

3. The appellant further claims that, under the amendment of 1903 to sections 131 and 132 of the Civil Code, the court has no power, at or before the time of rendering the interlocutory judgment of divorce, to make any inquiry, finding, or decree with respect to the property rights of the parties, or with respect to any other subject connected with the divorce, except the right of the complainant to a divorce. Section 131 on this point is as follows: "In actions for divorce the court must file its decision and conclusions of law as in other cases and if it determines that no divorce shall be granted, final judg-

EXHIBIT 3.2   *(Continued)*

ment must thereupon be entered accordingly. If it determines that the divorce ought to be granted an interlocutory judgment must be entered, declaring that the party in whose favor the court decides is entitled to a divorce." Section 132 provides that when "one year has expired after the entry of such interlocutory judgment, the court on motion of either party, or upon its own motion, may enter the final judgment granting the divorce, and such final judgment shall restore them to the status of single persons, and permit either to marry after the entry thereof; and such other and further relief as may be necessary to a complete disposition of the action. . . . The death of either party after the entry of the interlocutory judgment does not impair the power of the court to enter final judgment as hereinbefore provided; but such entry shall not validate any marriage contracted by either party before the entry of such final judgment, nor constitute any defense of any criminal prosecution made against either." As these provisions were made after the other sections of the code had been in force for many years, it was to be expected that the new provisions would not in all respects be consistent in language with other sections on the same subject. In section 146 the code speaks of a disposition of the community property "in case of the dissolution of the marriage." In section 147 the code declares that "the court in rendering a decree of divorce, must make such order for the disposition of the community property and of the homestead as in this chapter provided"; and in section 90 it declares that marriage is dissolved only by the judgment of a court of competent jurisdiction declaring a divorce. From these provisions it is argued by the appellant that the court's power to make a disposition of the property rights of the parties exists only at the time when the divorce judgment becomes final and that any act attempted to be accomplished before that, in the way of a trial or interlocutory judgment declaring the property rights or the rights to the custody of children, is *coram non judice* and void.

We do not think that the code provision requires such a narrow construction. When the history of legislation on the subject and the conditions existing at the time of the adoption of the amendment of 1903 are considered, the purpose, meaning, and effect of that amendment are not difficult to discover. While the law deems it necessary to provide that a divorce may be granted when conditions are such as to make the marriage relation intolerable, it is nevertheless true that the policy of the law does not favor the dissolution of marriages. It has been generally believed that many divorces were sought, not in good faith, but because a roving fancy had found another affinity more attractive, and that a dissolution was often desired solely for the purpose of forming a new marital connection. With the design of providing conditions under which it would be understood that ardent passions of this character must perforce have time to cool before a new marriage relation

(continues)

EXHIBIT 3.2   (*Continued*)

could be actually formed, the legislature, in 1897, enacted a law in effect providing that no marriage should be entered into by any divorced person, until at least one year had elapsed after the decree of divorce was rendered. (Stats. 1897, p. 34.) It had become customary to avoid the provisions of this act by the expedient of going to an adjacent state for the purpose of entering into a new marital relation. This court was compelled to hold that marriages contracted in another state were valid in this state, although they were entered into within less than a year after a divorce had been granted in this state to one of the parties. (*Estate of Wood,* 137 Cal. 129, [69 Pac. 900].) The purpose of the amendment of 1903 was to carry into effect the object attempted to be attained by the statute of 1897. To do this the expedient was adopted of delaying the final judgment in divorce cases for the period of one year after it was judicially ascertained that a divorce should be granted. By thus making the right to a divorce ineffective for the period of one year, it became impossible for the parties to contract a valid new marriage anywhere until at least a year after the trial of the action of divorce had taken place. Except so far as was necessary to accomplish this object, it was not the intent of the statute to change in any respect the practice and procedure in actions for divorce. We do not doubt that the court has the same power now that it has always had to try and determine the issues between the parties in a divorce action with respect to property and custody of children, and that this may, and generally should, be done at the same time as the issues with respect to the cause for divorce are tried and determined. Unquestionably the court would have power under the present law, as it always has had the power under previous laws, to postpone the trial and decision of the property rights and custody of the children to any reasonable time after the rendition of the judgment of divorce, whether interlocutory or final. The amendment has not changed its power in this respect. It is proper in all actions for divorce to try the entire action at the same time as the issues respecting divorce are tried and to give an interlocutory judgment declaring the rights of the parties with respect to property and children.

We commend the action of the court below in this case in declaring, in its interlocutory decree concerning the property, that the rights therein specified should become final at the time the decree of divorce became final. We are not called upon here to determine whether the adjudication of property rights would or would not have been final at the expiration of six months from the time of the entry of the interlocutory decree, if no appeal had been taken, and the parties had, before the expiration of one year and after the expiration of the six months, by mutual consent, procured an order from the court annulling the interlocutory decree of divorce; or whether such annullment would have had the effect of setting aside the decree relating to property rights and children. These questions are not involved in this case and it will be well to leave them for future disposition in some case where they are

EXHIBIT 3.2 *(Continued)*

---

directly presented. In the present case the court determined all the issues in one trial and rendered an interlocutory judgment declaring the rights of the parties upon all the issues, and providing that the same should in all respects become final only at the time when the decree of divorce became final, in the mean time allowing temporary alimony. We see no objection to this practice and commend it as not only within the power of the court but as a proper method of the exercise of that power.

The judgment as to the amount and value of the community property and as to the disposition thereof between the parties is reversed and the cause is remanded for a new trial and judgment upon that issue alone. In all other particulars the judgment is affirmed.

Angellotti, J., Sloss, J., Henshaw, J., Lorigan, J., and Melvin, J., concurred. On the thirtieth day of July, 1909, the court in Bank filed the following opinion and modification of the judgment:—THE COURT.

Since the filing of the opinion in this case, the plaintiff has asked that, instead of remanding the case for a new trial of the issues as to the property, the judgment be modified in regard thereto, and has filed a written consent that the defendant be allowed, as part of his separate estate, out of the cash on hand, interest at the rate of seven per cent on the $15,500 found to be the capital invested in his business. This removes the objection to directing a modification of the judgment. The defendant introduced no evidence to show that the capital invested was entitled to a greater return than legal interest, and in the absence of such evidence, the burden of proof being upon him, that would be the utmost he could claim. The wife would have been entitled to an opportunity to prove, if she could, that it earned a smaller proportion of the profits than legal interest, and, she being the respondent, it was for that reason considered necessary to order a new trial for that purpose. Her consent aforesaid avoids this necessity and leaves the case in such condition that a modification of the judgment will end the litigation with justice to both parties. (*Fox v. Hale & Norcross S. Mfg. Co.,* 122 Cal. 221, [54 Pac. 731].)

Interest at seven per cent on the $15,500 from April 19, 1900, the date of the marriage, to November 3, 1905, the time of the trial, amounts to $6012.70. Deducting this from $12,139.03, found to be the cash on hand at the time of the trial, leaves $6126.33, as the part of the cash belonging to the community. The plaintiff's three fifths of this is $3675.86 and the defendant's two fifths is $2450.47.

It is ordered that the judgment be modified by changing the respective statements of the shares of each in the cash on hand therein, so that the part relating to the plaintiff's share shall read as follows:—

(continues)

EXHIBIT 3.2 *(Continued)*

"2nd. The sum of three thousand six hundred and seventy-five and 86-100 dollars ($3675.86), in cash, being three fifths of the sum of $6126.33 in cash found by the supreme court to be community property of the plaintiff and defendant; and that no interest in defendant's separate property be awarded to plaintiff."

And so that the part relating to the defendant's share shall read as follows:—

"2nd. The sum of two thousand four hundred and fifty and 47-100 dollars ($2450.47), in cash, being two fifths of the sum found to be community property as aforesaid."

And that as so modified the judgment stand affirmed, the plaintiff to recover all costs.

Cal. 1909.

ANNA AGNES PEREIRA, Respondent, v. FRANK PEREIRA, Appellant.

A second California case from the District Court of Appeal that illustrates another method of dividing separate property from community labor is the *Van Camp* opinion. This case is included as Exhibit 3.3.

EXHIBIT 3.3   *Van Camp* Opinion

Van Camp v. Van Camp

District Court of Appeal, Second District, Division 1, California
Civ. No. 3603, Civ. No. 3604
53 CA 17, 199 P 885, CFLP §G.73

May 26, 1921.

EUPHRASIA VAN CAMP, Respondent, v. FRANK VAN CAMP, Appellant

APPEALS from a judgment of the Superior Court of Los Angeles County. Charles S. Crail, Judge. Affirmed and reversed.

Kemp & Clewett for Appellant in Civil No. 3603 and for Respondent in Civil No. 3604.

Fredericks & Hanna for Respondent in Civil No. 3603 and for Appellant in Civil No. 3604.

EXHIBIT 3.3 *(Continued)*

All the Justices concurred, except Wilbur, J., who was absent.

HEADNOTES

(1) DIVORCE—CONFLICT OF EVIDENCE—APPEAL.

Where in an action for divorce the evidence upon most of the issues is conflicting, the appellate court in considering the question as to whether the evidence is sufficient to sustain the findings is not permitted to weigh the testimony and determine as to where the preponderance lies.

(2) ID.—EXTREME CRUELTY—IMPROPER CONDUCT OF HUSBAND WITH CORESPONDENT.

—Acts tending to show improper relations of a husband with a corespondent may cause a wife sufficient mental suffering to constitute extreme cruelty.

(3) ID.—EXTREME CRUELTY—NATURE OF ACTS AND CONDUCT.

—Acts and conduct of either spouse, unjustifiable under a reasonable rule of marital behavior, which in any case may cause great physical suffering or mental torture, are sufficient to sustain a charge of extreme cruelty, although conduct which might amount to cruelty in case of a refined and sensitive spouse might not amount to such in the case of a person of no refinement and of a coarse nature.

(4) COMMUNITY PROPERTY—PRESUMPTION.

—All property in the possession of either husband or wife is deemed to be the community estate of the parties, notwithstanding the declaration of section 163 of the Civil Code that all property owned by the husband before marriage with the rents, issues, and profits thereof is his separate property, but such presumption is disputable and may be overcome by evidence to the contrary.

Whether profits accruing during marriage in connection with property belonging to separate estate of either spouse are community property, note, 31 L. R. A. (N. S.) 1092.

(5) ID.—MANAGEMENT OF CORPORATION—SALARY AND EXPENSES—INCOME FROM STOCK OWNED BEFORE MARRIAGE— SEPARATE PROPERTY OF HUSBAND.

—Where a husband at the time of his marriage was a man of large means, which included cash, notes, real estate, and corporate stock, and where during his marriage he devoted his exclusive attention to the management of a corporation for which he received a large salary and an additional amount for expenses incurred in the conduct of the business, his income during his married life outside of such salary and expenses was the rents,

(continues)

EXHIBIT 3.3   *(Continued)*

issues, and profits of his separate property owned by him before his marriage, and therefore his separate property, notwithstanding some of the income was from stock owned by him in the corporation and the result of his skillful management thereof.

(6) ID.—FAMILY SUPPORT—PAYMENT FROM COMMUNITY FUNDS—PRESUMPTION.

—In the absence of any evidence showing a different practice, the rule is that the community earnings of husband and wife are chargeable with the family support, and any amount expended for such purpose by either spouse is presumed to have been paid out of the community estate.

The facts are stated in the opinion of the court.

MAJORITY OPINION
THE COURT

—This is an action for divorce. Defendant Van Camp has appealed from a decree dissolving the marital bonds, and also from that portion of the judgment awarding to the plaintiff the sum of $60,000, and determining that certain real and personal property is the separate property of the wife. The judgment in favor of the wife for $60,000 was made upon the finding of the court that the community property was of the value of $90,000 and that the plaintiff was entitled to two-thirds thereof. There is a separate appeal taken by the wife from the judgment in so far as it fixes the value of the community estate, it being the contention of the plaintiff that the latter was of a value greatly in excess of $90,000. As the defendant's appeal involves contentions opposite to that of the plaintiff respecting the property judgment, we will consider the appeals together when that feature of the decree is given attention.

In her complaint the plaintiff first charged (on her information and belief) that the husband had committed adultery with a person who was named as corespondent, on two specific occasions, and at other times the dates of which were not stated. A course of improper conduct as occurring between the defendant and the corespondent was described in a separate cause of action and made the ground for a charge of extreme cruelty. As a part of this alleged cause of action it was also set forth that upon one occasion defendant had struck the plaintiff and called her "a damn fool." By reason of the acts and conduct of the defendant, as so described in the second alleged cause of action, plaintiff asserted that she had been caused "great and grievous mental suffering and anguish," and had been caused to "brood and worry to the point of distraction," and "that such mental suffering, anguish, brooding, and worry have seriously impaired the plaintiff's health and vitality." The court in its findings determined that the acts of adultery had not been committed but added to the findings touching these matters that "the plaintiff had probable and reasonable cause to believe" that defendant did commit the acts charged. It is urged that the findings are not sustained by

EXHIBIT 3.3 (*Continued*)

the evidence, either upon the divorce issues or as to the value of property belonging to the marital community. These contentions will be considered in the order named. In the year 1914 defendant Van Camp came from Indianapolis to Los Angeles. His family then consisted of a grown son. He was a man of large affairs and had been the directing head of an extensive packing establishment in Indianapolis bearing his name. He brought to California property of great value, consisting largely of cash and stock securities. After his arrival in Los Angeles he organized the Van Camp Sea Food Company. The company was capitalized with 2,000 shares of stock at a par value of $100 each. He became the president and general manager of the corporation and received up to January, 1918, a salary of $1,000 per month. This salary was increased on January 1, 1918, to $1,500 per month and so remained at all times subsequent thereto. The packing plant was located at the seaport town of San Pedro. More particular consideration will be given to the details of defendant's capital, his investments, earnings, and income when we later take up the points raised as against the finding of the court as to the value of the community holdings. We will here pass that subject with the observation that the packing company organized by Van Camp was a successful venture and produced large returns. In March of 1916 defendant Van Camp married the plaintiff, who was or had been an employee in the postoffice at San Pedro. Plaintiff was then twenty-one years of age; the defendant was about fifty-four years old. Immediately upon the marriage, defendant purchased a home in the city of Los Angeles, expending therefor about the sum of $15,000, and the deed to the place was made to the wife. Not long thereafter defendant delivered to the wife a certificate of deposit representing a cash credit of $10,000 and a deed to a lot at San Pedro. Defendant further provided each month for the plaintiff a cash allowance for household expenses which, at the time of the commencement of this proceeding, was $450; he also provided plaintiff with an automobile. The evidence goes to show that defendant was in the main liberal in the direction of gratifying all the wishes of his wife as to things desired for her pleasure and comfort. The mother of plaintiff resided at San Pedro and received partial support, at least, from the exchequer of Van Camp. [1] Considering the question as to whether the evidence is sufficient to sustain the findings of the court as to the facts upon which the decree of divorce is based, we are not permitted to weigh testimony and determine as to where the preponderance lies, for in the presence of a conflict such as appears here upon most of the issues, the determination of the trial judge as to facts must be deemed conclusive. The evidence then must be viewed from the standpoint that will give to it the strongest weight in sustaining the findings of the court. The record of the evidence is of large volume and in support of the plaintiff's case it shows that

(*continues*)

EXHIBIT 3.3 (*Continued*)

several years after the marriage of the parties, particularly in the year 1919, defendant Van Camp was often seen in the company of the corespondent, who was employed in the office of the Van Camp Company; that the two would be together in the automobile of defendant and that the frequency of their association in that manner was brought to the attention of plaintiff's family and others, and also reported to the plaintiff; that upon one of the earlier occasions plaintiff remonstrated with her husband and he admitted the wrongfulness of his conduct and promised not to repeat it; notwithstanding that promise he continued to conduct himself in the same manner with the corespondent; that he neglected the plaintiff in the home, became irritable and upon one occasion, when she took a paper from his hand and requested him to talk to her, struck her and called her "a damn fool"; that upon another occasion he drove in his automobile with the corespondent away from the traveled highway and into a thickly wooded grove, where he remained for a considerable time alone with the corespondent; that plaintiff at this time, in company with her mother and another person, pursued defendant into the grove and upbraided him with accusations of improper conduct, to which accusations he made the response that he had nothing to say; that plaintiff, prior to the alleged misconduct of the defendant had been well and not affected by illness of any kind, but that the knowledge of the alleged misdoings of the defendant so preyed upon her mind that she became nervous and ill; that she was unable to sleep and cried a great deal. There was sufficient corroboration of the particulars furnished to satisfy the requirement of the code. Defendant admitted the occurrence in the grove, when he was accosted by the wife. He claimed that he had merely stopped to eat fruit with the corespondent, but expressly declined to make any explanation as to why he had selected a secluded place away from the main thoroughfare. [2] Appellant makes the point that all of the acts found by the court to have been committed by him which tended to show improper relations with the corespondent were acts showing, if anything, only an adulterous intent, and that they were not available to the plaintiff for the purpose of establishing any cause of action except that of adultery. This contention rests upon the early cases of *Haskell v. Haskell,* 54 Cal. 262, and *Waldron v. Waldron,* 85 Cal. 251, [9 L. R. A. 487, 24 Pac. 649, 858]. These decisions do give decided aid to the contention, but are not now the law. (See *Barnes v. Barnes,* 95 Cal. 171, [16 L. R. A. 660, 30 Pac. 298]; *Wolff v. Wolff,* 102 Cal. 433, [36 Pac. 767, 1037].) [3] Acts and conduct of either spouse, unjustifiable under a reasonable rule of marital behavior, which in any case may cause great physical suffering or mental torture, are sufficient to sustain a charge of extreme cruelty. We state that as a general proposition, but it is subject always to the qualification that conduct which may in one case cause such suffering may not, in another, have the same effect. Thus the use of vulgar and profane epithets may, in the case of a highly cultured, refined, and sensitive woman, produce an effect of great mental

EXHIBIT 3.3 *(Continued)*

anguish; while the same conduct may not, in the case of a woman of no refinement and of coarse nature, have any such effect at all. Hence, in the first case the charge of extreme cruelty might be sustained by the evidence; in the second case it would not be. "Whether in any given case there has been inflicted this 'grievous mental suffering' is a pure question of fact, to be deduced from all the circumstances of each particular case, keeping always in view the intelligence, apparent refinement, and delicacy of sentiment of the complaining party; and no arbitrary rule of law as to what particular probative facts shall exist in order to justify a finding of the ultimate facts of its existence can be given." (*Barnes v. Barnes,* supra.) In the case before us, where a girl of twenty-one is shown to have married a man of fifty-four, we would be inclined to be very skeptical as to the truth of any claim that, by reason of the alleged acts of defendant toward the named corespondent, plaintiff's mental suffering was in anywise attributable to the fear alone that the bond of affection between her and her husband might be ruptured. The story, as it is told in the printed pages of the record, suggests strongly a marriage of convenience so far as the plaintiff is concerned. However, there are other factors to be considered, and under one phase of the case it cannot be said that the court was without warrant in finding that the plaintiff had suffered in the manner described in the complaint and findings. She presented a state of facts showing that the actions of defendant with and toward the alleged corespondent were noted by her family and others, and created comment and gossip, and that she was humiliated thereby and caused to suffer greatly in her mind. Whether or not her feeling toward her husband was one of lively affection, she was satisfied in her marital relations, her home was established and her future comfort apparently assured. The conduct of the husband, as the evidence shows and the findings determine it to have been, might well be said to have rendered intolerable a continuance of the marital partnership and to have caused the plaintiff to be humiliated and consequently disturbed in mind. That question was one peculiarly within the province of the trial judge to determine. The demeanor, appearance, and mental make-up of the complainant were all factors which would be proper to be considered, none of which can find much expression in the narrative of the testimony as it appears in cold type. And so we think, as we have already stated, that the case in its facts is put without the province of this court to draw conclusions on the question of cruelty different from those which have been assigned by the trial judge. In the foregoing we have made no attempt to set forth with any degree of detail the substance of the testimony which was presented at the trial. A much lengthier statement would be required if we were to make that effort, and, furthermore, it is only necessary that enough be stated to show that there was some substantial evidence presented by the plaintiff in support of

(continues)

EXHIBIT 3.3   *(Continued)*

the charge of cruelty as made in her complaint. We attach no significance to the phrase used by the trial judge in qualifying the finding negativing the adultery charges, which stated that while those charges were untrue plaintiff had reasonable cause to believe that they were true. This language was probably incorporated in the findings for the purpose only of showing that the adultery charges made by the plaintiff were not made with the idea of willfully imposing upon the court. The qualifying words might be eliminated from the findings altogether without affecting the conclusions in any respect. No errors of a substantial nature were committed by the lower court in receiving or rejecting evidence.

The community property allotment: It appears that during the existence of the marital relation defendant transferred and conveyed to plaintiff certain real estate of the value of $33,000, a certificate of deposit of $10,000, and a Liberty bond of the denomination of $5,000, making a total of $48,000, which property, together with certain personal property and household furnishings, the court found was the sole and separate estate of plaintiff. While there is a conflict in the testimony touching the question, the evidence was sufficient to show that all of said property so found to be the separate estate of plaintiff became such by gifts from defendant to plaintiff. As before stated, the court found that there was community property of the plaintiff and defendant Frank Van Camp of the value of $90,000, and by the judgment awarded plaintiff two- thirds of said sum. Defendant, as appellant, attacks this finding upon the ground that the evidence is insufficient to support the same, and plaintiff, on her appeal, insists that the evidence shows that the value of the community property of the parties was largely in excess of the amount found by the court. [4] Section 163 of the Civil Code provides that "all property owned by the husband before marriage . . . with the rents, issues and profits thereof, is his separate property." Notwithstanding this declaration, the rule is that all property in the possession of either husband or wife is deemed to be community estate of the parties. (*Freese v. Hibernia etc. Society,* 139 Cal. 392, [73 Pac. 172]; *Estate of Pepper,* 158 Cal. 619, [31 L. R. A. (N. S.) 1092, 112 Pac. 62].) Since, however, the presumption attending such possession is a disputable one, either spouse claiming to the contrary may controvert the presumption and offer evidence to overcome the same. [5] From the evidence offered touching the question, it appears without dispute that at the time of his marriage to plaintiff, defendant was a man of large means, which included cash, notes, real estate, and corporate stock; that at the time he was president and manager of a corporation known as the Van Camp Sea Food Company, to the management of the affairs of which he devoted his exclusive attention, and for the services so rendered to said corporation received therefrom, up to January, 1918, the sum of $1,000 per month, which, commencing with January, 1918, was increased to $1,500 per month; that in addition to such salary he received from said company during the period of the mari-

EXHIBIT 3.3 *(Continued)*

---

tal relation an additional sum of $12,203 for the purpose of meeting expenses incurred by him in connection with the business; that during the period in question he was engaged in no other business whatsoever, and, excepting the money so received from said corporation, he had no income other than that derived as rents, issues, and profits from the property owned by him at the time of his marriage. The total amount received by him from said corporation on account of salary and expense money during the existence of the marital relation was the sum of $69,203. It therefore follows that all other income, large or small and regardless of the amount thereof, must necessarily have been derived from the property which he owned at the time of his marriage. [6] In the absence of any evidence showing a different practice, and there is none, the rule is that the community earnings of husband and wife are chargeable with the family support. (*Estate of Cudworth,* 133 Cal. 462, [65 Pac. 1041].) Hence any amounts of money expended for such purpose by either spouse during the existence of the marital relation are presumed to have been paid out of the community estate. It appears that during such period defendant expended for the support of his family, and for income tax and premiums on policies of life insurance wherein his estate was made the beneficiary, the sum of $84,576. The premiums on his life insurance so paid were not a charge upon the community estate. Neither was the entire sum of $18,380 paid by defendant on account of income tax, a charge thereon. Just what proportion of said income tax should be charged to defendant's personal earnings is not made to appear; but conceding for the purpose of the argument that the community estate be deemed free from such burden and the entire sum so paid be imposed upon defendant's other income, and deducting both the life insurance premiums and income tax, the aggregate of which is $23,946, from the total of $84,576 so expended, leaves a balance of $60,630 as the amount actually expended for the community benefit and chargeable to his community earnings of $69,203. This leaves to the credit of the community estate the amount of $8,573, which sum, however, should be further reduced to the extent of the amount chargeable against it on account of its proportion of the income tax so paid by defendant. It thus appears that the evidence is insufficient to show the existence of a community estate of plaintiff and defendant of the value of $90,000, and since his earnings from personal service rendered did not exceed the sum of $69,203, the balance of his income, whatever it may have been, was necessarily derived from the rents, issues, and profits of the property which he owned at the time of his marriage. In our opinion, the evidence is as conclusive of that fact as though defendant had, upon proof of the property owned by him at the time of his marriage, shown the exact income derived therefrom. Hence, conceding, as argued by counsel for Mrs. Van Camp, that defendant at the time of the trial

(continues)

EXHIBIT 3.3   *(Continued)*

admitted the possession of cash, bonds, and other property acquired during the marriage, the value of which was in excess of the large income admittedly received during said time, nevertheless it cannot be said to have constituted community estate of the parties, but, for the reason that, as heretofore stated, his personal earnings having been conclusively fixed, any excess in value of property so acquired must be accredited to the income received from rents, issues, and profits of the separate estate, rather than to the income of the joint efforts of the community. And further, conceding that Van Camp, according to figures tabulated by counsel for the wife, accumulated (in addition to the amount received for his services from the corporation during the marriage and, as shown, exhausted in the payment of household expenses) property other than that owned at the time of the marriage, of the value of $241,000, such sum is largely offset by $141,000 received in dividends from the Van Camp Sea Food Company alone, while $48,000 was given to his wife, and a large sum on profits derived from sales of stock in said company, making a total approximating, if not equal to, the amount so claimed by plaintiff to have been received by him; all of which appears to have been the result of investments from his separate estate. Hence, assuming that defendant did not fully disclose the full amount of his separate income, which was in excess of that stated by him, and that he had acquired other property with such undisclosed income during the marriage, such property, since it was not acquired with his earnings, cannot be deemed community estate.

It is insisted by counsel for Mrs. Van Camp that the Van Camp Sea Food Company, if not a myth, was a mere agency through which defendant conducted his business, and since its enormous income was due to the skill and ability with which defendant conducted the business, the community estate should be accredited with all the profits derived therefrom in excess of seven per cent interest upon the capital which defendant had invested therein. In support of this contention she cites *Pereira v. Pereira*, 156 Cal. 1, [134 Am. St. Rep. 107, 23 L. R. A. (N. S.) 880, 103 Pac. 488], wherein it appeared that the husband at the time of the marriage had a separate estate of $15,500 invested in a business conducted by him. The trial court held that all moneys and profits derived by defendant after marriage through his personal management of such business belonged to the community estate. On an appeal by the husband, the supreme court, in discussing the question, said: "This capital was undoubtedly his separate estate. The fund remained in the business after marriage and was used by him in carrying it on. The separate property should have been credited with some amount as profit on this capital. It was not a losing business but a very profitable one. It is true that it is very clearly shown that the principal part of the large income was due to the personal character, energy, ability, and capacity of the husband. This share of the earnings was, of course,

EXHIBIT 3.3 (*Continued*)

community property. But without capital he could not have carried on the business. In the absence of circumstances showing a different result, it is to be presumed that some of the profits were justly due to the capital invested. There is nothing to show that all of it was due to defendant's efforts alone. The probable contribution of the capital to the income should have been determined from all the circumstances of the case, and as the business was profitable it would amount at least to the usual interest on a long investment well secured." In our opinion, the circumstances attending the *Pereira* case are not applicable to the facts involved herein. While it may be true that the success of the corporation of which defendant was president and manager was to a large extent due to his capacity and ability, nevertheless without the investment of his and other capital in the corporation he could not have conducted the business, and while he devoted his energies and personal efforts to making it a success, he was by the corporation paid what the evidence shows was an adequate salary, and for which another than himself with equal capacity could have been secured. Had such course been pursued and defendant contented himself merely with the receipt of dividends from the business, the character of the dividends as separate property could not have been questioned. Instead, however, of doing this, he entered upon the duties as manager of the corporation, gave his exclusive time and efforts thereto, for which he received first $12,000 and later $18,000 per year. The case presented is not unlike that involved in *Estate of Pepper,* 158 Cal. 619, [31 L. R. A. (N. S.) 1092, 112 Pac. 62], wherein it was held that the profits and earnings made by the husband after marriage in conducting the business of a nursery upon property owned by him at the time of his marriage was his separate property, notwithstanding the success of the venture required industry, skill, and attention. "It is impossible," said the court, "to apportion the crop so as to determine what share of it has come from the soil and what share from the exertions of man. The product must be treated as a whole, and, if it is the growth of land separately owned, it is the separate property of the owner of the land," citing *Diefendorff v. Hopkins,* 95 Cal. 343, [28 Pac. 265, 30 Pac. 549]. So, in the instant case, it is impossible to say what part of the enormous dividends paid by the Van Camp Sea Food Company should be apportioned to the skill and management thereof and what part should be apportioned to the investment of the capital and the favorable conditions under which the business was conducted. Furthermore, there is no merit in the contention that the corporation was a myth, or that it was a mere instrumentality through which defendant conducted his business. It was organized in June, 1914, long before defendant's marriage, with a capital of $200,000, consisting of 2,000 shares of the par value of $100 each, of which stock Van Camp at

(continues)

EXHIBIT 3.3 (*Continued*)

---

the time acquired 1,300 shares, Paul Eachus 500 shares, and F. H. Ford 200 shares, besides two shares distributed to others who, with the persons named, constituted the five directors of the corporation. Subsequently, for the sum of $20,000, defendant acquired the 200 shares of stock issued to Ford, and in March, 1915, for $35,000, he bought the stock issued to Paul Eachus. Later he sold 83 shares of his stock to Wilbur Wood, and, prior to his marriage, sold to his son 300 shares thereof for the sum of $45,000. At no time did he own more than 1,499 shares of the stock. The corporation was duly organized and constituted an entity separate and distinct from that of defendant. Even were it otherwise and, as claimed by plaintiff, a mere instrumentality for conducting defendant's business, nevertheless, in view of the fact that he was adequately paid by the corporation for his services, such compensation, under the holding in the case of *Estate of Pepper,* supra, must be deemed the extent of his personal earnings, and the balance of the profits derived from the business accredited to the use of the capital invested therein, in the same manner as though he had not been employed by the corporation.

The judgment as entered on the divorce issues is affirmed.

The judgment as to the amount and value of the community property and as to the disposition thereof between the parties is reversed and the cause is remanded for a new trial upon that issue alone; appellant Frank Van Camp to have his costs of appeal.

A petition to have the cause heard in the supreme court, after judgment in the district court of appeal, was denied by the supreme court on July 25, 1921.

All the Justices concurred, except Wilbur, J., who was absent.

Separate property, like in common law states, is property acquired by gift, inheritance, or prior to the marriage. It also includes property acquired during the marriage traceable to separate property. Separate property is not subject to division. In some states, the income from separate property is separate. In others, it belongs to the community estate. There is also disparity as to the point in time that the community or marital estate terminates for the purpose of accumulating assets. In some states, the ability to accumulate property terminates on the parties' separation. In others, it terminates when the divorce is final. Another example of how property is traced is detailed by the District Court of Appeal of Florida in the *Steiner* case. It is included as Exhibit 3.4

EXHIBIT 3.4   District Court of Appeal of Florida in the *Steiner* Case

---

IN THE DISTRICT COURT OF APPEAL OF FLORIDA
SECOND DISTRICT

Case No. 98-04130

DEBORAH H. STEINER,
Appellant,
v.
FRANKLIN W. STEINER,
Appellee.

Opinion filed November 17, 1999.

Appeal from the Circuit Court for Sarasota County; Deborah Ford-Kaus, Judge.

Mark Dungan of Icard, Merrill, Cullis, Timm, Furen & Ginsburg, P.A., Sarasota, for Appellant.

Douglas A. Wallace, Bradenton, for Appellee.

CAMPBELL, Acting Chief Judge.

Appellant/wife, Deborah H. Steiner, challenges the distribution of marital assets in the final judgment of dissolution of marriage. As we will explain, we affirm in part and reverse in part on the issues raised by the Wife. In addition, Appellee/husband, Franklin W. Steiner, cross-appeals the court's separate determination that the parties' antenuptial agreement was unenforceable. Because we conclude that the evidence supports the trial court's conclusion, we affirm on the Husband's cross-appeal. Additionally, because the parties agree that the judge erred in restricting removal of the parties' children from Florida, we direct that the trial court eliminate that provision on remand.

The principal issue raised by the Wife is whether a SunTrust bank account, maintained by the Husband jointly with his mother (who died some years ago), was a marital account, as to which the Wife would be entitled to share not only in the funds in the account, but also in the value of the payments made out of the account during the marriage. The trial court found that because the Wife was not listed on the account and the Husband did not hold the account jointly with the Wife, it was nonmarital, and, further that the funds deposited into the account, regardless of their source, did not become marital funds. This was error.

"In determining whether certain property is a marital asset, the question is not which party holds title to the asset." *Szemborski v. Szemborski*, 512 So. 2d 987, 988 (Fla. 5th DCA 1987). Marital assets are those acquired during the marriage, created or produced by the work efforts, services, or earn-

(continues)

EXHIBIT 3.4   (*Continued*)

ings of one or both spouses. *See Wright v. Wright,* 505 So. 2d 699 (Fla. 5th DCA 1987). Even if an account is titled in one spouse's name alone, it may become marital if both marital and nonmarital funds are commingled in that account. *See Adkins v. Adkins,* 650 So. 2d 61 (Fla. 3d DCA 1994).

In the instant case, the parties had two sources of income: wages from the Husband's employment and proceeds from three rental properties. The Husband deposited both types of income into the SunTrust account, which was the parties' only bank account. The way in which the Husband acquired and held these rental properties, both before and during the parties' marriage, is critical.

The Husband entered the marriage with three rental properties, the Webber Street property, the Sixth Street property, and a third property. All three properties were titled solely in the Husband's name. Shortly after the parties' marriage, the Husband sold the third rental property and used the profit from that sale to make a down payment on another rental property, the Ninth Street property. Also after the parties married, the Husband applied an additional portion of the profit from the sale of the third rental property to a down payment on the parties' marital home on Main Street. This brought the total number of properties the Husband owned to four. He kept all four properties titled in his name alone. The funds used to make the down payments on the Ninth Street property and the marital home could be properly traced back to the Husband's sale of that third rental property he had owned prior to the marriage. The record reveals that both parties participated in the management of the rental properties.

During the marriage, the parties used the SunTrust account for all of their banking transactions. All of the mortgage payments on the rental properties were paid out of the SunTrust account, and proceeds from the rental properties were deposited into the SunTrust account. Similarly, the Husband's earnings were deposited into the SunTrust account, and the parties' living expenses were paid out of that account. There was also some evidence that the Wife exercised signature authority on the SunTrust account from time to time.

First, we must agree with the trial court that, based on the above facts, the Webber Street and the Sixth Street properties, which the Husband had owned prior to the marriage and never in any way gifted to Wife, were nonmarital assets. Likewise, the marital home and the Ninth Street properties were nonmarital assets to the extent that their purchase prices were paid with proceeds that are traceable to the Husband's sale of the rental he had owned prior to the marriage.

However, we conclude that the rental income from these primarily non-marital assets was marital property because it was generated by the active participation and involvement of both parties; it was not obtained by merely passive appreciation in value, as argued by the Husband. To the contrary, the

---

EXHIBIT 3.4 *(Continued)*

---

parties had to maintain, advertise and otherwise actively manage the rental properties in order to produce the rental income. Because the record reveals that both the Husband and the Wife participated in this management, the rental income became marital property. *See Rosenfield v. Rosenfield,* 597 So. 2d 835 (Fla. 3d DCA 1992); *Moon v. Moon,* 594 So. 2d 819 (Fla. 1st DCA 1992).

When the Husband then deposited this marital property into the SunTrust account, commingled it with his earnings and paid the parties' living expenses out of that account, the SunTrust account itself became marital property. *See Stevens v. Stewart,* 651 So. 2d 1306 (Fla. 1st DCA 1995). Once the funds were commingled and used for joint expenses, they lost their separate character and became untraceable. *See Terreros v. Terreros,* 531 So. 2d 1058, 1060 (Fla. 3d DCA 1988).

Having concluded that the SunTrust account became a marital account, we necessarily also conclude that all principal mortgage reductions paid out of that account on the four properties became marital property. *See* § 61.075(5)(a)2., Fla. Stat. (1997). As a result, the court erred when it reduced the Wife's share of those reductions by an amount "commensurate with the percentage of time Wife participated in maintaining the rentals of the property during the marriage." The fact that one spouse may have a more active role in the accumulation of marital assets does not dictate that the marital partners should share in marital assets based on the degree of their role in this acquisition. *See Buttner v. Buttner,* 484 So. 2d 1265 (Fla. 4th DCA 1986).

We, therefore, reverse and remand the trial court's determination that the SunTrust account was nonmarital. On remand, the parties shall share equally in both the funds in the SunTrust account and the mortgage paydowns that were paid out of the SunTrust account. However, the amount of the paydowns traceable directly to the sale of the Husband's nonmarital Winn-Dixie stock shall not be included in the mortgage paydowns that the parties shall share equally. Furthermore, the parties agree that the trial judge erred in including in the final judgment a provision restricting removal of the parties' children from the state of Florida. Neither party requested such a restriction, and on remand it shall be eliminated. Finally, because we conclude that the evidence supports the court's conclusion on the parties' antenuptial agreement, we affirm on the Husband's cross-appeal.

Affirmed in part, reversed in part and remanded.

GREEN and DAVIS, JJ., Concur.

Changing the Character of Property

There are additional financial and accounting issues associated with separate property versus marital or community property. First, both property theories provide that if there is such commingling of the marital or community estate with the separate estate that the nature and amount of the property interests cannot be determined, the property *transmutes* into marital or community property.

It is possible that a change of character of separate property can occur, and it can become the separate property of the other party. There can be gifts of separate property from one to the other. There can also be a gift of marital or community property from one party to the other. This would cause the property gifted to become separate property. There may be a written agreement that is recognized under local law that causes the nature of the property to change. The financial adviser needs to have a complete understanding of how the local property laws work in his state.

Tracing

States with both common law and community property systems have tracing issues. These issues can be as simple as determining and documenting the source of funds used in an assets acquisition. It becomes more complex when the issues relate to tracing separate property into marital/community property, or tracing marital/ community property into separate property. Another California case that shows how property is transformed from community to separate is the *Lucas* case. It is presented as Exhibit 3.5.

EXHIBIT 3.5   *Lucas* Case

In re Marriage of Lucas

SUPREME COURT OF CALIFORNIA
L.A. No. 31254
27 C3d 808, 166 CR 853, 614 P2d 285, 1980 CFLR 1338, 1406, 1981 CFLR 1521, CFLP §§E.27-E.47

August 7, 1980

    IN RE THE MARRIAGE OF BRENDA G. AND GERALD E. LUCAS. GERALD E. LUCAS, APPELLANT, v. BRENDA G. LUCAS, RESPONDENT

    Superior Court of San Diego County, No. D 112880, Ross G. Tharp, Judge.
    Daniel W. Grindle, Gade, Grindle & Haynie and Goodwin & Grindle for Appellant.
    Robert T. Dierdorff for Respondent.

EXHIBIT 3.5 *(Continued)*

Opinion by Manuel, J., expressing the unanimous view of the court. Bird, C. J., Tobriner, J., Mosk, J., Clark, J., Richardson, J., and Newman, J., concurred.

Manuel

[Cal3d Page 811]

Gerald E. Lucas appeals from an interlocutory judgment dissolving his marriage to Brenda G. Lucas, awarding child custody, fixing spousal and child support and dividing property. Gerald contests only the trial court's determination of the parties' ownership interests in their residence and in a vehicle, both of which were purchased with a combination of community and separate funds. In this case we must resolve a conflict among the Courts of Appeal regarding the proper method of determining separate and community property interests in a single family dwelling acquired during the marriage with both separate property and community property funds.

Brenda and Gerald were married in March 1964 and lived together continuously until their separation in December 1976. At the time of their marriage Brenda was beneficiary of a trust. The trust corpus was distributed to her free of the trust in September 1964. She immediately established a revocable inter vivos trust of which she was trustor and beneficiary. The trust, conceded by Gerald to be Brenda's separate property, had a value of approximately $44,000 at the time of trial.

In November 1968, Brenda and Gerald bought a house for $23,300. Brenda used $6,351.57 from her trust for the down payment, and they assumed a loan of $16,948.43 for the balance of the purchase price. Title to the house was taken as "Gerald E. Lucas and Brenda G. Lucas, Husband and Wife as Joint Tenants." Brenda paid $2,962 from her trust funds for improvements to the property; the remainder of the expenses on the property was paid for with community funds. At the time [27 Cal3d Page 812] of trial the residence had a fair market value of approximately $56,250 and a loan balance of approximately $14,600, leaving a net equity of approximately $41,650. The community had reduced the principal by $2,052.32 and paid $6,801.14 in interest and $5,146.20 for taxes.

The trial court findings describe the parties' intent regarding ownership of the residence as follows: "The only discussions with regard to taking joint tenancy title to the property related to wife's understanding that title would pass to husband upon her death and that the children would benefit from this result; further, the parties contemplated that taking title in this manner would result in favorable tax consequences due to husband's veterans status. Wife did not intend to make a gift to the husband of any interest in the home purchased with her separate funds, nor did she know of any other legal signifi-

(continues)

EXHIBIT 3.5 (*Continued*)

cance of taking title to real property in the manner it was taken. Neither did husband intend to make a gift to wife of the payments made on the home from community funds during the period of ownership."

Brenda testified that she and Gerald did not discuss where the down payment would come from except to the extent that the payments would be higher if they did not use her trust fund and instead took a second trust deed on the house. Brenda said they had no agreement regarding the manner in which she would be disposing of the trust funds and that they did not discuss keeping the funds separate or using them to exhaust community debts. Brenda also testified that it was her intention at the time of the purchase to acquire the house for herself but that she did not discuss this with her husband.

In the interlocutory judgment entered in April 1978, the trial court deducted Brenda's $2,962 payment for improvements from the equity of $41,650.50 and then awarded a community property interest in the residence of 24.42 percent with a value of $9,477.50. (Footnote 1.) A separate property interest of 75.58 percent with a value of $29,241 was confirmed to Brenda.

The Courts of Appeal have taken conflicting approaches to the question of the proper method for determining the ownership interests in a residence purchased during the parties' marriage with both separate and community funds. In *In re Marriage of Bjornestad* (1974) 38 Cal. App. 3d 801 [27 Cal3d Page 813] [113 Cal. Rptr. 576], the Court of Appeal allowed only reimbursement for separate property contributions to the down payment on the purchase of the parties' residence. In *In re Marriage of Aufmuth* (1979) 89 Cal. App. 3d 446 [152 Cal. Rptr. 668], the Court of Appeal developed a scheme of pro rata apportionment of the equity appreciation between the separate and community property contributions to the purchase price. The Court of Appeal in *In re Marriage of Trantafello* (1979) 94 Cal. App. 3d 533 [156 Cal. Rptr. 556], however, held that the residence was entirely community in nature in the absence of any evidence of an agreement or understanding between the parties to the contrary.

The beginning point of analysis in each case was the nature of title taken by the parties. In *Bjornestad* and *Trantafello,* title was taken by husband and wife as joint tenants; in *Aufmuth,* it was taken as community property. Until modified by statute in 1965, there was a rebuttable presumption that the ownership interest in property was as stated in the title to it. (*Machado v. Machado* (1962) 58 Cal. 2d 501 [25 Cal. Rptr. 87, 375 P.2d 55]; *Gudelj v. Gudelj* (1953) 41 Cal. 2d 202 [259 P.2d 656]; *Socol v. King* (1950) 36 Cal. 2d 342 [223 P.2d 627]; *Tomaier v. Tomaier* (1944) 23 Cal. 2d 754 [146 P.2d 905].) Thus a residence purchased with community funds, but held by a husband and wife as joint tenants, was presumed to be separate property in which each spouse had a half interest. (See *Socol v. King,* supra, 36 Cal.

EXHIBIT 3.5   *(Continued)*

2d at pp. 345-347.) The presumption arising from the form of title could be overcome by evidence of an agreement or understanding between the parties that the interests were to be otherwise. (Ibid. *Gudelj v. Gudelj,* supra, 41 Cal. 2d at p. 212; *Machado v. Machado,* supra, 58 Cal. 2d at p. 506.) It could not be overcome, however, "solely by evidence as to the source of the funds used to purchase the property." (*Gudelj v. Gudelj,* supra, 41 Cal. 2d at p. 212.) Nor could it "be overcome by testimony of a hidden intention not disclosed to the other grantee at the time of the execution of the conveyance." (Ibid. *Socol v. King,* supra, 36 Cal. 2d at p. 346; *Machado v. Machado,* supra, 58 Cal. 2d at p. 506.)

The presumption arising from the form of title created problems upon divorce or separation when title to the parties' residence was held in joint tenancy. (Review of Selected 1965 Code Legislation (Cont. Ed. Bar) p. 40; Final Rep. of Assem. Interim Com. on Judiciary Relating to Domestic Relations (1965) pp. 121-122, 2 Appen. to Assem. J. (1965 Reg. Sess.) hereafter referred to as Domestic Relations Rep.) Unless the presumption of separate property created by the form of title could [27 Cal3d Page 814] be overcome by evidence of a common understanding or agreement to the contrary, a house so held could not be awarded to the wife as a family residence for her and the children. (Ibid.) In 1965 the Legislature considered various proposals to remedy this problem. The Legislature also noted that "husbands and wives take property in joint tenancy without legal counsel but primarily because deeds prepared by real estate brokers, escrow companies and by title companies are usually presented to the parties in joint tenancy form. The result is that they don't know what joint tenancy is, that they think it is community property, and then find out upon death or divorce that they didn't have what they thought they had all along and instead have something else which isn't what they had intended." (Domestic Relations Rep., p. 124.)

In 1965, in an attempt to solve these problems, the Legislature added the following provision to Civil Code section 164: "[When] a single family residence of a husband and wife is acquired by them during marriage as joint tenants, for the purpose of the division of such property upon divorce or separate maintenance only, the presumption is that such single family residence is the community property of said husband and wife." (Stats. 1965, ch. 1710, p. 3843; see now Civ. Code § 5110.) (Footnote 2.) The effect of this provision was to change the presumptive form of ownership to that more closely matching the intent and assumptions of most spouses who acquire and hold their residence in joint tenancy. (Review of Selected 1965 Code Legislation (Cont.Ed.Bar) pp. 40-41; Domestic Relations Rep., pp. 124-125.) There is no indication that the Legislature intended in any way to change the rules regarding the strength and type of evidence necessary

(continues)

EXHIBIT 3.5   (Continued)

to overcome the presumption arising from the form of title. (See Domestic Relations Rep., p. 124.)

The presumption arising from the form of title is to be distinguished from the general presumption set forth in Civil Code section 5110 that property acquired during marriage is community property. It is the affirmative act of specifying a form of ownership in the conveyance [27 Cal3d Page 815] of title that removes such property from the more general presumption. (See *Socol v. King,* supra, 36 Cal. 2d at p. 346.) It is because of this express designation of ownership that a greater showing is necessary to overcome the presumption arising therefrom than is necessary to overcome the more general presumption that property acquired during marriage is community property. In the latter situation, where there is no written indication of ownership interests as between the spouses, the general presumption of community property may be overcome simply by tracing the source of funds used to acquire the property to separate property. (See *In re Marriage of Mix* (1975) 14 Cal. 3d 604, 608-612 [122 Cal. Rptr. 79, 536 P.2d 479]; *Estate of Murphy* (1976) 15 Cal. 3d 907, 917-919 [126 Cal. Rptr. 820, 544 P.2d 956]; *See v. See* (1966) 64 Cal. 2d 778, 783 [51 Cal. Rptr. 888, 415 P.2d 776].) It is not necessary to show that the spouses understood or intended that property traceable to separate property should remain separate.

The rule requiring an understanding or agreement comes into play when the issue is whether the presumption arising from the form of title has been overcome. It is supported by sound policy considerations, and we decline to depart from it. To allow a lesser showing could result in unfairness to the spouse who has not made the separate property contribution. Unless the latter knows that the spouse contributing the separate property expects to be reimbursed or to acquire a separate property interest, he or she has no opportunity to attempt to preserve the joint ownership of the property by making other financing arrangements. The act of taking title in a joint and equal ownership form is inconsistent with an intention to preserve a separate property interest. Accordingly, the expectations of parties who take title jointly are best protected by presuming that the specified ownership interest is intended in the absence of an agreement or understanding to the contrary. We therefore resolve the conflict in Court of Appeal opinions by following *Trantafello* and disapproving *Aufmuth* and *Bjornestad* to the extent they are inconsistent with this opinion.

In the present case there is no evidence of an agreement or understanding that Brenda was to retain a separate property interest in the house. Nor is there any finding by the trial court on the question. The only findings in this regard are that neither party intended a gift to the other. Such evidence and findings are insufficient to rebut the presumption arising from title set forth in Civil Code section 5110. The trial court's determination must therefore be reversed. [27 Cal3d Page 816]

EXHIBIT 3.5 *(Continued)*

Neither the parties nor the court applied the correct rules to this case, and it is possible that had they done so the proof might have been different. In the interest of justice, therefore, the matter of the community or separate property character of the residence must be remanded for reconsideration in light of these rules.

If on reconsideration the house is found to be entirely community in nature, Brenda would also be barred from reimbursement for the separate property funds she contributed in the absence of an agreement therefor. It is a well-settled rule that a "party who uses his separate property for community purposes is entitled to reimbursement from the community or separate property of the other only if there is an agreement between the parties to that effect." (*See v. See,* supra, 64 Cal. 2d at p. 785; *Weinberg v. Weinberg* (1967) 67 Cal. 2d 557, 570 [63 Cal. Rptr. 13, 432 P.2d 709]; *In re Marriage of Epstein* (1979) 24 Cal. 3d 76, 82-86 [154 Cal. Rptr. 413, 592 P.2d 1165].) While the parties are married and living together it is presumed that, "unless an agreement between the parties specifies that the contributing party be reimbursed, a party who utilizes his separate property for community purposes intends a gift to the community." (*In re Marriage of Epstein,* supra, 24 Cal. 3d at p. 82.)

For guidance in the event that on reconsideration the court finds there was an understanding or agreement that Brenda was to retain a separate property interest in the residence, we discuss briefly the question of the proper method of calculating the community and separate interests. In these inflationary times when residential housing is undergoing enormous and rapid appreciation in value, we believe that the most equitable method of calculating the separate and community interests when the down payment was made with separate funds and the loan was based on a community or joint obligation is that set forth by Justice McGuire in *In re Marriage of Aufmuth,* supra, 89 Cal. App. 3d at pages 456-457. In brief, the *Aufmuth* formula gives the spouse who made the separate property down payment a separate property interest in the residence in the proportion that the down payment bears to the purchase price; the community acquires that percentage of the residence which the community loan bears to the purchase price. (Footnote 3.) [27 Cal3d Page 817]

If the trial court finds no agreement or understanding that Brenda was to retain a separate property interest in the residence, Brenda's contribution of $2,962 of separate funds for improvements should have no effect on the determination of the parties' interests, and the presumption of section 5110 is controlling. (*See v. See,* supra, 64 Cal. 2d at p. 783.) If there was an understanding that Brenda's separate interest should be maintained, but no separate understanding with respect to improvements, Brenda should

(continues)

EXHIBIT 3.5   (*Continued*)

receive no additional credit for her expenditure for improvements, for it may be presumed that she intended that they redound to both the community and her separate interest in the property. (Cf., *See v. See,* supra, 64 Cal. 2d at p. 785.)

Gerald also challenges the trial court's determination that a 1976 Harvest Mini-Motorhome, purchased in January 1976 for a cash price of $10,388, was Brenda's separate property. A community property vehicle was traded in on the purchase for an allowance of $2,567. An additional cash payment of $100 was made on the purchase from community funds. The cost of insurance and license fees ($474) added to the cash price of the motorhome, less the trade-in allowance and cash down payment, left a total unpaid balance of $8,195. That sum was paid by check drawn on Brenda's separate checking account. The community contributed 24.6 percent of the cost and Brenda contributed 75.4 percent of the cost of the vehicle. The fair market value of it at the time of trial was $9,000.

The purchase contract was made out in the name of Gerald alone, but title and registration were taken in Brenda's name only. Brenda wished to have title in her name alone, and Gerald did not object. The [27 Cal3d Page 818] motorhome was purchased for family use and was referred to and used by the parties as a "family vehicle."

The trial court confirmed the motorhome to Brenda as her separate property. The interlocutory judgment stated that Gerald "had a de minimus community property interest therein which was made a gift to respondent [Brenda] at the time of the purchase."

Contrary to Gerald's contention, the trial court's determination that he made a gift of his interest is supported by substantial evidence. Title was taken in Brenda's name alone. Gerald was aware of this and did not object. This evidence constitutes substantial support for the trial court's conclusion that Gerald was making a gift to Brenda of his community property interest in the motorhome. (See *In re Marriage of Frapwell* (1975) 49 Cal. App. 3d 597, 600-601 [122 Cal. Rptr. 718].)

The judgment is reversed insofar as it determines the respective interests of the parties in the residence and divides the community property.

It is affirmed in all other respects.

Disposition

It is affirmed in all other respects.

Opinion Footnotes

Footnote 1. The amounts stated in the interlocutory judgment differ slightly from those stated in the findings. The figures given are those stated in the judgment.

EXHIBIT 3.5 *(Continued)*

Footnote 2. Section 164 was repealed in 1969 in connection with the enactment of the Family Law Act. (Stats. 1969, ch. 1608, § 3, p. 3313.) It was replaced by section 5110 which contains an almost identical provision: "When a single-family residence of a husband and wife is acquired by them during marriage as joint tenants, for the purpose of the division of such property upon dissolution of marriage or legal separation only, the presumption is that such single-family residence is the community property of the husband and wife." Although section 164 was the applicable statute when the parties in this case purchased their house, as a matter of convenience, future references in this opinion will be to the current statute, section 5110.

Footnote 3. The value of those interests is computed by first determining the amount of capital appreciation, which is computed by subtracting the purchase price from the fair market value of the residence. The separate property interest would be determined by adding the amount of capital appreciation attributable to separate funds to the amount of equity paid by separate funds. The community interest would be the amount of capital appreciation attributable to community funds plus the amount of equity paid by community funds; the amount of equity paid by community funds is represented by the amount by which the principal balance on the loan has been reduced.

An example of an apportionment can be found in the case of a house purchased for $100,000, with the wife paying the entire down payment of $20,000 from separate property funds, and the community contributing the rest of the purchase price in the amount of a loan for $80,000. There would be a 20 percent separate property interest and an 80 percent community property interest in the house. Assume that the fair market value of the house at the time of trial is $175,000, resulting in a capital appreciation of $75,000, and the mortgage balance at the time of separation was $78,000. The value of the separate property interest would be $35,000, which represents the amount of capital appreciation attributable to the separate funds (20 percent of $75,000) added to the amount of equity paid by separate funds ($20,000). The net value of the community property interest would be $62,000, which represents the amount of capital appreciation attributable to community funds (80 percent of $75,000) added to the amount of equity paid by community funds ($80,000 minus $78,000).

Because the mixing of property often occurs over a lengthy marriage, there are significant issues of the amounts and nature of the records the parties may possess and whether, if not possessed by the parties, the records may be available from third parties. Banks and financial institutions may no longer have access to the information the parties may need to prove their appropriate interest in a particular piece of property. Sometimes the courts may allow non-documentary evidence to be presented by the parties themselves, but documentary evidence may carry more weight. The financial adviser can assist the party in recalling the types of information that may be helpful to proving the individual's interest in some property. There may also be collateral documentary evidence that is not of a financial nature to assist the parties in their claim.

The financial adviser must determine, on an asset-by-asset basis, whether marital/community, separate, or both sources of funds were used to acquire a particular asset. If marital/community funds were used, the court will likely divide the value of the property between the parties to the divorce. If separate funds were used, the court will award the property to the individual proved to be the separate source of the fund.

When there are issues of mixed ownership, and the property is not so commingled as to become marital/community property, there are several theories that are applied by the courts in dividing the value of the property. There are *apportionment* theories, *reimbursement* theories, and *lien* theories that divide the property. Apportionment theories allocate the percentage of ownership the parties may have in an asset, based on the proportion of the cost of the property contributed by the marital or community estate, and the proportion of the cost contributed by the separate estate, applied to the current fair market value of the property.

Reimbursement theories first determine the nature of the property as being marital/community or separate. Identifying the source of the funds used to acquire the property most often makes this determination. Second, the amount of the different character funds or labor invested in the property is computed. Then the non-ownership estate is reimbursed for the contributions of labor or funds made to improve the property. In some instances, interest or other computed return is added to the reimbursement. There is another form of reimbursement theory that considers whether the marital estate/community estate or the separate estate has advanced funds, which may not be invested in property, which should be returned. These theories can range from marital/community funds being used to pay separate income taxes to separate income being used to subsidize marital/community expenses. Some courts look at these theories with some degree of restraint. In many cases, the court may rule that the parties agreed to spend the financial resources, and that those resources are now gone. In other jurisdictions, there may be reimbursements due. A case that illustrates the reasoning courts may apply to these types of issues was decided by the Supreme Court of California in the *See* case. It is included as Exhibit 3.6.

EXHIBIT 3.6   Supreme Court of California, *See v. See* Case

See v. See

SUPREME COURT OF CALIFORNIA IN BANK
L.A. No. 27754.
64 C2d 778, 51 CR 888, 415 P2d 776, CFLP §D.80
July 1, 1966

LAURANCE A. SEE, PLAINTIFF AND APPELLANT, v. ELIZABETH LEE SEE, DEFENDANT AND APPELLANT.

APPEALS from a judgment of the Superior Court of Los Angeles County. Frederick W. Mahl, Jr., Judge. Reversed in part and affirmed in part.

Crowley & Goffin, Arthur J. Crowley and Ron Swearinger for Plaintiff and Appellant.

Stanley N. Gleis for Defendant and Appellant.

Traynor

[64 Cal2d Page 781]

TRAYNOR, C.J. Plaintiff Laurance A. See and cross-complainant Elizabeth Lee See appeal from an interlocutory judgment that grants each a divorce. Laurance attacks the finding that he was guilty of extreme cruelty, the granting of a divorce to Elizabeth, and the award to her of permanent alimony of $5,400 per month. Elizabeth attacks the finding that there was no community property at the time of the divorce. Neither party contests the provisions regarding custody and support of the three minor children.

The parties were married on October 17, 1941, and they separated about May 10, 1962. Throughout the marriage they were residents of California, and Laurance was employed by a family-controlled corporation, See's Candies, Inc. For most of that period he also served as president of its

(continues)

EXHIBIT 3.6   (*Continued*)

wholly-owned subsidiary, See's Candy Shops, Inc. In the twenty-one years of the marriage he received more than $1,000,000 in salaries from the two corporations.

The trial court did not err in finding that plaintiff's actions constituted extreme cruelty. That finding was made upon consideration of all the circumstances of the case in light of the "intelligence, refinement, and delicacy of sentiment of the complaining party" (*Nunes v. Nunes,* 62 Cal. 2d 33, 36 [41 Cal. Rptr. 5, 396 P.2d 37]) and is supported by substantial [64 Cal2d Page 782] evidence. When repeated instances of offensive conduct are offered to establish cruelty, it is not necessary that each be corroborated. The determination of the sufficiency of corroborating evidence is within the sound discretion of the trial court. (*Id.* at p. 37.)

Nor did the trial court abuse its discretion in awarding alimony to Elizabeth. Alimony may be awarded to either party even though a divorce is granted to both. (*Mueller v. Mueller,* 44 Cal. 2d 527, 530 [282 P.2d 869]; *DeBurgh v. DeBurgh,* 39 Cal. 2d 858, 874 [250 P.2d 598].) We do not reach plaintiff's contention that the alimony award was excessive. Since that part of the judgment must be reversed for reasons that appear hereafter, the considerations that prompted the amount of the award may no longer be relevant.

Laurance had a personal account on the books of See's Candies, Inc., denominated Account 13. Throughout the marriage his annual salary from See's Candies, Inc., which was $60,000 at the time of the divorce, was credited to this account and many family expenses were paid by checks drawn on it. To maintain a credit balance in Account 13, Laurance from time to time transferred funds to it from an account at the Security First National Bank, hereafter called the Security Account.

The funds deposited in the Security Account came primarily from Laurance's separate property. On occasion he deposited his annual $15,000 salary from See's Candy Shops, Inc., in that account as a "reserve against taxes" on that salary. Thus there was a commingling of community property and separate property in both the Security Account and Account 13. Funds from the Security Account were sometimes used to pay community expenses and also to purchase some of the assets held in Laurance's name at the time of the divorce proceedings.

Over Elizabeth's objection, the trial court followed a theory advanced by Laurance that a proven excess of community expenses over community income during the marriage establishes that there has been no acquisition of property with community funds.

Such a theory, without support in either statutory or case law of this state, would disrupt the California community property system. It would transform a wife's interest in the community property from a "present, existing and equal interest" as specified by Civil Code section 161a, into an inchoate

EXHIBIT 3.6 *(Continued)*

expectancy to be realized only if upon termination of [64 Cal2d Page 783] the marriage the community income fortuitously exceeded community expenditures. It would engender uncertainties as to testamentary and *inter vivos* dispositions, income, estate and gift taxation, and claims against property.

The character of property as separate or community is determined at the time of its acquisition. (*In re Miller,* 31 Cal. 2d 191, 197 [187 P.2d 722]; *Siberell v. Siberell,* 214 Cal. 767, 770 [7 P.2d 1003]; *Bias v. Reed,* 169 Cal. 33, 42 [145 P. 516]. If it is community property when acquired, it remains so throughout the marriage unless the spouses agree to change its nature or the spouse charged with its management makes a gift of it to the other. (*Odone v. Marzocchi,* 34 Cal. 2d 431, 435 [211 P.2d 297, 212 P.2d 233, 17 A.L.R.2d 1109]; *Mears v. Mears,* 180 Cal. App. 2d 484, 499 [4 Cal. Rptr. 618].)

Property acquired by purchase during a marriage is presumed to be community property, and the burden is on the spouse asserting its separate character to overcome the presumption. (*Estate of Niccolls,* 164 Cal. 368 [129 P. 278]; *Thomasset v. Thomasset,* 122 Cal. App. 2d 116, 123 [264 P.2d 626]. The presumption applies when a husband purchases property during the marriage with funds from an undisclosed or disputed source, such as an account or fund in which he has commingled his separate funds with community funds. (*Estate of Neilson,* 57 Cal. 2d 733, 742 [22 Cal. Rptr. 1, 371 P.2d 745]. He may trace the source of the property to his separate funds and overcome the presumption with evidence that community expenses exceeded community income at the time of acquisition. If he proves that at that time all community income was exhausted by family expenses, he establishes that the property was purchased with separate funds. (*Estate of Neilson,* supra, at p. 742; *Thomasset v. Thomasett,* supra, at p. 127.) Only when, through no fault of the husband, it is not possible to ascertain the balance of income and expenditures at the time property was acquired, can recapitulation of the total community expenses and income throughout the marriage be used to establish the character of the property. Thus, in *Estate of Ades,* 81 Cal. App. 2d 334 [184 P.2d 1], relied on by plaintiff, this method of tracing was used to establish that assets discovered after the husband's death had been acquired before the marriage. The question was not presented as to the balance of income and expenditures at any specific time during the marriage. In *Estate of Arstein,* 56 Cal. 2d 239 [14 Cal. Rptr. 809, 364 P.2d 33], relied on by plaintiff, the husband's skill [64 Cal2d Page 784] and industry in managing his separate property was the source of all community income during the marriage. Not until the trial could a determination be made as to what proportion of the total income was attributable to the husband's skill and industry. In *Thomasset v. Thomasset,* supra, 122 Cal. App. 2d 116, the court made clear that the time of acquisition of disputed property is decisive. "An accountant

(continues)

EXHIBIT 3.6 *(Continued)*

testified that at the time the various items adjudged to be defendant's separate property were purchased, there were no community funds available. . . . The evidence [shows] . . . that at the time the property was purchased the community funds had been exhausted. . . ." (*Id.* at p. 127.) Anything to the contrary in *Patterson v. Patterson,* 242 Cal. App. 2d [51 Cal. Rptr. 339], is disapproved.

A husband who commingles the property of the community with his separate property, but fails to keep adequate records cannot invoke the burden of record keeping as a justification for a recapitulation of income and expenses at the termination of the marriage that disregards any acquisitions that may have been made during the marriage with community funds. If funds used for acquisitions during marriage cannot otherwise be traced to their source and the husband who has commingled property is unable to establish that there was a deficit in the community accounts when the assets were purchased, the presumption controls that property acquired by purchase during marriage is community property. The husband may protect his separate property by not commingling community and separate assets and income. Once he commingles, he assumes the burden of keeping records adequate to establish the balance of community income and expenditures at the time an asset is acquired with commingled property.

The trial court also followed the theory that a husband who expends his separate property for community expenses is entitled to reimbursement from community assets. This theory likewise lacks support in the statutory or case law of this state. A husband is required to support his wife and family. (Civ. Code, §§ 155, 196, 242). Indeed, husband and wife assume mutual obligations of support upon marriage. These obligations are not conditioned on the existence of community property or income. The duty to support imposed upon husbands by Civil Code section 155 and upon wives by Civil Code section 176 requires the use of separate property of the parties when there is no community property. There is no right to reimbursement under the statutes. [64 Cal2d Page 785]

Likewise a husband who elects to use his separate property instead of community property to meet community expenses cannot claim reimbursement. In the absence of an agreement to the contrary, the use of his separate property by a husband for community purposes is a gift to the community. The considerations that underlie the rule denying reimbursement to either the community or the husband's separate estate for funds expended to improve a wife's separate property (*Dunn v. Mullan,* 211 Cal. 583, 589 [296 P. 604, 77 A.L.R. 1015]) apply with equal force here. The husband has both management and control of the community property (Civ. Code, §§ 172, 172a) along with the right to select the place and mode of living. (Civ. Code, § 156.) His

EXHIBIT 3.6 *(Continued)*

use of separate property to maintain a standard of living that cannot be maintained with community resources alone no more entitles him to reimbursement from after-acquired community assets than it would from existing community assets.

Nor can we approve the recognition of an exception, a right to reimbursement of separate funds expended for community purposes at a time when a community bank account is exhausted. (*Kenney v. Kenney,* 128 Cal. App. 2d 128, 136 [274 P.2d 951]; *Thomasset v. Thomasett,* supra, 122 Cal. App. 2d 116, 126; *Hill v. Hill,* 82 Cal. App. 2d 682, 698 [187 P.2d 28]; cf. *Mears v. Mears,* supra, 180 Cal. App. 2d 484, 508.) Although this exception was restricted to recovery from the same community account when replenished, there is no statutory basis for it, and the court that first declared it cited no authority to support it. Such an exception conflicts with the long-standing rule that a wife who uses her separate funds in payment of family expenses without agreement regarding repayment cannot require her husband to reimburse her. (*Ives v. Connacher,* 162 Cal. 174, 177 [121 P. 394]; *Blackburn v. Blackburn,* 160 Cal. App. 2d 301, 304 [324 P.2d 971]; *Thomson v. Thomson,* 81 Cal. App. 678 [254 P. 644]; cf. *Haseltine v. Haseltine,* 203 Cal. App. 2d 48 [21 Cal. Rptr. 238].) Nor is a wife required to reimburse her husband in the converse situation, particularly since the husband has the control and management of community expenses and resources. The basic rule is that the party who uses his separate property for community purposes is entitled to reimbursement from the community or separate property of the other only if there is an agreement between the parties to that effect. To the extent that they conflict with this rule *Mears v. Mears,* supra, 180 Cal. App. 2d 484; *Kenney v. Kenney,* supra, 128 Cal. App. 2d [64 Cal2d Page 786] 128; *Thomasset v. Thomasset,* supra, 122 Cal. App. 2d 116; and *Hill v. Hill,* 82 Cal. App. 2d 682 [187 P.2d 28], are disapproved.

Elizabeth makes several additional assignments of error relative to specific assets in existence on the dissolution of the marriage but not found to be community property. The record does not afford a basis for determining the nature of these assets, with the exception of Laurance's interest in the profit-sharing trusts of the two See corporations. His interest in these funds arose by virtue of his employment and was irrevocable at the time of the divorce. It was therefore unquestionably a community property asset.

Plaintiff has not met his burden of proving an excess of community expenses over community income at the times the other assets purchased during the marriage were acquired. The part of the judgment finding them to be his separate property is therefore reversed. Since the property issues were tried on the theory that the nature of the property could be determined

(continues)

EXHIBIT 3.6   *(Continued)*

---

by proving total community income and expenditures and since the parties may have additional evidence that would otherwise have been presented, plaintiff's failure to overcome the presumption that the assets are community property is not conclusive. We therefore remand the case for retrial of the property issues. Since the court considered the lack of community property a significant factor in determining the amount of the alimony award, that part of the judgment is also reversed.

The judgment is affirmed in all other respects. Elizabeth shall recover her costs on both appeals.

McComb, J., Peters, J., Tobriner, J., Peek, J., Mosk, J., and Burke, J., concurred.

Lien theories attribute a liability against the property for different character funds or labor invested in the property and provides for a return on that liability. Depending upon its character, upon property division, the liability and the accrued return on that investment are awarded as an asset to one of the parties.

These theories demonstrate how appreciation or other growth in value from the acquisition of mixed character property. The date of the marriage, and the date of divorce, is divided in different ways in different jurisdictions.

There are other problems that exist any time a couple mixes property with other property that is not of the same nature. When property is mixed, there are immediately questions of how the ownership accounting should be determined. The division and character of the sources of funds used to purchase property becomes an issue. There is no question most accountants would believe an allocation of ownership could be performed, but the methodology can be disputed. It becomes a question of what system is used. When a financial account exists that has mixed funds, and there is an investment made out of the account, there are a number of systems that can be applied to determine the nature of the investment.

If the account was clearly established as a separate account or a marital/community account, it can be argued that the nature of the account at establishment clearly determines the nature of an investment made from the account. Therefore, an investment made from a separate account would be a separate investment. This theory comes under attack when mixed funds are introduced into the account. Once that occurs, the character of the investment becomes unclear. Once the account has mixed funds, there are any numbers of theories that can be applied to determine the character of an asset acquired from the account.

If the source of funds was a separate account and there were sufficient separate funds in the account to fund an investment, then clearly the investment could be separate property. This could be the case even if there were also marital/community funds in the same account. A contrary argument could be made that the investment was owned in proportion to the nature and amount of the funds that existed in the account at the date of the acquisition of the asset. There is the argument that if the account were separate, a first-in-first-out method of tracing would be used. Therefore, to the extent separate funds were available, they are used until exhausted to acquire the asset. If there are not sufficient separate funds in the account to pay for the assets, then the balance of the assets is owned by the marital/community estate. There is also the contrary argument that the last funds deposited in the account would be used first to make the investment. Even more outside the financial advisers' area of expertise is the argument that there is a fiduciary responsibility by each party to the marital/community estate. Maybe the party making the investment owed the marital/community estate the first right to make the investment. This would assume there were sufficient marital/community funds available to make the investment. This would more closely conform to the standards legally established for business executives and members of corporate boards of directors. It raises the issue of whether parties in a relationship owe each other the duty to maximize their relationship's value.

There are also property characterization issues when debt is used to acquire property. There is a question whether the funds that come from the debt are marital or community, or whether they are separate. Each jurisdiction will have its own rules on these matters. The determination may be made based upon issues such as whether the lender was notified of the nature of the loan in advance of it being made, or whether there were sufficient same character assets and income to support the debt. Assuming one can determine the proper characterization of the loan, the manner in which the debt affects the property division may center on the nature of the funds used to pay down the debt.

Various jurisdictions may consider the support of a spouse in obtaining a degree or professional license to create a property interest in the spouse's future income. There are other jurisdictions that consider degrees and licenses to be personal in nature and as such separate, if they are considered property at all. A case that details some of the issues that may be considered in such a determination is the Supreme Court of California case of *Sullivan*. It is included as Exhibit 3.7.

EXHIBIT 3.7   Supreme Court of California, Case of *Sullivan*

In re Marriage of Sullivan

SUPREME COURT OF CALIFORNIA
L.A. No. 31653
37 C3d 762, 209 CR 354, 691 P2d 1020, 1982 CFLR 1994, 1985 CFLR 2698, CFLP §§G.67.10-G.67.13

December 31, 1984

IN RE THE MARRIAGE OF JANET LINNEA AND MARK JAYE SULLI-VAN. MARK JAYE SULLIVAN, APPELLANT, v. JANET LINNEA SULLIVAN, APPELLANT

Superior Court of Orange County, No. D-147767, John K. Trotter, Jr., Judge, and Robert A. Schwamb, Temporary Judge. (Footnote)

Sorenson & Meek, Morris J. Sorenson and Max Goodman for Appellant Husband.

Fred J. Hiestand and Hassard, Bonnington, Rogers & Huber as Amici Curiae on behalf of Appellant Husband.

Patricia Herzog for Appellant Wife.

Linda S. Mullenix, Phyllis Alden Truby, Grace Ganz Blumberg, Marti Ann Draper, Carol S. Boyk, Gassner & Gassner, Beverly Jean Gassner, Covington & Crowe, Donald G. Haslam, Jean D. Marcucci and Judi Oser as Amici Curiae on behalf of Appellant Wife.

Opinion by Bird, C. J., with Kaus, Broussard, Reynoso and Grodin, JJ., concurring. Separate concurring and dissenting opinion by Mosk, J. Bird [37 Cal3d Page 765]

EXHIBIT 3.7 *(Continued)*

I.

Is a spouse, who has made economic sacrifices to enable the other spouse to obtain a professional education, entitled to any compensation for his or her contribution upon dissolution of the marriage?

Janet and Mark Sullivan were married in September of 1967. The following year, Mark (respondent) entered medical school at Irvine and Janet (appellant) began her final year of undergraduate college at UCLA. (Footnote 1.)

Appellant gives the following abbreviated account of the ensuing years. (Footnote 2.) From 1968 through 1971, respondent attended medical school. Until 1969, appellant worked part time while completing her undergraduate education. After graduation, she obtained a full-time position which she held through 1971.

In 1972, respondent began his internship at Portland, Oregon. Appellant gave up her full-time job to accompany him there. Shortly after the move, she obtained part-time employment.

The couple's daughter, Treisa, was born in May of 1974. Appellant ceased work until 1975 when she resumed part-time employment. From [37 Cal3d Page 766] 1976 through 1977, she worked full-time. During this period, respondent completed his residency.

Both parties then moved back to California. Shortly afterward, they separated. In August 1978, respondent petitioned for dissolution of the marriage.

During the marriage, the couple had accumulated some used furniture and two automobiles, both with payments outstanding. This property was disposed of by agreement. Appellant received $500, some used furniture and her automobile, including the obligation to complete the payments.

At the dissolution proceeding, appellant sought to introduce evidence of the value of respondent's medical education. She argued that the education was obtained by the joint efforts and sacrifices of the couple, that it constituted the greatest asset of the marriage, and that—accordingly—both parties should share in its benefits.

The superior court rejected these arguments and granted respondent's motion *in limine* to exclude all evidence pertaining to the value of the education. At the same time, the court granted partial summary judgment to the effect that respondent's education did not constitute community property. The court indicated that it was barred from awarding appellant any compensation for her contribution to respondent's education by the rule of *In re Marriage of Aufmuth* (1979) 89 Cal. App. 3d 446, 461 [152 Cal. Rptr. 668] (professional education does not constitute community property).

In May of 1980, the court issued its interlocutory judgment of dissolution. Appellant was awarded no spousal support, but the court reserved juris-

(continues)

EXHIBIT 3.7   *(Continued)*

diction for five years to modify that determination. The parties were awarded joint custody of their daughter. Respondent was ordered to pay appellant $250 per month for child support and to reimburse her for half the cost of the child's medical insurance. Finally, the court directed respondent to pay appellant $1,250 in attorney fees and $1,000 in costs.

Both parties appealed.

II.

This court originally granted a hearing in this case primarily to determine whether a spouse, who has made economic sacrifices to enable the other spouse to obtain an education, is entitled to compensation upon dissolution of the marriage. While the case was pending before this court, the [37 Cal3d Page 767] Legislature amended the Family Law Act to provide compensation in all cases not yet final on January 1, 1985. (Stats. 1984, ch. 1661, §§ 2-4.) Footnote 3.)

The amendments provide for the community to be reimbursed, absent an express written agreement to the contrary, for "community contributions to education or training of a party that substantially enhances the earning capacity of the party." (Civ. Code, § 4800.3, added by Stats. 1984, ch. 1661, § 2.) The compensable community contributions are defined as "payments made with community property for education or training or for the repayment of a loan incurred for education or training." (Ibid.) The reimbursement award may be reduced or modified where an injustice would otherwise result. (Ibid.) (Footnote 4.) [37 Cal3d Page 768]

In addition to providing for reimbursement, the amendments require the court to consider, in awarding spousal support, "the extent to which the supported spouse contributed to the attainment of an education, training, or a license by the other spouse." (Civ. Code, § 4801, as amended by Stats. 1984, ch. 1661, § 3.)

Since the property settlement in the present proceeding will not be final on January 1, 1985 (see Cal. Rules of Court, rule 24(a)), appellant is entitled to the benefit of the new amendments. (Stats. 1984, ch. 1661, § 4.) The trial court did not, of course, make the findings necessary to determine whether and in what amount reimbursement and/or support should be awarded under these provisions since they were not in existence at that time. Accordingly, the judgment denying any compensation for contributions to education must be reversed.

III.

Respondent has cross-appealed from that portion of the trial court's judgment ordering him to pay $1,250 for appellant's attorney fees and $1,000 for her costs. He contends that the decision was an abuse of the trial court's discretion.

EXHIBIT 3.7 (*Continued*)

Civil Code section 4370 provides that "[in] respect to services rendered or costs incurred after the entry of judgment, the court may award such costs and attorneys' fees as may be reasonably necessary to maintain or defend any subsequent proceeding . . . ." The purpose of the award is to provide one of the parties, if necessary, with an amount adequate to properly litigate the controversy. (*In re Marriage of Popenhager* (1979) 99 Cal. App. 3d 514, 525 [160 Cal. Rptr. 379]; *In re Marriage of Aufmuth,* supra, 89 Cal. App. 3d at p. 466.)

In making its determination as to whether or not attorney fees and costs should be awarded, the trial court considers the respective needs and incomes of the parties. (*In re Marriage of Popenhager,* supra, 99 Cal. App. 3d at p. 525; *In re Marriage of Janssen* (1975) 48 Cal. App. 3d 425, 428 [121 Cal. Rptr. 701].) Further, the trial court is not restricted in its assessment of ability to pay to a consideration of salary alone, but may consider all the evidence concerning the parties' income, assets and abilities. (*Meagher v. Meagher* (1961) 190 Cal. App. 2d 62, 64 [11 Cal. Rptr. 650]; *Estes v. Estes* (1958) 158 Cal. App. 2d 94, 98 [322 P.2d 238].

Finally, a motion for attorney fees and costs in a dissolution proceeding is left to the sound discretion of the trial court. (*Stewart v. Stewart* (1909) 156 Cal. 651, 656 [105 P. 955]; *In re Marriage of Cueva* (1978) 86 Cal. App. 3d 290, 296 [37 Cal3d Page 769] [149 Cal. Rptr. 918].) In the absence of a clear showing of abuse, its determination will not be disturbed on appeal. (Ibid.; *In re Marriage of Janssen,* supra, 48 Cal. App. 3d at p. 428.) "[The] trial court's order will be overturned only if, considering all the evidence viewed most favorably in support of its order, no judge could reasonably make the order made. [Citations.]" (*In re Marriage of Cueva,* supra, 86 Cal. App. 3d at p. 296.)

Review of the total financial situation of each of the parties reveals that there is substantial evidence to support the trial court's order. The record reflects that the trial court considered the financial statements of both the appellant and respondent before making its award. Appellant's financial statement disclosed a net monthly income that was several hundred dollars less than her monthly expenses. Further, appellant's total separate property assets amounted to even less than her net monthly income. According to her statement, then, appellant's assets would have been depleted within a matter of months and her expenses would continue to exceed her net income.

Respondent's financial statement, prepared in the spring of 1980, also reflected monthly expenses which exceeded his net monthly income by over $800. Similarly, respondent's assets, although greater than appellant's, would also have been depleted within a few months if his income and expenses remained the same.

(*continues*)

EXHIBIT 3.7   *(Continued)*

However, the court also had before it a comparative statement of respondent's business revenue and expenditures for the years 1978 and 1979, respondent's first two years of medical practice. Significantly, this comparative statement demonstrated that the fees which respondent collected during his second year of practice were more than double the fees he collected during the first. His annual net income increased by over $40,000 in one year. On the other hand, there was no corresponding statement or testimony to indicate any likelihood of an increase in appellant's income.

Given this evidence, this court can only conclude that the trial court made the reasonable inference that respondent's burgeoning medical practice would continue to flourish and that his income would increase dramatically. The facts of this case fall woefully short of establishing any abuse of discretion by the trial court. "[The] cases have frequently and uniformly held that the court may base its decision on the [paying spouse's] ability to earn, rather than his [or her] current earnings . . ." for the simple reason that in cases such as this, current earnings give a grossly distorted view of the paying spouse's financial ability. (*Meagher v. Meagher,* supra, 190 Cal. App. 2d at p. 64.) [37 Cal3d Page 770]

IV.

That portion of the judgment ordering respondent to pay appellant's costs and attorney fees is affirmed. The judgment denying compensation for contributions to spousal education is reversed and the cause remanded for further proceedings consistent with the views expressed in this opinion. Appellant to recover costs on both appeals.

Disposition

That portion of the judgment ordering respondent to pay appellant's costs and attorney fees is affirmed. The judgment denying compensation for contributions to spousal education is reversed and the cause remanded for further proceedings consistent with the views expressed in this opinion. Appellant to recover costs on both appeals.

MOSK, J. While I agree this matter should be returned to the trial court for consideration in the light of recent legislation, I fear that inappropriate language in the majority opinion may mislead the bench and bar. Several times in the majority opinion—indeed, in framing a question at the outset—there is reference to "compensation" for contributions to education. I must assume the repetition of that term was calculated and not inadvertent.

At no place in the relevant legislation does the word "compensation" appear. With clarity and precision, the Legislature referred instead to "reimbursement." The terms are not synonymous; there is a significant distinction that extends beyond mere semantics. Reimbursement implies re -payment of a debt or obligation; that is what the Legislature obviously contemplated.

EXHIBIT 3.7   (*Continued*)

Compensation, on the other hand, may be payment in any sum for any lawful purpose; the Legislature also obviously did not intend to give such a blank check to trial courts.

Furthermore, the majority, in their creative reference to "compensation," fail to emphasize to whom it is to be paid. It is not to an individual spouse, in response to the initial query of the majority. The Legislature was crystal clear: reimbursement is to be made to the community. The community consists of both the husband and the wife, not one or the other. Thus when reimbursement is made to the community, that reclaimed community asset should be divided between the husband and wife in the same manner as all other community property.

I point out that the issue framed in this case does not involve the element of spousal support. That is to be awarded generally on the basis of the needs of one spouse and the ability of the other to pay, although a number of other factors may be considered. (Civ. Code, § 4801.) The only issue raised by the appellant in these proceedings is whether acquired knowledge and education are a species of property subject to monetary division. The Legislature has now answered that question in the negative.

To review the legislation: Civil Code section 4800.3, subdivision (b)(1), provides "The community shall be reimbursed for community contributions [37 Cal3d Page 771] to education or training of a party that substantially enhances the earning capacity of the party. The amount reimbursed shall be with interest . . . ." Subdivision (c) provides "The reimbursement and assignment required by this section shall be reduced or modified . . . ." Subdivision (d) is even more precise: " Reimbursement for community contributions and assignment of loans pursuant to this section is the exclusive remedy of the community or a party for the education or training and any resulting enhancement of the earning capacity of a party." (Italics added.)

One searches in vain in the statute for a single use of the word "compensation." Thus I find it curious that the majority choose to employ that term rather than to consistently adhere to "reimbursement," the only monetary claim authorized by the Legislature. I trust that trial courts will not be misled into making awards of any sums for any purpose other than that permitted in what the Legislature described with remarkable emphasis as "the exclusive remedy."

General Footnotes
[53] Footnote. Pursuant to Constitution, article VI, section 21.

(*continues*)

EXHIBIT 3.7   *(Continued)*

Opinion Footnotes

Footnote 1. Both parties appealed from the judgment. However, Janet appealed on the issue that prompted this court to grant a hearing. Therefore, Janet will be referred to as appellant and Mark as respondent.

Footnote 2. This account is contained in appellant's trial brief, which was added to the record on appeal by stipulation, and which was before the trial court at the time of its rulings on the motions at issue here. Respondent has stated that he does not object to the use of these facts as general background.

It is not disputed that respondent obtained his professional education during the marriage or that appellant worked to support the couple. Also undisputed are the facts relating to the couple's property settlement and to the dissolution proceedings. (See post, at p. 766.)

Footnote 3. Chapter 1661 amended sections 4800 and 4801 of the Civil Code and added section 4800.3. At the time of filing of this opinion, the changes had not been published in code form. Accordingly, the citations in this opinion are to session and chapter number.

Footnote 4. The reimbursement provision states in full: "Section 4800.3 is added to the Civil Code, to read:

"4800.3. (a) As used in this section, 'community contributions to education or training' means payments made with community property for education or training or for the repayment of a loan incurred for education or training. "(b) Subject to the limitations provided in this section, upon dissolution of marriage or legal separation: "(1) The community shall be reimbursed for community contributions to education or training of a party that substantially enhances the earning capacity of the party. The amount reimbursed shall be with interest at the legal rate, accruing from the end of the calendar year in which the contributions were made. "(2) A loan incurred during marriage for the education or training of a party shall not be included among the liabilities of the community for the purpose of division pursuant to Section 4800 but shall be assigned for payment by the party. "(3) The reimbursement and assignment required by this section shall be reduced or modified to the extent circumstances render such a disposition unjust, including but not limited to any of the following: "(1) The community has substantially benefited from the education, training, or loan incurred for the education or training of the party. There is a rebuttable presumption, affecting the burden of proof, that the community has not substantially benefited from community contributions to the education or training made less than 10 years before the commencement of the proceeding, and that the community has substantially benefited from community contributions to the education or training made more than 10 years before the commencement of the proceeding. "(2) The education or training received by the party is offset by the education or training received

---

EXHIBIT 3.7 *(Continued)*

---

by the other party for which community contributions have been made. "(3) The education or training enables the party receiving the education or training to engage in gainful employment that substantially reduces the need of the party for support that would otherwise be required. "(4) Reimbursement for community contributions and assignment of loans pursuant to this section is the exclusive remedy of the community or a party for the education or training and any resulting enhancement of the earning capacity of a party. However, nothing in this subdivision shall limit consideration of the effect of the education, training, or enhancement, or the amount reimbursed pursuant to this section, on the circumstances of the parties for the purpose of an order for support pursuant to Section 4801. "(5) This section is subject to an express written agreement of the parties to the contrary."

There are many accounting issues and valuation issues that must be dealt with by financial experts as a result of these various systems of property characterization. Experts must, without exception, become familiar with the law that exists in the states where they practice.

FAMILY-LIMITED PARTNERSHIPS

Estate planners, looking for ways to reduce the estate and gift tax effects on transfers of property to heirs, seized upon discounts as a mechanism for drastically reducing the fair market value of transferred assets. By doing so, they were able to substantially reduce estate and gift taxes. They created limited partnerships, open only to family members, grantors, and the objects of their bounty, and transferred significant marital assets into them. Revenue Ruling 93–12 opened the door to this new estate-planning tool called the family-limited partnership. In its conventional form, the family-limited partnership allows individuals to continue to control their estates, but to potentially decrease the value of assets included in their estates by the 30 to 70 percent minority and marketability discount afforded by this structure. There are advisers who have their clients claim larger reductions.

Thereafter, the owners of the assets, typically mom and dad, would gift or bequest the limited-partnership interests to their children. Since these were nonmarketable, minority interests in the limited partnership, the fair market value of the transfers of the interests were determined after the application of those discounts. The discounts allow the grantors to gift more property without gift tax, to significantly reduce any gift tax payable, and to significantly reduce the value of the assets included in their estates. Oftentimes, there is no business purpose for these partnerships except the avoidance of the potential tax liabilities.

Revenue Ruling 93-12 states that for gift tax purposes business *control* should be considered in determining the value of an ownership interest transferred from one family member to another. This ruling acquiesces to the Tax Court's decision in *Estate of Lee v Commissioner* 69TC 860(1978). It gives up the Internal Revenue Service's position that control be determined based on family attribution rules, which position imputed ownership for control purposes among members of a family. The result of this imputation was that minority valuation discounts were not applicable. Most states are unclear about the consequences or impact of the family-limited partnership upon the division of property in a marital dissolution.

The estate planners had to assume, and rightly so, that the Internal Revenue Service was not going to favor these entities. Financial advisers can expect the divorce courts to behave similarly. Initially, predictions were that these entities would be attacked because of their lack of legitimate business purpose and perhaps be disregarded by the courts as a sham. The Internal Revenue Service has made such attacks, but the courts have taken different roads.

Interesting issues arise when the estate-planning mechanism of the family-limited partnership is viewed with an eye to the possibility of a divorce of the founding participants. As the Tax Court has observed, these tax avoidance vehicles obviously, at the very least, alter the legal relationships between the participants and their heirs, family members, and creditors. The overriding purposes of such partnerships involve the drastic reduction in value of property passed to heirs and the resultant tax savings. These results are achieved while still allowing the hypothetical husband and wife to exercise virtually complete control over the assets of the partnership during their lives. When working with a founding-family-limited partnership party to a divorce lawsuit, the overriding problem faced by the financial adviser is what is the nature and value of the interest they and their spouse may own.

Once a family-limited partnership is created, is it ever possible to extricate the parties from continued, lifelong involvement with one another, particularly when the bulk of their assets are the property of the partnership? If it is not possible to separate the individuals from the partnership, does the domestic relations court have the jurisdiction to impose its ruling against the partnership, which is typically not a party to the divorce lawsuit? If the court does not have such power, what other methods may be imposed to impart an equitable division of property by the court?

Does the necessity of continued involvement in the partnership by the divorcing parties create a potential risk of liability to extramarital partners if the partnership assets are improperly managed due to lack of consensus or irrational decisions? Perhaps the extramarital partners have an interest in keeping the partnership intact and, as such, could interfere with the divorce process.

Should one possible alternative of the court be awarding mutual control of the partnership to the divorcing couple? If mutual control is not desirable or to be avoided, is the noncontrolling spouse entitled to a greater interest in the marital estate to compensate for the lack of control of the asset? Put another way, are discounts legally or practically applicable when considering the value of partnership interests for property distribution purposes? There is no question that the restrictions written into the partnership agreements cause the sum of the fair market value of the individual partnership interests to be substantially less than the value of the underlying partnership property.

Would partnership law, the partnership agreement, or state property division law allow one party to control, in spite of the other party's ownership, a larger percentage of the general partners' interests?

How do the rights of the extramarital partners or the partnership agreement affect the ability to leave one's spouse or another in a controlling position, or to even allocate their respective interests in the divorce proceeding? For example, would local law allow the conversion of a portion of the general partner's interest to a limited partner's interest (with or without the cooperation of extramarital partners)? Does the agreement or applicable law even allow the partition of the interests? What are the tax effects of such machinations?

Would the proposal of a partition of the spouses' interest create an opportunity for other partners to dissolve the partnership or take control? Would *dissolution on divorce* provisions in a family-limited partnership organic document increase the risk of the Internal Revenue Service or Tax Court disregarding the entity?

Does an estate planner, an attorney, or financial adviser, implementing a family limited partnership, have a duty to fully inform married parties of the extent of the potential changes in their legal relationships, and how those changes may impact their marital property rights? Should these advisers fully consider the possible ramifications of a subsequent divorce when advising or assisting in the implementation of a family-limited partnership?

These questions probably do not exhaust the potential issues involved in divorcing participants. The most current and timely law on these matters currently comes from the Tax Court. When advising clients, financial advisers should review the current status of these entities in both the divorce and tax courts. Attached is a checklist detailing information that may be helpful when working with a family-limited partnership.

Disclosure Requirements for Gift Tax Returns

Of interest to financial advisers and to parties to divorces attempting to value assets that may have been transferred by a gift, is a requirement issued by the Internal Revenue Service related to disclosure on gift tax returns. This regulation requires significant valuation information be disclosed on the face of the return. If the disclosure requirement is not met, a complete appraisal of the property by a qualified appraiser must be attached. The statute of limitation fails to toll as the penalty for failing to attach the required information or report. Parties that fail to include the required information will be subject to examination forever.

Internal Revenue Service Regulation 301-6501(c)–1 applies to gifts made after December 31, 1996 for which the gift tax return for such year is filed after December 3, 1999. This regulation requires disclosure of a detailed description of the method used to value any interest transferred in an entity not actively traded. A description must be provided for any discount claimed in valuing the interests in the entity or any assets owned by such entity. Any restrictions related to the transferred property considered in the valuation must be disclosed along with a description of any discounts, such as discounts for blockage, minority or fractional interests, and lack of marketability. The disclosure must also include the value of 100 percent of the entity, any discounts in valuing the entity or any assets owned by the entity, the pro rata portion of the entity subject to the transfer, and the fair market value of the transferred interest as reported on the return.

The regulation allows the submission of appraisals in lieu of the above-required disclosure. An individual who holds himself out as an appraiser must perform the appraisal. The individual must have qualifications including background, experience, education, and membership in professional appraisal organizations and be qualified to make appraisals of the type of property being valued. The individual must not be the donor, donee, or be employed by the donor or the donee, or be a family member of either. The appraisal must detail the type of information related to the valuation as described in this paper.

There will be significant valuation information disclosed if gift tax returns have been filed by the parties since the implementation of this regulation. This information can be an important source of valuation data that is independent from the divorce. This information can be especially useful to the financial adviser. There may be additional information requested during the appraisal process. In addition to the information above, there may be some instances where the advisers will request general ledgers, accounting journals, payroll tax returns, sales tax returns, bank statements, cancelled checks, and other such documentation.

TAXATION OF PROPERTY TRANSFERS

The transfer of property incident to a divorce falls within the provisions of Internal Revenue Code Section 1041. There is no gain or loss recognized on the transfer and the basis of the property is not adjusted for the valuation in the property settlement. This was not the case prior to the implementation of the Code Section. Prior to the implementation, gains and losses could be recognized upon the culmination of property settlements pursuant to a divorce. While this result has been eliminated for divorcing couples, the possibility still exists for couples dividing property acquired during non-traditional relationships.

Revenue Rules—Incident to a divorce. A transfer of property is *incident to the divorce* if it:

- Occurs within 1 year after the date the marriage ends, or
- Is related to the cessation of the marriage. (*Internal Revenue Code Section 1041(c)*.)

Transfers are related to the cessation of the marriage if they are made pursuant to a divorce or separation instrument and occur within six years of the marriage's end. For this purpose, a *divorce or separation instrument* includes a modification or amendment of the instrument. In addition, annulments and cessation of marriages that are void from the beginning because of state law violations are considered divorces for purposes of Internal Revenue Code Section 1041.

Transfers that are not pursuant to a divorce or separation instrument, or that occur more than six years after the marriage ends are presumed not related to the marriage's end. Showing the transfer was made to divide property owned by the former spouses when the marriage ended may rebut this presumption. Temporary Regulation Section 1.1041–1T(b), Question and Answer 7 and 8.

REDEMPTION OF STOCK IN A CLOSELY HELD CORPORATION

In most divorces involving businesses, the business is the most valuable asset in the couple's estate. As a result, the assets that are available to equalize the party's estate typically are inside the business, or will be earned by the business in the future. One common method of equalizing these marital estates has been to transfer corporate cash and notes to the nonemployee spouse in exchange for that individual's interest in the corporation.

The income taxation consequences of that type of transaction were unsettled for a number of years. In some cases, the nonemployee spouse was treated as redeeming stock from the corporation and was taxed on the gain.

In other circumstances, the cash and property received by the nonemployee spouse was treated as qualifying under Internal Revenue Code Section 1041 and no tax was charged. Under Temporary Income Tax Regulation 1.1041-1T(c), Question and Answer Nine, the Internal Revenue Service has declared that there are three situations in which transfers to third parties on behalf of a spouse could qualify under §1041. These situations are:

1. Where the transfer to a third party is required by the divorce or separation instrument.
2. Where the transfer to a third party is pursuant to the written request of the other spouse.
3. Where the transferor receives from the other spouse a ratification or written consent to the transfer to the third party.

It is important to note that, when one of these conditions is met, Question and Answer Nine specifically provides that the transfer of property will be deemed to have been made directly to the nontransferring spouse, who is then deemed to have immediately transferred the property to the third party. The constructive transfer from the non-transferring spouse to the third party is "not a transaction that qualifies for non-recognition of gain under Section 1041."

This position by the Internal Revenue Service led to another potential taxable event. The deemed constructive transfer to the nontransferring spouse triggers this event. When the deemed transfer comes from a corporation with retained profits, the Internal Revenue Service has attempted to treat the transfer as a dividend to the non-transferring spouse. In addition, they argued the interest paid by the corporation on the deferred portion of the transfer was not deductible as a business expense and was part of the dividend the remaining shareholder received.

In several of the cases tried, the Internal Revenue Service argued all of these positions in the same case. While they were successful in some circumstances, in others, the courts found there was no taxable event to any of the parties. In August 2002, the Internal Revenue Service issued a Proposed Amendment of 1.1041–1T. This amendment proposes that the result contemplated in Question and Answer Nine would not apply to transfers in which a new proposed Section 1.1041-2 does apply.

Section 1.1041-2, as proposed, gives the attorney drafting the agreement the option of determining how the proceeds will be taxed. Depending on the wording in the document, the transfer can be taxed as a redemption by the nonshareholder spouse, or as a dividend paid to the shareholder spouse. By following the provisions in the Proposed Regulation, not only can the attorney determine which party will be taxed, he can insure that the other party will not be taxed. There is another provision in the Proposed Regulation that states the determination of tax treatment can be made by written agreement by both spouses no later than the timely filing of the nontransferor spouse's income tax return for the year that includes the redemption.

This provides a real example of a circumstance where the parties to the divorce may want to settle their case, rather than present such a complex tax issue to a judge to make a ruling. By settling the case, they can determine the taxation of the redemption and insure their attorney properly drafts the documents to implement the agreement. Otherwise, in some cases, the judge may not address the issue. In others, the judge may rule which party should be taxed. The judge will always attempt to rule in accordance with the local laws, which may or may not be in the best interest of the divorcing couple.

The determination of the nature, valuation, and distribution of property are at the core of the divorce process. The financial adviser has an obligation to his client to understand the financial consequences of each of these processes in the local jurisdiction to insure the client has timely advice regarding the division of the marital/community estate.

CHAPTER 4

The Valuation of Businesses in Divorce Litigation

BUSINESS VALUATION

The valuation of a business for purposes of dividing property between spouses is a frequent source of litigation. Generally, the valuation method appropriate for domestic relations litigation is determined by local case law. For this reason, opinions rendered by valuation specialists for this purpose are determinations of "fair value" as opposed to "fair market value." In a domestic relations case, there is no willing buyer, one party may have limited information, and the other is typically ordered by the court to purchase their spouse's interest in the business. As a result of these differences, the term "fair value" was created.

In the case of businesses started during the marriage, the value determined by the court will be used in the property division. Multiple valuations may be required in some jurisdictions where the increase in value of separate property is considered to be marital or community property. In these cases, a valuation must be performed at the date of marriage with a second valuation performed at the appropriate dissolution date. In these states, the difference in the values becomes a part of the property that will be divided by the court. In other states, the value of the labor performed for a business versus the compensation for that labor becomes a factor. If the business is separate property and labor is used to enhance the business' value without being properly compensated, the amount of undercompensation may become marital or community property.

Valuation advisers may come from a variety of disciplines. They can be Certified Public Accountants, without other certification, but

97

possibly may be a member of the American Institute of Certified Public Accountants, or a Certified Public Accountant/Accredited in Business Valuation by the American Institute of Certified Public Accountants. Other certifications are available from the National Association of Certified Valuation Analysts, the American Society of Appraisers (from any academic discipline), or the Institute of Business Appraisers (also from any academic discipline). The American Society of Appraisers, National Association of Certified Valuation Analysts, and the Institute of Business Appraisers each have formal valuation standards that have been adopted by the organizations. The American Institute of Certified Public Accountants is in the process of formalizing standards that were released in the fall of 2002. Each of these standards contain, or will contain, report-writing rules that prescribe the written presentation of the valuation analysis and the conclusions reached by the valuator. The members of these organizations must comply with the standards of their membership organization. The American Society of Appraisers also requires compliance with the Appraisal Foundation's Uniform Standards of Professional Appraisal Practice (USPAP). These standards (USPAP) are adopted by the federal courts and are required to be followed by all experts in federal cases. Further, the financial adviser should also be aware that the Internal Revenue Service has adopted internal standards that are patterned after the National Association of Certified Valuation Analysts' standards. While the standards in place are not identical, they bear such similarity as to appear so to the layperson. In addition, the Department of Labor and the local court system in the advisers' jurisdiction may have standards that apply to valuation or expert witness engagements. In certain settings, the Federal Rules of Civil Procedure may also be relevant as many jurisdictions have adopted those rules as their own. If not, the adviser must be aware of the local rules that have been adopted. All of these standards, except the Federal Rules of Civil Procedure and standards in those jurisdictions adopting their own rules, do not require the valuator to issue a formal written report in valuation engagements resulting from litigation. Local law and rules may, however, require some form of report or exhibits. The remainder of this chapter describes the general current state of the standards and provides information that will assist the evaluation of work performed by others in domestic relations matters.

STANDARDS

All of the governing organizations that preside over the business valuation discipline recognize that Internal Revenue Ruling 59–60 provides the core of current valuation theory. By following the analysis detailed in the elements of this ruling, the adviser has a checklist that can be used to determine if proper methodologies have been used in any appraisal reviewed.

In addition, the American Society of Appraisers, the National Association of Certified Valuation Analysts, and the Institute of Business Appraisers all have detailed written standards. The American Institute of Certified Public Accountants is in the process of developing standards. Each of these organizations' published standards are very similar to each other and will provide the financial adviser with detailed information regarding the valuation and reporting process.

The Uniform Standards of Professional Appraisal Practice Standard Nine addresses the substantive aspects of business and intangible appraisal, and Standard Ten addresses written reports. These standards provide the financial adviser with the general framework for a complete valuation analysis. The remaining portions of the Uniform Standards of Professional Appraisal Practice deal with the valuation of assets other than businesses.

Valuations may vary in form and content depending on the purpose or use of the valuation, the size and complexity of the business interest being valued, and the form of presentation chosen by the adviser.

Purpose of the Valuation and Key Valuation Issues

When a valuation analysis is performed, the purpose or reason for the valuation and any key valuation issues are normally discussed in a transmittal letter, executive summary, or opinion letter. A summary of the information considered, the analysis performed, and the conclusions of value are presented. This summary details the client or individual for whom the valuation has been performed, identifies the entity being valued, and discloses the purpose and intended use of the valuation. It discusses the definition of the standard and premise of value, the date at which the business interest is being valued, and the date the report is issued. It identifies and describes the business interest being valued, including any rights or restrictions related to that interest, and identifies any assumptions, limiting conditions, or scope limitations that were a factor in the analysis. Finally, it will detail any limitations on the use of the report and contain the signature of the evaluator or the evaluator's firm. An executive summary or opinion letter is not intended to stand alone and should clearly refer to the report to discourage its use separate and apart from the report.

Limiting Conditions

Every valuation is subject to limiting conditions and assumptions. Some valuations are constrained by scope limitations. These occur when the valuator is unable to complete all of the steps that would normally be included in a complete valuation. The limiting conditions, assumptions, and scope limitations are disclosed in the body of the report. These conditions are sometimes presented in a stand-alone appendix to the report, or can be presented in the summary or opinion letter. In divorce litigation, these limitations become important, as they may provide fruit for cross-examination of an opposing expert. Realizing this, the valuation adviser should carefully consider the limitations that may apply to the valuation to not limit the effectiveness of the report. Limiting conditions should always include defining the premise of value, the standard of value, and the purpose of the report. Other limiting conditions can include a statement of independence that confirms that the valuator has no future or contemplated interest in the business being valued, a statement that the valuator has no obligation to update the report for events and circumstances occurring subsequent to the date of the report, or a statement reflecting the valuator's reliance on information and representations furnished by management without any further verification as to its veracity. They also include a restriction that the report is only valid for the date and purpose specified, a statement of reliance on the work of other professionals (e.g., an equipment appraiser), and a statement that business valuations may be based on future earnings potential that may or may not materialize. In domestic relations cases, local law will determine the valuation date. It may be the date of divorce, the date of separation, or some other imposed date. Failure to utilize the proper date can render an adviser's work worthless.

Summary of Valuation Findings

The conclusion of value will be clearly expressed in the report, normally both in the summary opinion letter and in the body of the report. In a divorce court, where no report is produced, the expert should be ready to verbally support conclusions of value and support all of the elements that would normally be contained in a written report.

Firm and Valuator Experience and Qualifications

The valuator who is primarily responsible for the conclusions of value must be identified in the body of the report. The valuator's training and experience will be discussed to provide the reader with information that enables the determination of the valuator's qualifications. In litigation, the valuator qualifications will be detailed in their qualification as an expert witness. More than one valuator may be identified in the valuation of a business. Even if one valuator ultimately forms the conclusion of value, the other valuation advisers may have collaborative input into one or more key assumptions or conclusions used in the process. It is not unusual for multiple professionals working on the same project to reach a consensus on the conclusion of value. In addition, there may be a discussion of a firm's expertise and valuation experience to provide the user of the report additional information regarding the capabilities and qualifications of the valuation team.

Valuation Approaches

Fair market value is the price that a buyer could reasonably be expected to accept if the assets were exposed for sale on the open market for a reasonable period of time, both buyer and seller being in possession of the pertinent facts, and neither being under compulsion to consummate the transaction. In addition, court decisions frequently state the hypothetical buyer and seller are assumed to be able, as well as willing, to consummate a transfer. Fundamental to this concept of fair market value is the assumption that there exists for the business an open market in which there are a number of potential buyers and sellers, each seller offering property more or less similar to that whose value is being determined by the appraiser. Obviously, such conditions may not exist with respect to a given entity. The open marketing of a company is frequently undesirable because of confidentiality issues. It is also unlikely that any similar businesses will be for sale at the time the valuation is being performed.

It must be understood that the appraisal environment is different from a business sale environment, where the company is actually put on the market. Recognition must be given to the fact that businesses are bought and sold for a price after lengthy disclosure and negotiation. Many times, the actual transactions are the result of conditions that are outside the definition of fair market value. Examples could include a seller forced to sell for reasons of ill health, or a purchaser acquiring a business to gain some competitive advantage that may not be available to other purchasers in the market place. The appraiser's role is to estimate the value based on a hypothetical purchaser and seller who never exist in reality. Numerous conditions may have an influence upon price in actual transactions that would not affect the theoretical fair market value. The purpose of a valuation is to determine this theoretical market value. It is probable that in hundreds of hypothetical sales between actual buyers and sellers, the business will not sell for the price estimated by a valuation adviser. It is, however, the goal of the valuation adviser to determine the most likely sale value, given the assumptions detailed in the definition of fair market value.

The valuation report should affirmatively state what premise of value is being used. These include a valuation as a going concern, a liquidating business, a synergistic, or investment value. Each of these premises will result in a different conclusion of value for the identical business. At one extreme of the range of possible sale values is liquidation value, at the other is a synergistic value that would be offered by a specialized and identifiable purchaser. Neither extreme represents the fair market value the appraiser seeks to estimate.

In addition, the report should affirmatively state the standard of value being used. The standard will typically either be fair market value or fair value. The fair market value standard assumes the facts and circumstances contemplated in the definition of fair market value. The fair value standard assumes something different. This includes a valuation based on federal or state statutes, or applicable case law. Most domestic relations valuations are based on a standard of fair value, because of the absence of a willing buyer or seller.

VALUATION METHODOLOGIES

The valuation methodologies utilized in a valuation analysis are selected based on the purpose of the valuation and the individual facts and circumstances regarding the company. The valuation adviser not only understands the valuation methods utilized in a valuation performed, but also any potential methods that could have been considered and were not used. The adviser should be able to discuss the facts considered, when choosing or rejecting methodologies. Evaluation of this information and analysis becomes the input for three separate and distinct approaches to value.

The market approach is a determination of the value at which all, or a portion of, the company would be sold on the open market. The valuation is based on information derived from the sale of all, or part of, similar businesses. This approach to value has its basis in the principle of substitution. At what value are similar assets selling?

Prior to using any method of valuation, the adviser must adjust the balance sheet and income statement of the company being valued to make the information comparable with a hypothetical company to be run by a hypothetical investor. These adjustments, sometimes called *normalization adjustments,* must be made in any method of valuation prior to any analysis being performed. These adjustments are designed to bring the assets and liabilities to fair market value and to adjust the income statement to eliminate the owner's personal and subjective influence on the expenses. One of the most common adjustments made is related to analysis of the compensation of the owners. Seldom do owners pay themselves at market rates and typically the amount of compensation they may take depends on their cash flow needs and income tax concerns.

Sources of comparable salary information include the Bureau of Labor Statistics, industry associations, and various Internet employment sites. *Carlson v. Carlson* is a case that illustrates some of the legal issues encountered when making adjustments for compensation. In *Carlson v. Carlson,* the North Carolina Court of Appeals ruled on the use of national surveys when determining the appropriate salary for a cardiologist. The complete text of the case is attached as Exhibit 4.1. The entire text of the case is included, giving the reader a view of the types of issues argued in domestic relations cases.

EXHIBIT 4.1   North Carolina Court of Appeals

NO. COA96–1098
NORTH CAROLINA COURT OF APPEALS

Filed: 5 August 1997

ERIC B. CARLSON,
Plaintiff
v.

Pitt County
No. 91-CVD-2310

PATRICIA A. CARLSON (HARRINGTON),
Defendant

ERIC B. CARLSON, Plaintiff
v.

Pitt County
No. 92-CVD-2191

PATRICIA A. CARLSON (HARRINGTON),
Defendant

Appeal by plaintiff from order entered 4 October 1995 nunc pro tunc 15 April 1995 by Judge David A. Leech in Pitt County District Court. Heard in the Court of Appeals 19 May 1997.

Ward and Smith, P.A., by Shelli Stoker Stillerman and John M. Martin, for plaintiff appellant.

Edward P. Hausle, P.A., by Edward P. Hausle, for defendant appellee.

SMITH, Judge.

Plaintiff and defendant were married on 1 June 1975, separated on 10 October 1991, and divorced on 15 December 1992. Prior to receiving evidence at an equitable distribution hearing, the parties made numerous stipulations regarding the identity, classification, valuation and distribution of a

EXHIBIT 4.1 (*Continued*)

substantial amount of property. On 24 October 1994, an equitable distribution trial was held with regard to the property issues on which the parties were unable to agree. This appeal pertains specifically to the methodology employed by the trial court in determining the value of two marital assets, a ten-acre tract of land and plaintiff's medical practice.

Plaintiff is a cardiologist trained in the highly specialized field of interventional cardiology, a sub-specialty of invasive cardiology. Invasive cardiologists perform diagnostic procedures, such as coronary catheterization, to determine whether a patient has heart disease or blockages in the arteries. Interventional cardiologists are trained to perform the same diagnostic procedures as invasive cardiologists, and in addition perform therapeutic treatments designed to remove blockages from the arteries.

Plaintiff was employed by Quadrangle Medical Specialists, P.A. from 1987 until he resigned in January 1989 and established his own cardiology practice known as Eastern Cardiology. Plaintiff selected a site located in a medical park on Stantonsburg Road in Pitt County (hereinafter Stantonsburg property) on which to build his medical offices.

In January 1990, plaintiff purchased the Stantonsburg property from Park West Properties for $389,000.00. Plaintiff's deed included a provision requiring the grantor to construct an access road from a public highway at the grantee's request. The cost of the road construction would be shared by the grantor and grantee, with the grantee's portion not to exceed $25,000.00.

Pursuant to an equitable distribution order entered 4 October 1995 *nunc pro tunc* 15 April 1995, the trial judge made numerous findings of fact valuing the marital assets of the parties. We turn first to the contested finding regarding the valuation of the Stantonsburg property.

[1] The trial court found as a fact that the value of the Stantonsburg property was $300,000.00. In addition the court made the following finding to which plaintiff assigns error:

24. (i) The deed of conveyance to plaintiff required the grantees to build an access road from Stantonsburg Road back to Plaintiff's ten-acre tract. The Court finds from the evidence presented that the cost to build this road, which would have to be built in order to get to plaintiff's land, was estimated to be no less than $75,000.00. The deed required the grantee, plaintiff, to pay up to, but no more than, $25,000.00 toward the road construction costs. The Court finds as a fact that the value of plaintiff's land is increased over the $30,000.00-per-acre value because the deed to plaintiff required the grantor to spend a sum (which the Court finds would be not less than $75,000.00 for the road), which is greater than the maximum ($25,000.00) plaintiff has to spend to build the road. The value of plaintiff's land is therefore increased because of the obligation of the grantor to build this road for plaintiff, and the increased value is $50,000.

(*continues*)

EXHIBIT 4.1 *(Continued)*

(i) [sic] Therefore, the gross fair market value of the 10 acres was $350,000.

Plaintiff contends that because the access road was never actually constructed, the trial court improperly based its valuation of the Stantonsburg property upon a fact not in existence at the date of separation.

N.C. Gen. Stat. § 50-21(b) (1995) provides that "[f]or purposes of equitable distribution, marital property shall be valued as of the date of the separation of the parties." In making a determination as to net market value of a marital asset, the trial court is required to only consider evidence of the value of the property as of the date of separation. *Christensen v. Christensen,* 101 N.C. App. 47, 55, 398 S.E.2d 634, 639 (1990). As of 10 October 1991, the date of separation, the access road had not been constructed. The evidence of the value the grantor's *promise* to build the road may have added to the land was mere speculation and improperly considered by the trial court. However, defendant contends that the trial court properly considered evidence of the promise to build a road because the *obligation* was a fact in existence as of the date of separation.

Prior to ordering an equitable distribution of marital property, the trial judge is required to calculate the net fair market value of the property. *Beightol v. Beightol,* 90 N.C. App. 58, 63, 367 S.E.2d 347, 350, *disc. review denied,* 323 N.C. 171, 373 S.E.2d 104 (1988). "*Fair market value* is defined as the price which a willing buyer would pay to purchase the asset on the open market from a willing seller, with neither party being under any compulsion to complete the transaction." Brett R. Turner, *Equitable Distribution of Property* § 7.03, at 505 (2d. ed. 1994). The trial court calculates the *net* fair market value, by reducing the fair market value of the property by the value of any debts that are attached to the asset. *Id.* at 505.

In this case, the trial court first determined the fair market value of the Stantonsburg property to be $300,000.00. The court then added $75,000.00 representing the cost of the road construction and then subtracted the $25,000.00 debt plaintiff would incur as a result of the improvement; calculating a net added value of $50,000.00.

The case *sub judice* is analogous to equitable distribution actions in which some trial courts have erroneously reduced the value of an asset by the cost of projected expenses associated with a possible future sale of the asset. The majority of jurisdictions hold that when determining the net fair market value of an asset, "the court should deduct only debts which are reasonably certain to exist in the near future." *Id.* at 506. Accordingly, most jurisdictions hold that costs associated with hypothetical sales of assets should not be subtracted from the fair market value of the property. See e.g. *McDaniel v. McDaniel,* 829 P.2d 303 (Alaska 1992); *Taber v. Taber,* 626 So. 2d 1089 (Fla. Dist. Ct. App. 1993); *In re Benkendorf,* 252 Ill. App. 3d 429, 624 N.E.2d 1241 (1993); *Goodwin v. Goodwin,* 640 So. 2d 173 (Fla. Dist. Ct. App.

EXHIBIT 4.1 *(Continued)*

1994). When an actual sale of an asset is not imminent, "expenses of sale are hypothetical liabilities which may well never be incurred." Turner, supra § 7.03 n.73 (Supp. 1996).

Moreover, the expenses of a future sale of an asset are uncertain in both occurrence and amount. *Id.* For example, the property owner may die and thus never sell the asset. *Id.* In any event, even if the sale does take place in the future, unless the sale is imminent, there is no reasonable basis upon which to predict the amount of expenses related to the sale. *Id.*

The majority rule precluding the deduction of expenses associated with future sales is equally applicable to the facts of this case. Plaintiff presented evidence showing that on several occasions he made oral and written demands to Park West requesting construction of the access road. Yet, as of the date of the equitable distribution hearing, a full three years after the date of separation, plaintiff was unaware of any plans to begin road construction on the Stantonsburg property. In fact, plaintiff ultimately decided to select another site on which to locate his medical practice due to the failure of Park West to provide the promised road.

In making a determination as to the fair market value of the Stantonsburg property, the trial court must ascertain the price a willing buyer would pay to purchase the land on the open market from a willing seller as of the date of the parties' separation. The value, if any, of the obligation to build an access road on the property is intrinsic to the fair market price and should have been included in the trial court's fair market valuation of the real property. The trial court's findings of fact numbered 24(i) and (i) [sic] are vacated and the case is remanded for a determination of the fair market value of the Stantonsburg property on the date of separation, to include the value, if any, of the obligation to construct a road to the property.

[2] Next, we examine plaintiff's assignment of error regarding the trial court's valuation of plaintiff's medical practice, particularly the "goodwill" component of the practice. Goodwill, the most difficult element of a professional practice to value, is "commonly defined as the expectation of continued public patronage." *Poore v. Poore,* 75 N.C. App. 414, 420, 331 S.E.2d 266 271, *disc. review denied,* 314 N.C. 543, 335 S.E.2d 316 (1985). "It is an intangible asset which defies precise definition and valuation." *Id.* "There is no set rule for determining the value of the goodwill of a professional practice; rather, each case must be determined in light of its own particular facts." *Id.* at 421, 331 S.E.2d at 271 (citations omitted). If it appears that the trial court, based on competent evidence and a sound valuation method, reasonably approximated the goodwill value of plaintiff's medical practice, that valuation will not be disturbed on appeal. *Id.* at 422, 331 S.E.2d at 272.

(continues)

EXHIBIT 4.1 *(Continued)*

The record shows that the trial court carefully considered the evidence presented by three different experts and determined that "capitalization of excess earnings" was the appropriate method for determining the fair market value of plaintiff's medical practice. This Court has described the capital excess earnings method as a proper and legitimate means of measuring the present value of goodwill. *Id.* at 421, 331 S.E.2d at 271. Under this approach, the trial court first determines the difference between plaintiff's actual earnings and the earnings of the "average" similarly situated physician. *Turner,* supra § 7.07, at 533; see also *Poore,* 75 N.C. App. at 421-422, 331 S.E.2d at 271-72. The difference between the compared earnings is then multiplied by a number (the factor) between one and five to yield the final value. *Turner,* supra § 7.07, at 533. The accuracy of this approach depends significantly upon the accuracy of the "average" statistics used in the comparison. *Id.* at 535.

Plaintiff contends that the trial judge committed reversible error by utilizing information regarding the average salaries of invasive cardiologists as published in a national survey entitled *Physician Compensation and Production Survey: 1992 Report Based on 1991 Data* (hereinafter *"Physician Survey"*) to make a determination as to the average salary of a similarly situated physician. Plaintiff contends that the trial court was required to utilize evidence presented as to the average salary of interventional cardiologists in Pitt County. We disagree.

The trial court relied on the testimony and evidence presented by Edward Strange, plaintiff's expert in the field of evaluation of medical practices. Mr. Strange testified that in calculating the goodwill component of plaintiff's medical practice, he relied on the *Physician Survey* because it was the only salary survey he could find that gathered information regarding the specialty of invasive cardiology. He also testified that it was a very good source because it included information on fringe benefits and compensation amounts "in terms of total production" as well as general compensation information.

To ascertain the salary of a physician similarly situated to plaintiff, Mr. Strange adopted the *Physician Survey* salary for an invasive cardiologist in the 90th percentile. Mr. Strange explained in his *Valuation Report,* that he used the 90th percentile column because he believed that the "conditions for earning ability in Greenville, North Carolina for invasive cardiologists would be represented in the upper strata." During direct examination, he noted that the salary he selected was somewhat lower than the average earnings reported by Pitt County interventional cardiologists.

In finding the goodwill component of plaintiff's medical practice, the trial judge rejected utilizing either the salary of the invasive cardiologist in the 90th percentile or the average salary of Pitt County interventional cardiologists. Rather, he determined the similarly situated physician salary by relying on the average salary of an invasive cardiologist in the 75th percentile as reported in the *Physician Survey.* In selecting the disputed salary, the trial judge explained his reasoning as follows:

EXHIBIT 4.1 (*Continued*)

[Finding #28(c)] . . . The Court finds from the evidence that a similarly situated invasive cardiologist would earn $418,000.00 per year. This salary figure is higher (in the 75th percentile) than the medial salary, because the plaintiff is a very hard-working individual, who strives to perfection, and who is ambitious in the best sense of the word. He is skilled in marketing his practice, and he is a "hard-driving" physician. The Court finds that Dr. Carlson also possesses an exceptionally higher level of skill than other invasive cardiologists. . . .

[T]he average income of interventional cardiologists practicing in Pitt County should not be considered because this group represents too small of a statistical sample, and all of the interventional cardiologists practicing in Pitt County may have practice good will . . .

[T]he Court does not find these physicians to be similarly situated, because a comparison of plaintiff to approximately six cardiologists in Pitt County provides too small a statistical basis or sample for this Court to find this comparison meaningful or reliable in finding the similarly situated physician. Additionally, Dr. Carlson actively markets his practice with advertising, clinics, and the like, and there is no evidence that the other Pitt County physicians market at all, much less to the degree of Dr. Carlson.

Plaintiff objects to the trial court's finding that the number of interventional cardiologists in Pitt County was too small a sample to provide a useful comparison. He contends the trial judge was required to utilize the average salaries of local interventional cardiologists. We disagree.

Other courts have approved of the use of national statistics in determining the goodwill component of a business valuation "[w]here the number of businesses in the field is small and the market is essentially nationwide" or a "small local sample size prevents collection of reliable information." *Turner,* supra § 7.07 at 536; see e.g. *In re Bookout,* 833 P.2d 800 (Colo. Ct. App. 1991) (using American Physical Therapists Association survey data); *Clark v. Clark,* 782 S.W.2d 56 (Ky. Ct. App. 1990) (using American Medical Association survey of obstetrical practices data). Given the facts and circumstances of this case, the trial judge did not abuse his discretion by utilizing national salary statistics to calculate the goodwill component of plaintiff's medical practice.

The trial court reasonably approximated the goodwill value of plaintiff's medical practice on the basis of competent evidence and a sound valuation method. The court's findings and conclusions with regard to the valuation of plaintiff's professional practice will not be disturbed on appeal.

Vacated and remanded in part, affirmed in part.

Judges EAGLES and McGEE concur.

Adjustments may also be made to account for differences in industry practices, to make the statements conform to generally accepted accounting principles, and to adjust related party transactions to a fair value as determined by the marketplace.

One of the most subjective components of the market methodology is the determination of which companies to use as guidelines. The most efficient data used comes from the public marketplace where there are market quotes readily available, and there is copious disclosure of each entity's financial condition. It is difficult, however, to find public companies with comparable size, financial structure, or marketplace. There is often information in the disclosures made by public companies of the details of purchases of private companies that may meet the adviser's comparability standards.

Alternatives to the public markets include privately developed databases that accumulate information from the sale of privately held firms. This information, when used, must be purchased from the developers. Private databases may provide data on the sale of more comparable businesses, but there is seldom the level of detailed financial information that is available from the public companies.

An additional issue in using the market method of valuation is the nature of the interest being valued opposed to the nature of the comparable interest used. Most interests being valued are controlling or minority interests, but are typically nonmarketable. A public firm's pricing is primarily minority marketable interests. If the private databases are used, the interests are controlling nonmarketable interests. When there are differences in the nature of the property being valued, adjustments must be made at some level of the valuation. These adjustments may impact the normalization adjustments, the capitalization rates, or the discounts used.

The market approach is used when there is reliable financial information available from a business, and there is comparable company financial information available to the financial adviser. The Internal Revenue Service prefers this method of valuation be considered in tax-based appraisals.

The cost or asset-based approach is a determination of the fair market value of the company's assets net of existing liabilities. The fair market value of the individual assets is determined based on replacement cost, adjusted downward to recognize the age and physical deterioration of the assets. There can also be upward adjustments for assets not recorded on the books of the company.

These adjustments are the same as the normalization adjustments referred to in the market method discussion. Totaling the value of the assets and deducting the amount of the liabilities yields the value of the company, under the cost method. This approach to value has its basis in the principle of duplication. What would it cost to acquire the assets of the company with similar financing in place?

The adjustments made to reflect the asset values include adjustments to correct for accounting methods, as well as adjustments to bring assets to a fair market value. Examples of accounting adjustments can include adjusting an inventory to its most recent cost, or eliminating capitalized organization costs from the balance sheet. A fair market value adjustment could be increasing the value of real estate on the balance sheet to the appraised value. If there are significant assets on the balance sheet for which there is not current valuation information available, third party appraisals of those assets may be required. Third-party appraisals are used with real estate, farms, ranches, oil properties, gas properties, other mineral interests, and collectibles. Those appraised values are then included in the valuation adviser's analysis.

The cost approach is more often used if a company is not profitable, the industry is depressed, or the value of a company is typically measured by the value of its assets. Examples could include real estate or natural resource holding companies.

The income approach is based on the determination of the present value of the future stream of income that will be realized by the company. After the income stream to be utilized is determined, a capitalization or discount rate is applied. From this analysis, the value of the business is determined. This approach to value has its basis in the theory of return on investment. What amount of future income would be expected by the hypothetical investor to justify a present cash outlay?

One of the initial decisions to be made when using the income method of valuation is which earnings stream should be utilized. The theoretical basis of this method relies on valuing future earnings, but many companies do not prepare forecasts or projections containing that information. As a result, the valuator may use historical earnings and trends as a proxy for the future projections. In addition, the marketplace values future cash flow, while most small businesses prepare financial statements using the income tax basis or generally accepted accounting principles basis of accounting. The adviser must determine which information to use prior to proceeding with the valuation. Different streams can produce different results. Many times, the adviser will use earnings as a proxy for cash flow.

Once the earnings stream to be used has been identified, it must be normalized to eliminate subjective income and expense. The owner of the business may cause the business to rent a facility from the owner at an inflated value, or may take high or low salaries depending on personal income tax situations. The valuation adviser must make a hypothetical determination of what expense levels a competent employee manager would impose on the business, and what the business would yield to a hypothetical absentee owner. After these normalization adjustments are performed, the cash flow or earnings stream can be valued by applying a capitalization or discount rate.

Capitalization or discount rates represent the rate of return that the hypothetical investor would expect on an investment in the business being valued. There are several methodologies for developing the capitalization or discount rate. In the most accepted and utilized method, rates are formulated using a build-up methodology, also called the capital asset pricing model (CAPM). This analysis begins by determining the historical rate derived in the market place from investments in long-term treasury securities. Added to this rate are an equity risk premium based on historical returns in the public marketplace, a small company premium to convert the equity risk premium to the bottom decile of company size, and a premium for the specific risks associated with the company being valued. The formulation of the specific risk factor should be based on the actual risks associated with the company being valued. Risk factors external to the company that should be evaluated include the condition and expectations for the general economy, the condition and expectations for the company's industry, and the competitive environment of the company's industry. Internal risk factors include the size and form of the company, the general expectations, financial condition, history of the earnings, competitive position, quality and depth of management, and quality of the workforce of the company. The build-up method provides a capitalization rate yielding a marketable minority interest.

Sometimes, after the rate has been developed it is adjusted by a factor called beta. Beta is a numerical multiplier determined as the result of economic study that adjusts the overall market risk to industry specific risk. The adjustment is determined based on the volatility of specific industries in comparison to the public market as a whole. Many valuators ignore beta when valuing small closely held businesses, considering it inappropriate for the businesses being valued.

Capitalization rates are applied to single period earnings to determine the value of the earnings stream. Discount rates are applied to future streams of income to determine the net present value of the earnings stream. Either can be applied to earnings or cash flows. When evaluating future streams of income with level growth, the capitalization rate can be computed by subtracting the growth rate in the earnings from the discount rate.

A capitalization rate can be expressed a number of ways. It is the reciprocal multiplier which, when applied to income, determines the principal amount of investment necessary to yield the stated income. It is the rate of return the hypothetical investor would expect when making an investment in the particular type of business, taking into account the appropriate risk factors and similar alternative investments. It is determined and modified to reflect a pre- or post-tax rate, a marketable or nonmarketable rate, or a controlling or minority rate. Many errors are discovered in valuation reports because the valuator uses the incorrect rate for the interest being valued.

When analyzing and normalizing a company's balance sheet and income statement, there are a number of items that require the specific attention of the adviser. These items include, but are not limited to:

- Adequacy of all allowance and reserve accounts.
- Allowance for doubtful accounts receivable.
- Reserves for self-insurance.
- Pension liabilities.
- Inventory accounting methods.
- FIFO, LIFO, and other methods.
- Write-down and write-off policies.
- Depreciation methods and schedules.

- Depletion.
- Treatment of intangibles.
- Capitalization versus expensing of various costs.
- Timing of recognition of revenues and expenses.
- Contract work.
- Installment sales.
- Sales involving actual or contingent liabilities.
- Prior-period adjustments.
- Accounting for leases.
- Accounting for certain tax aspects.
- Investment tax credits.
- Tax loss carryforwards.
- Treatment of interests in affiliates.
- Extraordinary or nonrecurring items.
- Ordinary versus extraordinary items.
- Other nonrecurring items.
- Discontinued operations.
- Operating versus nonoperating items.
- Management compensation and perquisites.
- Transactions involving company insiders.
- Contingent assets and liabilities.
- Adjustments to asset valuations.
- Marketable securities.
- Other assets.
- Tax aspects of valuation.
- Cost of enjoying property.
- Built-in tax liabilities.
- Any assets not required for the operation of the business.

The valuation of the appropriate salary expense for the business owner and family members is often disputed. The valuation adviser should pay particular attention to receiving sufficient information to be able to value the cost of a hypothetical, appropriately skilled replacement employee. Information for comparable salaries is available from a number of sources, including the federal government, state agencies, and headhunting firms.

The lack of complete and accurate information is one of the important aspects a valuation adviser must accept when working in domestic relations litigation. It is not unusual for the spouse outside the business to be able to discover all the information the valuation adviser may request. It is also not unusual for the spouse inside the business to control the information provided to the adviser. In both of these circumstances, the adviser can proceed, but must disclose the limitations of the scope of the work that can be performed.

ANALYSIS OF THE BUSINESS

Revenue Ruling 59–60 details eight primary factors that must be considered for income tax purposes when valuing a closely held business. All the governing appraisal bodies have accepted these criteria as the underlying basis for the reporting standards they have adopted. In valuing the interests of closely held businesses where market quotations are not available, all available financial data and all relevant factors that may impact the fair market value should be considered. No general formula may be given that is applicable to all valuation situations. The ruling details the following factors that are set forth as being important in determining the value of a business interest.

First, the nature of the business and the history of the enterprise from its inception must be considered. To understand and evaluate the risk associated with a business, it is important to know its past stability, rate of growth, and diversity of operations. This history includes the nature of the business, its products or services, details of operating and investment assets, and an understanding of its capital structure, plant, facilities, sales, and management. If an enterprise has changed its form of organization but has carried on the same or similar operations of its predecessor, the history of the former enterprise should also be considered. A business can change dramatically over the years, but valuations are date specific. The valuator should capture this information and communicate the organizational and financial history of the company preceding the date of the valuation. The valuator must gather sufficient information to understand the company's industry, its line of business, and the conduct of the business. This will include information about wholesalers, manufacturers, retailers, and service providers. Information should be gathered regarding the locations of business, personnel, and suppliers. The company's form of organization, history of the business, and the capital structure that supports the entity require reporting and analysis. The owners and their ownership interests should be detailed and understood. Competing ownership interests should be identified. Management depth and capabilities need to be evaluated. Key employees require identification, as well as plans that may exist for the succession of management.

Second, the general economic outlook and the conditions and outlook of the specific industry in which the business enterprise competes are factors in what the value of a business may be. What are the future prospects of competitive industries and of competitors within the particular industry in which the business operates? What are the indicated price trends in the marketplace for commodities utilized by the business and for securities in the business's industry? The valuator should understand the general economic outlook and the outlook of the specific industry. The knowledge and analysis of the national, regional, and local economy as it relates to the industry should be performed with a focus on which elements impact the value of the company. The work performed should provide an understanding of the firm's markets and the company's competitors. Sources of this information include:

- National Data.
  - Bureau of Labor Statistics.
  - WEFA Industrial Monitor. (Formerly Wharton Economic Forecasting Associates)
  - Bureau of Economic Analysis.
  - Federal Reserve Bulletin.
  - Standard and Poors Statistical Service.
- Regional and Local Data.
  - Local sources of economic research.
  - City planning Internet sites.
  - State profile sites.
  - State taxation sites.
  - U.S. Census data on retail trade.
  - U.S. Census data on wholesale trade.
  - U.S. Census data on service industries.
  - U.S. Census data on manufacturing industries.
- Industry Data.
  - Various Internet financial sites.
  - WEFA Industrial Monitor.
  - Integra Information Resources.

- Standard and Poors Industrial Surveys.
- Trade associations.
- Risk Management Associates (RMA) Annual Statement Studies.
- Financial studies of small business.
- The Almanac of Business and Financial Ratios.

Third, the book value of the company and the financial condition of the business are significant indicators of its value. Comparative annual balance sheets will detail the company's liquid position, the net book value of its fixed assets, working capital, long-term indebtedness, capital structure, and net worth. By analyzing historic and comparative balance sheets, the valuation adviser can gain an understanding of the current and historical trends in the company's financial condition. Many times, the individual performing the valuation will adjust these statements to reflect the fair market value of the assets and liabilities listed, as well as adding those that have been omitted. These adjustments are prepared to allow the analysis of the combined fair market value of the net assets of the entity and to support the valuator's asset-based conclusions of value.

Fourth, the past, present, and future earnings capacity of the company provide information that is relevant in determining a company's value. Income statements for the proceeding several years should show gross income, expenses, interest, taxes, depreciation, and amortization, yielding net income. Future earnings capacity is a primary factor in determining the value of a business. Information concerning past income can become a predictive factor in projecting future income. These predictions become a component of an adviser's income valuation opinion. Through quantitative analysis, the valuator can address the financial position of the company, its history, current operations, prospects for the future, and its financial strengths, weaknesses, and performance compared with its peers. The ratio analysis and comparison of the company to its peers should be subjected to a detailed study to provide a basis for the valuator's opinion of the financial condition of the company in comparison to its peers.

Fifth, if a corporation is being valued, the dividend-paying history and capacity of the company, or in a noncorporate entity, the history of the company in providing a cash return to its owners, is an indicator of value. It may be necessary for a company to retain a portion of its profits for growth and expansion. Dividends or distributions paid in the past may or may not bear a relationship to the current paying capacity of the entity. The prior payments may have been determined by the income needs or tax concerns of the stockholders and may not be reflective of the entity's current ability to pay.

Sixth, the extent of goodwill or other intangible values of the business are factors that must be considered in valuing a business. Goodwill is reflected in a company's earning capacity. Its value is traditionally determined based on the excess of the entity's net income over a fair return on its net tangible assets. This excess earnings capacity may be a reflection of the reputation of the business, brand names, leases, patents, copyrights, successful operations over a period of time in a particular locality, or any number of other intangibles. Many times these intangibles are not reflected on the company's balance sheet and must be added by the adviser to properly access a company's worth.

Seventh, the proportionate value of any recent sales of the company and the percentage interest of the business that changed hands are information that must be considered by the valuation adviser. If the sales are not arm's-length transactions, are forced sales, distress sales, isolated sales in small amounts, or a large percentage of ownership interest is transferred, prices of these sales may or may not represent the fair market value of the business. A controlling interest may have justified a higher value per unit than a minority interest, and other transfers may not involve a willing seller. These historical transactions may, however, reflect an indication of market value if they are arm's-length, are of similar interest, and are in a close proximity to the date of valuation.

Eighth, the market value of the stocks of companies engaged in the same or similar lines of business that have shares actively traded either on an exchange or in the over-the- counter markets must be evaluated in the adviser's analysis. The prices of listed stocks of corporations engaged in the same or a similar line of business and actively traded by the public are considered first. If sufficient similar listed stocks cannot be found, other comparable companies that have stock actively traded in the over-the-counter market may be used. In addition, closely held company transactions can be used if they can be located. In determining whether other corporations are comparable, consideration should be given to factors in addition to their lines of business. The classes of stocks and debentures outstanding and whether their business is declining or increasing are factors that may impact comparability. The size of the comparable company, as defined by sales and total asset size, may be considered. Many valuation advisers consider companies that are more than ten times larger than the company being valued as not being comparable. Revenue Ruling 59–60 requires consideration of "the market price of interests of enterprises engaged in the same or a similar line of business having interests actively traded in a free or open market." The valuation adviser should have conducted a comprehensive search for appropriate guideline companies. The study of any valuation should consider the steps taken in the search for comparable companies, the research sources considered, and the results of the search.

If guideline companies were identified as potentially comparable, whether or not they were ultimately used as value indicators, the valuator should affirmatively consider and be prepared to discuss the similarities and dissimilarities of the guideline companies. Factors considered can include industry similarity, size of the entity, historical financial trends, prospective growth, financial risk, capitalization, operating risk, and management depth. There are a number of sources available in which to research comparable sales. The public marketplace can be researched using sources such as the brokerage firms, Securities and Exchange Commission filings, and various independent financial sites on the Internet. In addition, data recording the sales of smaller closely held businesses are accumulated in several national databases. These include *Pratt's Stats* and the Institute of Business Appraiser's "Market Database". These databases can provide useful information on business sales of smaller and possibly more comparable businesses. When a comparable company is located and to be used for the valuation, it is called a guideline company. If no guideline companies are found, the valuation adviser should be prepared to affirmatively describe the factors that prevented the location of comparable companies.

Revenue Ruling 68–609 was one of the first valuation rulings issued after 59–60. It details a method to compute the value of intangibles in a going concern. The excess earnings methodology is used in the ruling, but has not gained general acceptance in the valuation community. The exception is the valuation of professional practices. This method has become the predominant method in those valuations. It continues to be a valid methodology for tax valuations. The methodology utilizes the adjusted (normalized) earnings capacity of an organization and reduces those earnings by a "return" on the tangible assets of the business. The excess of those earnings is then capitalized to determine the "intangible value" of the business. That intangible value is then added to the other adjusted (normalized) asset values of the business to determine the fair market value of the entity as a whole under the cost method of valuation. This analysis values a nonmarketable controlling interest.

The rate of return applied to the adjusted assets as described in Revenue Ruling 68–609 itself is stated to be a rate of return on a long-term safe investment, such as 20-year Treasury Securities. The valuation community, however, generally uses comparable rates for return on assets reported to third parties by similar businesses.

The capitalization rate utilized is adjusted appropriately for pre- or posttax earnings, marketability, and the minority or control position being valued.

The determination of the value of the goodwill is important in many jurisdictions. Some require the valuation adviser to further divide the intangible value into the amount attributable to the business versus the amount attributable to the owner. In some states, the amount attributable to the owner is considered to be separate property.

The value of any business must be based upon numerous considerations, all of which contribute to the determination of a fair return on the willing buyer's investment.

CONTROL VERSUS MINORITY INTERESTS AND OTHER DISCOUNTS AND PREMIUMS

When a conclusion of value is reached for an entity, the valuator must consider whether it is proper to apply a discount or a premium to reach the fair market value of the interest being valued. Part of the decision rests with the valuation method utilized and the nature of the value resulting from that method. For example, if the method produces the value of a controlling nonmarketable interest and that is the nature of the interest being valued, no discounts or premiums may be appropriate. However, if there is a difference in the nature of the valuation method's result and the nature of the interest being valued, discounts or premiums will be required. Once it is determined that discounts or premiums are needed, the magnitude is impacted by the degree of control (minority, controlling, or swing vote) and the degree of marketability of the interest. Other factors that may require a discount or a premium can include voting rights, blockage, key person reliance, and portfolio risk. These discounts or premiums can be substantial. The valuator must use significant professional judgment in determining the nature and magnitude of any premiums or discounts that are to be applied. The adviser must be prepared to discuss the factors considered when determining and quantifying any discounts and premiums.

It is not unusual for an adviser to rely upon various historical academic studies to assist in the quantification of premiums or discounts. The subjects of these studies include restricted stock, initial public offerings, and floated public offerings. Premiums and discounts must be developed based on the interest in the company being valued and the interest's individual character.

DETERMINATION OF VALUE

The value determined is based on the analysis of the accumulated research and the adviser's professional judgment. When the adviser presents the conclusion of value, the valuator must be prepared to present and discuss the historical information reviewed, the research performed, the analysis performed, and the conclusions reached. The conclusion can be presented as a point of value, range of value, or relationship of value where two interests are being compared.

Financial advisers working on divorce cases in which the valuation of a closely held business is an issue can provide significant value to the client. If the adviser understands the unique factors that impact the value of a business, the adviser can assist the litigant in investigating and determining how the business's specific circumstances impact that value. If the adviser has intimate knowledge of the business, the service can be rendered whether or not the adviser specializes in valuation. An adviser that has specialized in business valuation may perform the appraisal of the entity and be called as a testifying expert. Exhibit 4.2 includes an example of an engagement letter used in business valuations. Exhibits 4.3 and 4.4 show document and information requests for business valuations and professional practice valuations.

EXHIBIT 4.2   Business Valuation Engagement Letter

(DATE)

(Client)
(Address)
(Address)
(City)

Dear (Client):

This letter is to confirm our understanding of the terms and objectives of the engagement of our firm for valuation of Company. We will estimate the fair market value, on a controlling interest basis, of this company as of (Date) for purposes of (State Purpose). We will perform various analytical review procedures of the Company's latest five (5) years financial statements and perform other procedures that we consider necessary to accomplish this purpose.

The objective of our valuation will be to estimate the fair market value of (Company). The term "fair market value" is defined as follows:

The price at which the property would change hands between a willing buyer and a willing seller, neither being under a compulsion to buy or sell and both having reasonable knowledge of relevant facts.

Although our valuation is intended to estimate fair market value, we assume no responsibility for a seller's or buyer's inability to obtain a purchase contract at that price. Users of business valuations should be aware that business valuations may be based on certain hypothetical values of assets and/or future earnings potential that may or may not materialize. Therefore, the actual asset values and future period earnings will vary from the projections and amount used in this valuation, and the variations may be material.

The valuation will be based on what we consider to be the most appropriate method of valuation in the circumstances. In performing our valuation, we will be relying on the accuracy and reliability of your historical financial statements, forecasts of future operations, or other financial data of your company. We will not audit, compile, or review your financial statements, forecasts, or other data, and we will not express an opinion or any form of assurance on them. At the conclusion of the engagement, we will ask you to sign a representation letter on the accuracy and reliability of the financial information used

EXHIBIT 4.2 (*Continued*)

in the engagement. Our engagement cannot be relied on to disclose errors, irregularities, or illegal acts, including fraud or defalcations, that may exist.

In developing our value estimate, it may be necessary to use the services of outside appraisers to establish the value of property and equipment. The costs of such outside appraisers will be billed to you in addition to our fees. We will reveal to you the need for such outside appraisals, the identity of the outside appraiser, and the expected cost prior to obtaining any such outside appraisals, should any become necessary.

We will document the results of the engagement in a formal report. We understand that our valuation conclusion will be used for (Purpose). The distribution of our report is restricted to the internal use of the management of (Company) for the stated purpose and, accordingly, will not be distributed to outside parties to obtain credit or for any other purposes, nor will additional copies of our report be made without our permission. To the extent our report is relied upon by any other party for any purpose other than as described herein, you agree to indemnify and hold The financial adviser harmless from any liability to such party based upon such party's reliance upon our report.

We have no responsibility to update our valuation report for events and circumstances that occur after the date of its issuance. If for any reason we are unable to complete the valuation engagement, we will not issue a report as a result of the engagement.

Our fees will be based upon our standard hourly rates, which range from $40 per hour to $225 per hour, depending upon the level of the individual performing the task. Our fees, plus any out of pocket expenses, will be billed on a monthly basis and are payable upon receipt. Our valuation report will state that our fee is not contingent on the value determined by this engagement. We agree that the liability of The financial adviser for any damages suffered by you as a result of any errors or omissions in our report will be limited to the amount of our fee for this engagement.

Billings become delinquent if not paid within 30 days of the invoice date. Any amounts not paid within 30 days will be assessed a late charge of 1.5% per month. If billings are past due, we will stop all work until your account is brought current, or withdraw from this engagement. You acknowledge and agree that we are not required to continue work in the event of your failure to pay on a timely basis for services rendered as required by this engagement letter. You further acknowledge and agree that, in the event we stop work or withdraw from this engagement as a result of your failure to pay on a timely basis for services rendered as required by this engagement letter, we shall not be liable to you or any other party for any damages that occur as a result of our ceasing to render services.

(*continues*)

EXHIBIT 4.2   *(Continued)*

The fee estimate is for the valuation and valuation report and does not include any services that may be required to defend our valuation report in litigation, including conferences, depositions, court appearances, and testimony. Fees for such services, if required, will be billed at our standard hourly rates and covered under an additional engagement letter.

We agree that any dispute over fees charged by us will be submitted for resolution by arbitration in accordance with the rules of the American Arbitration Association. Such arbitration shall be binding and final. IN AGREEING TO ARBITRATION, WE BOTH ACKNOWLEDGE THAT, IN THE EVENT OF A DISPUTE OVER FEES, EACH OF US IS GIVING UP THE RIGHT TO HAVE THE DISPUTE DECIDED IN A COURT OF LAW BEFORE A JUDGE OR JURY AND INSTEAD WE ARE ACCEPTING THE USE OF ARBITRATION FOR RESOLUTION. In the event an arbitration or litigation (including but not limited to any proceeding to compel arbitration) is initiated to resolve or settle any dispute or claim between the parties, the prevailing party shall be entitled to recover from the non-prevailing party or parties its reasonable costs, including but not limited to reasonable attorney's fees. This agreement shall be governed by and construed in accordance with the laws of the State of New Mexico.

We sincerely appreciate this opportunity to be of service to you. If you agree with the foregoing terms, please sign the copy of this letter where indicated and return it to us. We will deliver a draft of our valuation report to you for your factual review within six weeks of our receipt of all information necessary to conduct this engagement. We have enclosed a Document and Information Request List describing the information necessary to complete our valuation.

Very truly yours,

THE FINANCIAL ADVISER

Name and title

Enclosures

ACCEPTED AND APPROVED:

This letter correctly sets forth the understanding of (Client).

(Client)

by _____

Title _____

Date: _____

EXHIBIT 4.3 Business Valuation

BUSINESS VALUATION
DOCUMENTS AND INFORMATION REQUEST
VALUATION DATE: (VALUATION DATE)

In order for a financial adviser to render a meaningful opinion relating to the estimate of value of the company, it is important that as much of the following information be supplied as may be available. In the event certain information is not available as of the valuation date, please provide this information for the time period as close to the valuation date as possible.

Financial Statements

1. Provide annual financial statements for the last five years.
2. Provide interim financial statements for the period ending closest to the valuation date.
3. Provide a balance sheet as of the valuation date, if it is not included in items 1 and 2.
4. Provide federal and state income tax returns for the business for prior five years. State income tax returns, if applicable.
5. Provide copies of any forecasts or projections of future earnings, sales or other financial data that include periods after the valuation date.
6. List any subsidiaries or other businesses in which the subject company has an ownership interest, together with their financial statements and tax returns for the five years prior the valuation date and the period ended closest to the valuation date.

Other Financial Data

7. List cash accounts and any significant cash investments as shown on the business's balance sheets provided in items 1,2, and 6.
8. Provide and aged accounts receivable listing as shown on the business's balance sheets provided in items 1,2, and 6. Include management's estimate of the amount of receivables on the list that will not be collected and an explanation of how those amounts are determined.
9. List items comprising inventory including the quantity, description, and cost of the individual items and detail of the method of pricing the inventory as of valuation date.
10. Provide a fixed asset register or depreciation schedule to include all company owned real estate and equipment, dates of acquisition, cost of the assets, depreciation method, useful life, and the accumulated depreciation of each.
11. List all items comprising significant other assets as shown on the business's balance sheet provided in items 1,2, and 6.

(continues)

EXHIBIT 4.3 *(Continued)*

12. Provide an accounts payable listing as of the valuation date that supports the financial statements provided and items 1,2, and 6.
13. Provide a detailed analysis of liabilities as shown on the business's balance sheets provided in items 1,2, and 6.
14. Provide a list of notes payable and other interest-bearing debt as shown on the business's balance sheets provided in items 1,2, and 6. Include copies of all related notes, mortgages, and amortization schedules.
15. List all items comprising significant other liability balances as shown on the business's balance sheets provided in items 1,2, and 6.
16. Provide copies of any sales, capital, or operating budgets that project for periods post valuation date.
17. Provide copies of any formalized business plans developed within the prior five years.
18. Provide a schedule of the amounts and nature of officers', relatives', and owners' compensation. Detail how each individual's compensation is determined and when it is paid.
19. Schedule any company owned life insurance on the lives of key employees, related parties, or owners.
20. Provide any relevant reports of other professionals, such as:
    a. Appraisals of any assets of the company, and
    b. Reports of any other consultants that include information relevant to the business.

Other Operating Data

21. Provide brochures, price lists, catalogs, or other product information that detail the products and services sold by the business.
22. List all owners, showing the percentage and nature of the interests owned by each person.
23. Provide a copy of the business's organizational chart or a written description of the organization.
24. List the five largest customers over the past three years and the total amount of sales to each of those customers in each year. Provide details and copies of any agreements and contracts with those customers.
25. Provide a narrative detailing the company's product lines and how those lines developed.
26. Describe the company's customer base.
27. Provide a narrative detailing the company's customer base, including how customers are developed.
28. What factors outside of your control impact sales?
29. How large is your market place, both geographically and in dollars?
30. How many competitors do you have?
31. How do you rank among your competitors?
32. How are your products priced?

EXHIBIT 4.3 *(Continued)*

33. What are your typical terms of sale?
34. Why do your customers buy your products?
35. Describe how your sales force is compensated.
36. Does your customer base buy your products from only your company or from several companies? What determines their loyalty?
37. Describe how the products are marketed and sold to the customers.
38. Does your customer base require you to competitively bid and, if so, describe the process?
39. List the amount of sales and gross profit by major product line.
40. Explain which product lines' sales are growing or declining and at what rate.
41. Are there patents, trade secrets, or contracts in place that prevent competitors from selling items in your product lines?
42. Who are your competitors and how do they compete?
43. List the five largest suppliers over the past three years and the total amount purchased from each of those suppliers in each year. Provide details and copies of any agreements and contracts with those suppliers.
44. Describe the company's products and services including their uses, advantages, and disadvantages.
45. Provide a narrative detailing the company's suppliers including how suppliers are developed.
46. Describe how the products listed are distributed to the customers.
47. Describe how long it takes from the order of products to their receipt by the company.
48. Are any suppliers the company's sole source of product?
49. How stable is the pricing received from suppliers?
50. Are the suppliers financially sound?
51. List all known parties related to the business including relatives, subsidiaries, and affiliates that do business or are employed by the company. List the details of any transactions the business has with those related parties.

Legal Documents

52. Provide copies of documentation of leases and loans whether receivable or payable.
53. Provide copies of business organic documents (Articles of Incorporation, Bylaws, Partnership Agreements, Articles of Organization, Operating Agreements, etc.) to include information detailing the business's legal structure, name, date of formation, state in which formed, and sufficient information to understand the ownership and structure of the invested and retained capital existing on the valuation date. If the business is a corporation, the information would include the number of shares of stock issued, authorized, it's par value, and any other classes of equity.

(continues)

EXHIBIT 4.3   *(Continued)*

54. Provide copies of any agreements between the owners of the business.
55. Provide details of any stock options, rights, warrants, or deferred compensation plans not provided elsewhere.
56. Provide minutes of the board of director, partner, or member meetings for the prior five-year period.
57. Provide copies of any buy-sell agreements or written offers to purchase the entire company or any portion thereof that were received within the prior five years.
58. Provide copies of key managers', owners', and key employees' employment contracts.
59. Provide copies of any sales or purchasing contracts or agreements that will impact the future operations of the business.
60. Provide details of any current litigation, including pending or threatened lawsuits.
61. Provide details of all employee benefit plans, including pension plans, profit sharing plans, and employee stock option plans, including the documents establishing the benefit, as well as previous five years of tax returns filed that are related to the benefit. If any plans are defined benefit plans, provide copies of the most recent five years of actuarial reports.
62. Provide any collective bargaining agreements or details of any potential unionization of the business.
63. Provide copies of reports of examination issued by any governmental agency such as EPA, OSHA, IRS, and EEOC.
64. Provide the prior years attorney's fee invoices or billing statements.

Other Company Data

65. List any patents, copyrights, trademarks, or other similar intangibles. Provide copies of related legal documents and details of how the items are listed in the accounting records.
66. Describe any federal or state regulations that impact the company's business.
67. Detail any contingent liabilities, including guarantees, warranties, or other off-balance sheet financing such as letters of credit as of the valuation date.
68. Provide resumes or summaries of the background and experience of all key personnel.
69. List the members and qualifications of the company's board of directors and describe how active the board may be in company governance.
70. Provide copies of property tax assessments and insurance policies covering the businesses property.

EXHIBIT 4.3   *(Continued)*

71. Provide a listing of each location maintained by the company and the primary business activity conducted at each location.
72. How hard is it for others to start a business like yours?
73. What are the current product trends in your industry and how will they impact your business.
74. Describe the history and evolution of the employees of the business.
75. How hard is it to find employees to work in your business?
76. If the business uses temporary workers or subcontractors, describe their use and relationship with the company.
77. How are the employees compensated?
78. Are there any officers or employees that would be difficult to replace?
79. Detail the history and evolution of any acquisitions the business has made.
80. Detail the history and evolution of the ownership of the business.
81. How soon, and at what cost, will the company's equipment and facilities require replacement?
82. Given the current equipment and facilities, how close is the business to its maximum capacity?
83. List any key dates or events in the company's history.
84. Are there any environmental issues associated with the business?

Industry Data

85. List any trade associations that are related to the companies business, whether or not the business is a member.
86. List any trade publications related to the company's business.
87. List the business's standard industrial classification code.
88. Provide copies of any financial surveys that are available related to the company's line of business.

There may be additional information requested during the appraisal process. In addition to the information above, there may be some instances where we will request general ledgers, accounting journals, payroll tax returns, sales tax returns, bank statements, cancelled checks, and other such documentation.

EXHIBIT 4.4   Practice Valuation

PRACTICE VALUATION
PROFESSIONAL PRACTICE DOCUMENTS AND
INFORMATION REQUEST
VALUATION DATE: (VALUATION DATE)

In order for a financial adviser to render a meaningful opinion relating to the estimate of value of the practice, it is important that as much of the following information be supplied as may be available. In the event certain information is not available as of the valuation date, please provide this information for the time period as close to the valuation date as possible.

Financial Statements

1. Provide annual financial statements for the last five years.
2. Provide interim financial statements for the period ending closest to the valuation date.
3. Provide a balance sheet as of the valuation date if it is not included in items 1 and 2.
4. Provide federal and state income tax returns for the practice for prior five years. State income tax returns, if applicable.
5. Provide copies of any forecasts or projections of future earnings, fees or other financial data that include periods after the valuation date.
6. List any subsidiaries or other businesses in which the subject practice has an ownership interest, together with their financial statements and tax returns for the five years prior the valuation date and the period ended closest to the valuation date.

Other Financial Data

7. List cash accounts and any significant cash investments as shown on the business's balance sheets provided in items 1,2, and 6.
8. Provide an aged accounts receivable listing as shown on the practice balance sheets provided in items 1,2, and 6. Include management's estimate of the amount of receivables on the list that will not be collected and an explanation of how those amounts are determined.
9. List items comprising professional supplies and inventory including the quantity, description, and cost of the individual items and detail of the method of pricing the items as of valuation date.
10. Provide a fixed asset register or depreciation schedule to include all practice-owned real estate and equipment, dates of acquisition, cost of the assets, depreciation method, useful life, and the accumulated depreciation of each.
11. List all items comprising significant other assets as shown on the practice's balance sheet provided in items 1,2, and 6.

EXHIBIT 4.4   *(Continued)*

12. Provide an accounts payable listing as of the valuation date that supports the financial statements provided and items 1,2, and 6.
13. Provide a detailed analysis of liabilities as shown on the practice balance sheets provided in items 1,2, and 6.
14. Provide a list of notes payable and other interest-bearing debt as shown on the practice balance sheets provided in items 1,2, and 6. Include copies of all related notes, mortgages, and amortization schedules.
15. List all items comprising significant other liability balances as shown on the practice balance sheets provided in items 1,2, and 6.
16. Provide copies of any fee, capital, or operating budgets that project for the period's postvaluation date.
17. Provide copies of any formalized business plans developed within the prior five years.
18. Provide a schedule of the amounts and nature of officers', relatives', and owners' compensation. Detail how each individual's compensation is determined and when it is paid.
19. Schedule any company owned life insurance on the lives of key employees, related parties, or owners.
20. Provide any relevant reports of other professionals, such as:
    a. Appraisals of any assets of the company, and
    b. Reports of any other consultants that include information relevant to the business.

Other Operating Data

21. List all owners, showing the percentage and nature of the interests owned by each person.
22. Provide a copy of the practice's organizational chart, or a written description of the organization.
23. Describe the practice's client or patient base.
24. How large is your marketplace, both geographically and in dollars?
25. Describe the services performed by the practice, including the service mix.
26. Detail the fees in dollars generated by each service.
27. Which area of service is growing the most and which the least? Why?
28. Is the revenue generated by the practice seasonal or cyclical? If so, describe how and why.
29. How does the practice charge for services?
30. Provide a copy of the practice's fee schedule.
31. If there is unbilled work in process, describe how it is accumulated and what amounts will be billed and collected.
32. What hours does the practice keep?

(continues)

EXHIBIT 4.4 *(Continued)*

33. What are the working hours of each professional?
34. Describe what marketing activities are utilized to attract business.
35. If a medical or dental practice:
   a. Describe the source of patients and what percentage come from professional referrals
   b. Detail the revenue dollars referred to the practice from any source referring in excess of 10% of the practices fees.
   c. Describe the contractual relationships that exist in the practice with third party payers or providers, including the amounts of fees generated by each relationship, the duration of the contract, and the reimbursement percentage paid by each.
   d. If there are capitation contracts, describe how the practice manages the risk of providing patient care in exchange for a fixed fee.
   e. Describe any expected change in the practice's third party payer relationships and how those changes will impact the practice.
   f. If the practice performs procedures, how many are performed each week?
   g. If the practice performs procedures, describe the procedures and indicate any that are dominant.
   h. Provide details of practice revenue for the latest twelve months broken down by CPT code.
   i. Provide details of the practice's professional charges, adjustments, and collections monthly for the latest 36 months, including breakdown by third party payer if possible.
   j. How many active patients are there in the practice?
   k. How many patients are seen each week?
   l. Are patients seen for one or two visits or are they seen regularly once a patient.
36. If a veterinary practice:
   a. What types of animals does the practice treat?
   b. Detail the amount of revenue by each type treated.
   c. How many active clients are there in the practice?
37. How many competitors do you have?
38. How do you rank among your competitors?
39. Are there patents, trade secrets, or contracts in place that prevent competitors from selling services in your marketplace?
40. Who are your competitors and how do they compete?
41. Provide a narrative detailing the company's suppliers, including how suppliers are developed.
42. Are any suppliers the company's sole source of any product?
43. How stable is the pricing received from suppliers?
44. Are the suppliers financially sound?

EXHIBIT 4.4   *(Continued)*

45. List all known parties related to the business, including relatives, sub-sidiaries, and affiliates that do business or are employed by the company. List the details of any transactions the business has with those related parties.

Legal Documents

46. Provide copies of documentation of leases and loans whether receivable or payable.
47. Provide copies of the practice organic documents (Articles of Incorporation, Bylaws, Partnership Agreements, Articles of Organization, Operating Agreements, etc.) to include information detailing the practice's legal structure, name, date of formation, state in which formed, and sufficient information to understand the ownership and structure of the invested and retained capital existing on the valuation date. If the practice is a corporation, the information would include the number of shares of stock issued, authorized, its par value, and any other classes of equity.
48. Provide copies of any agreements between the owners of the practice.
49. Provide details of any stock options, rights, warrants, or deferred compensation plans not provided elsewhere.
50. Provide minutes of the board of director, partner, or member meetings for the prior five-year period.
51. Provide copies of any buy-sell agreements or written offers to purchase the entire practice or any portion thereof that were received within the prior five years.
52. Provide copies of key managers', owners', and key employees' employment agreements.
53. Provide copies of any documents detailing the admission or buy out of any professional in the practice for the previous five years.
54. Provide copies of any contracts or agreements that will impact the future operations of the practice.
55. Provide details of any current litigation, including pending or threatened lawsuits.
56. Provide details of all employee benefit plans, including pension plans, profit sharing plans, and employee stock option plans, including the documents establishing the benefit, as well as previous five years of tax returns filed that are related to the benefit. If any plans are defined benefit plans, provide copies of the most recent five years of actuarial reports.
57. Provide copies of reports of examination issued by any governmental agency such as EPA, OSHA, IRS, and EEOC.
58. Provide the prior years attorney's fee invoices or billing statements.

(continues)

EXHIBIT 4.4   *(Continued)*

Other Practice Data

59. List any patents, copyrights, trademarks, or other similar intangibles. Provide copies of related legal documents and details of how the items are listed in the accounting records.
60. Detail any contingent liabilities, including guarantees, warranties, or other off-balance sheet financing such as letters of credit as of the valuation date.
61. Provide resumes or summaries of the background and experience of all key personnel.
62. Provide copies of property tax assessments and insurance policies covering the practice property.
63. Provide a listing of each location maintained by the practice and the primary activity conducted at each location.
64. What are the current trends in your profession and how will they impact your practice?
65. Describe the history and evolution of the employees of the practice.
66. How are the employees compensated?
67. How are the practice professionals compensated?
68. How many associates has the practice employed for the past five-year period?
69. Are there any employees that would be difficult to replace?
70. Detail the history and evolution of any acquisitions the practice has made.
71. Detail the history and evolution of the ownership of the practice.
72. How soon and at what cost will the practice equipment and facilities require replacement?
73. Given the current professionals, equipment, and facilities, how close is the practice to its maximum capacity?
74. List any key dates or events in the practice's history.

Professional Data

75. List any professional or trade associations that are related to the practice, whether or not a member.
76. List any professional or trade publications related to the practice.
77. Provide copies of any financial surveys that are available related to the practice.

There may be additional information requested during the appraisal process. In addition to the information above, there may be some instances where we will request general ledgers, accounting journals, payroll tax returns, sales tax returns, bank statements, cancelled checks, and other such documentation.

CHAPTER 5

The Valuation and Division of Retirement Plans in Divorce Litigation

RETIREMENT PLANS

Retirement plans may be the largest assets that a couple accumulates during the marriage. As a result of the magnitude of the retirement assets, couples can battle fiercely over their value and distribution. Dividing these plans requires a great deal of care. Most plans have large potential tax liabilities that can suddenly become due if the division is not properly documented. In addition to dealing with the income tax rules, each plan has its own set of requirements that must be met. Next, there is the issue of valuation. Many plans have vesting schedules that may or may not apply for a domestic relations valuation. The only document, other than the summary plan description, required to value a defined contribution plan is typically a participant statement that details the balance in the account on a particular date and a proration of earnings through the appropriate date. Other plans are defined benefit plans that specify the amount and timing of a future benefit that will be received. The valuation of these plans requires that statistical or actuarial methods be applied to the benefit stream. The final issue encountered with retirement plans is the issue of distribution. Can the assets of the plan be currently transferred from one spouse to the other, or must the benefits be divided when they ultimately are paid? Many times the plan itself will answer this question, and, in some circumstances, the parties to the divorce can make their own decision.

TYPES OF QUALIFIED PLANS

Qualified plans are those that meet the requirements of Section 401 of the Internal Revenue Code. Plans that qualify under this section achieve certain benefits that are valuable to both the employer establishing the plan as well as the employee participant in the plan. Contributions made to the plan are immediately deductible by the employer and the investments in the plan grow free of income taxation until withdrawn. Because of these benefits, many employers establish qualified plans for the benefit of their employees.

The most common type of plan encountered by the financial adviser is the defined contribution plan. These plans can be profit sharing plans, employee wage deferral plans, or pension plans. The essence of these plans is that contributions are deposited, investments made, and when the time comes the participant receives the balance in the account. As a result, the participant's balance in the account is easy to determine and is not normally the subject of dispute.

The source of the contributions may be the employer, the employee, or both. Some plans accept rollovers of amounts from the employee's prior employer's plan. The trustee of the plan typically makes the investments. Some plans, however, allow the participants to self-direct investments.

Almost all retirement plans have a waiting period that employees must meet prior to participation in a plan. Once the waiting period has expired and the employee becomes a participant, plans have vesting schedules that determine the employee's rights to employer contributions. It is normal that any employee contributions are immediately vested. These schedules can provide a period of time-pass, prior to the employee having an interest in the employer contributions. Once vesting begins, the employee gains the right to an incremental nonforfeitable percentage of the employer's contributions. This vesting continues over several periods until the employee becomes completely vested. Since the employee may not have a right to all of the balance in the retirement account at the time of the divorce, disputes arise over what is the appropriate amount to divide. There are jurisdictions that strictly apply the vested percentage to the participant's balance and divide the result. There are others that may ignore the vesting schedules altogether and divide the participant's account balance.

Many small or closely held businesses have retirement plans. It is not unusual for these plans to be designed to maximize the benefits received by the owner group. When a member of that group divorces, the courts may disregard the plan's provisions. It is not unusual for courts to ignore vesting schedules when valuing participant's interests in divorces of an owner-employee. Other restrictive provisions may also be ignored as the court may determine that the owner maintains the control and enjoyment of the assets despite the restrictive provisions of the retirement plan. Plans of unrelated employers are a different matter. It is presumed by most courts that the restrictive provisions of retirement plans are there for the benefit of the employer and not for the benefit of a party to a divorce.

The valuation of defined contribution plans is complicated by the plan's tax attributes. When funds are withdrawn from the plan, a taxable event occurs. The only exception is permitted borrowings. For this reason, a dollar inside the plan may not be equal to a dollar outside of the plan. The various courts are divided on the impact of this deferred income tax liability on the value of the participant's interest. Some courts will divide the amount computed that would be received after deducting income taxes. Other jurisdictions consider the amount, timing, and payment of the tax to be speculative and disregard its existence.

The next most common plans encountered are defined benefit plans. Very large employers used these types of plans for years to provide for their employee's pensions. They have, however, fallen out of favor with most large employers because of their high cost. They continue to be used in some circumstances by high-earning professionals to set aside large sums of tax-deferred funds for the future.

Defined benefit plans allow the high income individual to defer much greater amounts than the defined contribution plan. An actuary determines the amount of funding that is required in a defined benefit plan. The determination is based on life expectancies, disability probability, and assumed investment returns. The assumptions made can cause wide swings in the amounts of required contributions. These plans are subject to the same type of waiting periods, vesting, and owner employee issues as the defined contribution plans.

The benefits from these plans are typically expressed in terms of a monthly payment to be paid, on the occurrence of a specified event, for a specified period of time. The monthly payment may be specified by pay grade or may be computed; for example, the total annual payment will be 60 percent of the average of the highest five years' earnings. Events triggering the payments can be the achievement of a milestone such as the attainment of age sixty-five, or can be a moving target such as the payment commencing when the sum of the employee's age and years of service reach the total of eighty-five. The term of the payments can be for a specified term, such as ten years, or can be for the remainder of the individual's and survivor's lives.

Because the benefits that will be received under defined benefit plans are contingent on a number of factors, their current valuation is frequently disputed in divorce cases. Benefits payable over a participant's life span will depend on how long the individual survives. The amounts to be paid are contingent on the employee reaching the prescribed retirement milestone. In some circumstances, if the employee dies, or is disabled prior to retirement, different or no benefits may be paid. Because of these contingencies, statistical probability and actuarial methods are used to value these types of plans. The use of simple present value computations to determine the value of defined contribution plans now is used in a minority of cases.

Some jurisdictions prefer to disburse the proceeds from defined benefit plans, if and when they are received. This pay-as-it-comes-in system eliminates all of the contingencies associated with the receipt of the ultimate benefit, but it forces the non-employee spouse to wait until the employee spouse retires to receive a benefit. Some courts may express a preference for a *lump sum* or *cash value* distribution of all property interests at the time of dissolution in order to ease the transition of the parties after dissolution and to minimize future contact and conflict between divorcing spouses. Courts may also allow the use of the pay-as-it-comes-in or reserved jurisdiction method of dividing property in circumstances that are at the discretion of the trial court, or in which the parties agree.

Most defined benefit plans provide the employee and the employee's spouse with the opportunity to provide a survivor's benefit if the employee predeceases the spouse. In these cases, the employee accepts a reduced benefit in exchange for more reduced benefit to be paid to the surviving spouse. The amount and timing of these reductions can impact the current value of the plan. For these reasons, a financial adviser can assist a divorcing party by determining if it may make sense to insure the life of the ex-spouse in exchange for a higher benefit during the employee's life. Many times it will cost less to insure in an amount to cover the survivor benefit than the financial cost of the benefit reduction.

Employee stock ownership plans are a type of defined contribution profit sharing plan. They are established by employers with the express intent of investing in the shares of the employer corporation. While the investments in these plans are not diversified, they are, for most respects, operated in the same manner as other qualified plans. In a rare situation, the financial adviser may encounter a circumstance in which an employee stock ownership plan has been used as an exit strategy to sell an individual's interest in a closely held business. There are provisions that allow an owner to dispose of the ownership of a closely held business by selling to an employee stock ownership plan. When this occurs and the owner invests the proceeds in qualified securities, there is a deferral of the tax on the gain realized from the sale. The qualified securities then retain the income tax basis the owner possessed in the stock of the closely held business. In these cases, the financial adviser may find high value investments with little or no basis. As discovered previously, when there is a large unrealized tax gain built into an asset, its valuation can be a challenge and may be dictated by local law.

GOVERNMENTAL PLANS

All military and some federal and state-funded retirement plans are forms of defined benefit plans. The remainder of the plans are a form of defined contribution plan. As they are not provided for in Internal Revenue Code Section 401, they are not considered to be qualified plans. This is despite the fact that they share most of the same characteristics as qualified plans. Depending on their nature, these plans are valued in the same manner as the qualified defined contribution and defined benefit plans. In a case that illustrates some of the legal issues argued when dealing with government retirement plans, the Superior Court of New Jersey in *La Sala v. La*

Sala ruled that the nonemployee spouse could not anticipate benefits from the state retirement system. The nonemployee spouse must wait for the employee to attain the rights to the benefits before the nonemployee spouse could receive a share of those benefits. The entire text of the case is included to allow the reader to understand the types of legal issues argued in domestic relations litigation. See Exhibit 5.1.

EXHIBIT 5.1   *La Sala* Case, Superior Court of New Jersey

SUPERIOR COURT OF NEW JERSEY
APPELLATE DIVISION
DOCKET NO. A-5512-98T5

KARLEEN LA SALA,
Plaintiff-Respondent,
v.
ALFRED LA SALA,
Defendant,
and
POLICE AND FIREMEN'S
RETIREMENT SYSTEM,
Appellant.

Argued October 16, 2000–Decided November 3, 2000
Before Judges Wefing, Cuff and Lefelt.

On appeal from the Superior Court of New Jersey, Chancery Division, Family Part, Hudson County, whose opinion is reported in *324 N.J. Super. 264* (Ch. Div. 1999)

Susanne Culliton, Deputy Attorney General, argued the cause for appellant (John J. Farmer, Jr., Attorney General, attorney; Nancy C. Kaplan, Assistant Attorney General, of counsel; Ms. Culliton, on the brief).

Richard Seltzer argued the cause for respondent.

The opinion of the court was delivered by LEFELT, J.A.D.

EXHIBIT 5.1 *(Continued)*

Plaintiff Karleen LaSala and defendant Alfred LaSala were in the midst of a divorce proceeding when plaintiff requested equitable distribution of defendant's Police and Firemen's pension before defendant retired. The trial court divorced the parties on April 19, 1999 and directed the Board of Trustees of the Police and Firemen's Retirement System ("PFRS") to commence immediate monthly payments to plaintiff and to continue these payments for the remainder of her life or until one-half the value of defendant's pension has been paid, whichever comes first. The trial court's written decision explaining the pension distribution was published at *La Sala v. La Sala (See footnote 1), 324 N.J. Super. 265,* 285 (Ch. Div. 1999). PFRS now appeals, and we reverse.

Plaintiff and defendant were married on May 18, 1968. After twenty-eight years of marriage, plaintiff filed for divorce on February 14, 1996. The parties had three children, all of whom are emancipated. Defendant is fifty-three years old and is Deputy Chief of the Jersey City Fire Department. Because defendant has thirty-years of service, he is fully vested in his pension, but defendant has no present plans to retire.

Plaintiff re-entered the work force in 1984 when the parties' youngest child began attending school. Plaintiff's full time employment continued until 1994 when she lost her job due to downsizing by her employer. Since that time her employment has been sporadic and at modest compensation. Plaintiff is a high school graduate with limited job skills.

During their marriage, the parties acquired only two assets of any significance, the marital home and defendant's PFRS pension. Excluding defendant's pension, the parties' net worth is just slightly in excess of $12,000. The trial judge established $669,000 as the value of defendant's pension, as of February 14, 1996, the date plaintiff filed her divorce complaint. The value was derived from calculations used by the Division of Pensions to estimate the amount of funds that must be transferred to the retirement account when a member retires.

Because plaintiff sought, before defendant's retirement, either a lump sum or other equitable distribution of her interest in defendant's pension, the judge, upon plaintiff's motion, joined PFRS as a party to the litigation. After conducting a plenary hearing on the distribution of defendant's pension, the trial court ordered PFRS to commence monthly payments to plaintiff for the remainder of her life or until she received the maximum benefit of $334,500, one-half the value of defendant's pension. The trial court stayed its judgment, and only PFRS appealed. No party has challenged the value established for defendant's pension, though PFRS does take the position that neither defendant nor plaintiff is entitled to the present value of defendant's retirement allowance. The issue presented by this appeal, thus, is whether the trial court

(continues)

EXHIBIT 5.1   *(Continued)*

erred by ordering PFRS to distribute plaintiff's share of defendant's pension before defendant's retirement.

The trial court has discretion in allocating marital assets to the parties in equitable distribution. *Borodinsky v. Borodinsky, 162 N.J. Super. 437,* 443-44 (App. Div. 1978). We review distributions to determine whether the court has abused its discretion. *Ibid.* Thus, we will affirm an equitable distribution as long as the trial court could reasonably have reached its result from the evidence presented, and the award is not distorted by legal or factual mistake. *Perkins v. Perkins, 159 N.J. Super. 243,* 247-48 (App. Div. 1978). However, "[a] trial court's interpretation of the law and the legal consequences that flow from established facts are not entitled to any special deference." *Manalapan Realty v. Township Comm., 140 N.J. 366,* 378 (1995).

The trial court, in this case, was concerned that plaintiff would become destitute unless it directed the immediate distribution of plaintiff's share of defendant's pension. *La Sala,* supra, 324 *N.J. Super.* at 285. The judge, in effect, made plaintiff "a limited member of PFRS." *Id.* at 284. According to the trial court, plaintiff was not entitled to a lump sum payment by PFRS, but she was entitled to make two choices: (1) "withdraw her share of the contributions[,] . . . waive the pension, . . . [and] receive only her proportionate share of the contributions made during coverture"; or (2) "receive the pension . . . payable in monthly installments [from PFRS], capped by her distributive share, $334,500." *Ibid.* Our problem with this result is that the trial court has granted plaintiff rights in defendant's pension that no member of PFRS enjoys.

PFRS is a pooled annuity defined benefit fund. Only a member's contributions are attributable to the member. All of the remaining assets are "pooled" for the entire system. Under the current statute, therefore, only when defendant retires will he be entitled to his pension. Until he retires, he has no present right to a retirement benefit.

Defendant's pension, until he retires, is also contingent upon separation from service and withdrawal from the retirement system. N.J.S.A. 43:16A-11 to 11.1. His pension may also be completely or partially forfeited "for misconduct occurring during the member's public service." N.J.S.A. 43:1-3b. The only immediate right defendant enjoys is the right to borrow up to one-half of his accumulated contributions to the retirement system. N.J.S.A. 43:16A-16.1. Should defendant die, there is no statutory provision to continue his benefits to his spouse. The remaining funds allocated to defendant's pension would upon his death be returned to the fund.

In 1967 the PFRS statute was significantly amended by L. 1967, c. 250, § 31, repealing N.J.S.A. 43:16A-12, which permitted PFRS members to elect a form of retirement that would provide a survivor annuity to a designated beneficiary. Under this form of retirement, the member received a reduced benefit in exchange for the survivor annuity.

EXHIBIT 5.1 *(Continued)*

Instead, after the 1967 amendment, PFRS provides a separate "widow's pension," which supplies a life annuity to the member's surviving spouse without additional contributions by the member or reduction in the member's retirement benefits. N.J.S.A. 43:16A-12.1. The "widow's pension" constitutes a fixed percentage of the member's "average final compensation." *Ibid.* According to the statute, however, a widow is a "woman to whom a member or retirant was married at least one year before the date of his death and to whom he continued to be married until the date of his death and who has not remarried." N.J.S.A. 43:16A- 1(24). A recent amendment to this provision now requires that the woman be married to the member "on the date of his death." L. 1999, c. 428, § 1, effective January 18, 2000. Thus, to be entitled to a widow's pension, the widow must have been married to the member on the day he died and not remarried. No provision is included for divorced spouses, and as a result of the divorce, plaintiff is no longer eligible for the "widow's pension."

PFRS does, however, allow for any named beneficiary to receive a life insurance benefit under N.J.S.A. 43:16A-12.3, and in the case of death during service, a return of pension contributions upon the member's death. N.J.S.A. 43:16A-9(1). Thus, under the existing PFRS statute, should defendant die before retiring, any beneficiary will be entitled to a return of pension contributions and the life insurance benefit.

Upon retirement, defendant would receive monthly payments of the retirement allowance. N.J.S.A. 43:16A-12.2. A PFRS member who has accrued twenty-five years of service may retire regardless of age at sixty-five-percent of final salary. N.J.S.A. 43:16A-11.1. At thirty years of service, the member may retire at seventy-percent of final salary. *Ibid.* Further, these monthly pension benefits cease upon the retiree's death, and the only benefits that are available, upon the member's death, are the "widow's pension" and life insurance benefit. No one questions plaintiff's right to equitable distribution, under N.J.S.A. 2A:34-23, of defendant's pension. *Kruger v. Kruger,* 73 N.J. 464 (1977). It is well recognized in this state that a spouse's pension, acquired during the marriage, is subject to equitable distribution upon divorce. *Moore v. Moore,* 114 N.J. 147,155 (1989). Because employee pensions often are accrued by the parties' joint efforts during the marriage, pension benefits paid after divorce can be equitably distributed. *Ibid.* The distribution normally requires the spouse's share, as determined under *Painter v. Painter,* 65 N.J. 196 (1974), to be multiplied by a coverture fraction. *Whitfield v. Whitfield,* 222 N.J. Super. 36, 48 (App. Div. 1987).

It is the judge's function to develop an appropriate equitable distribution method. Over the years, three methods have generally been utilized to distribute pensions: (1) "deferred distribution," where payment occurs after the

(continues)

EXHIBIT 5.1   (*Continued*)

retiring spouse begins receiving benefits; (2) "immediate offset or payment," which utilizes existing assets to either offset or pay the benefit; and (3) "partial deferred distribution," which entails a "current valuation award of the appropriate share of the non-contingent portion of the pension and a deferred distribution of the share of the contingent benefits if and when they are paid to the employee spouse." *Moore v. Moore*, supra, 114 N.J. at 161.

The problem confronting the trial judge was obviously the parties' lack of assets. If the parties had enough assets to affect an offset of plaintiff's claim against defendant's pension, then such a distribution would be possible. *Moore*, supra, 114 N.J. at 160. If defendant were retired, then plaintiff could receive her equitable share on a monthly basis, like defendant, directly from PFRS. See *Cleveland v. Board of Trustees, Police and Firemen's Retirement System*, 229 N.J. Super. 156 (App. Div. 1988).

Here, however, the trial court basically established an immediate payout by PFRS of a portion of defendant's pension. Because defendant himself has no present right to the pension benefits, plaintiff also has no present right, and the trial court's distribution was unauthorized. Should defendant die before he retires, his beneficiary would be entitled only to defendant's contributions and the life insurance benefit. Moreover, any loans by the member from his contributions would be deducted from any money due upon defendant's retirement or death. While defendant is entitled to a monthly benefit upon retirement, once he dies, there is no requirement to continue payment of the benefit.

The trial judge believed that because the legislature created the "widow's pension," the Legislature clearly and unmistakenly demonstrated an intent to provide for the future financial security of a dependent spouse surviving a PFRS member. Further, since the additional benefits were provided without an adjustment to the funding mechanism, it is clear that the Legislature intended to subordinate actuarial soundness to the accomplishment of this specific, significant public purpose.

[*La Sala,* supra, 324 N.J. Super. at 273]

We disagree with the breadth of this statement and the application of this rationale to a divorced spouse. The legislative language is clear and does not include a divorced spouse within the definition of "widow." We have previously determined that "a court cannot balance [the] equities by taking a portion of a widow's statutory entitlement and giving it to a former spouse." *Seavey v. Long*, 303 N.J. Super. 153, 160 (App. Div. 1997). The legislature created the widow's benefit in such a way that the member cannot control the designation of benefits upon his or her death. Defendant cannot designate a beneficiary to receive the "widow's benefit." *Id.* at 158. The benefit is controlled by statute, and once plaintiff and defendant divorced, plaintiff ceased to be a surviving spouse under N.J.S.A. 43:16A- 12.1.

EXHIBIT 5.1 *(Continued)*

We cannot ascribe to the Legislature by its enactment of the "widow's pension" an intention to provide for the future financial security of a surviving divorced spouse. We are required to enforce the legislative intent as written, "and not according to some supposed unexpressed intention." *Lehmann v. Kanane,* 88 N.J. Super. 262, 265 (App. Div.), certif. denied, 45 N.J. 591 (1965).

Moreover, pension benefits for police and fire fighters will be jeopardized in the future if the fund is not "'maintained upon a sound actuarial basis.'" *Brown v. Township of Old Bridge,* 319 N.J. Super. 476, 498 (App. Div.), certif. denied, 162 N.J. 131 (1999) (quoting *Seire v. Police and Fire Pension Comm'n of Orange,* 6 N.J. 586, 591 (1951)). The fund must be administered "in accordance with sound actuarial principles and experience." *Consolidated Police & Firemen's Pension Fund Comm'n v. City of Passaic,* 23 N.J. 645, 655 (1957). We cannot agree that by adopting the "widow's pension," the legislature intended to overlook actuarial soundness to provide a benefit for divorced spouses.

The trial court recognized that no precedent supported plaintiff's request for immediate payout of defendant's PFRS pension. He did note that "several of our sister states have adopted a variant form of immediate payout." *La Sala,* supra, 324 N.J. Super. at 278. The judge cited *Furia v. Furia (Furia I),* 638 A.2d 548 (R.I. 1994); *Furia v. Furia (Furia II),* 692 A.2d 327 (R.I. 1997); *Rowe v. Rowe,* 480 S.E.2d 760 (Va. App. 1997); and *Gilmore v. Gilmore,* 629 P.2d 1 (Cal. 1981). Under these cases, however, the member spouse was required to pay the distributive share of his or her pension to the non-member spouse in regular installments out of current pre-retirement income. Thus, as the trial judge also recognized, none of these foreign cases support requiring the system to make an immediate pension payout, as was ordered in the instant matter. None of the cases required the retirement fund to make a payment that was not set forth in the controlling statute.

In this case, we conclude that the trial court's form of immediate distribution is not legally possible. Plaintiff has no right through the guise of equitable distribution to have any marital asset enhanced. Plaintiff's equitable share of defendant's pension must be determined "in accordance with the plan formula." *Marx v. Marx,* 265 N.J. Super. 418, 428 (Ch. Div. 1993). A court may not re-write the pension statute under the guise of doing equity. The terms of the plan determine the parties' rights and entitlements. We may not vary the basic terms of the pension plan or confer benefits beyond those contemplated by the plan. Rather, distribution schemes must "conform to the plan's essential purpose." *Weir v. Weir,* 173 N.J. Super. 130, 135 (Ch. Div. 1980). Trial courts, in fashioning equitable distribution, must be sensitive to whatever limitations exist in the nature of the particular asset being considered.

(continues)

EXHIBIT 5.1 *(Continued)*

We are, of course, sympathetic to the admirable goals that motivated the trial court. We accept that plaintiff is in need of immediate income, and thus waiting until defendant retires to distribute his pension might be less than satisfactory. But, a court may satisfy a party's needs only in a lawful manner.

On remand, we suggest that the trial court consider other methods of generating immediate income for plaintiff. For example, defendant has an outstanding loan balance of $28,782.93. He may borrow an additional $19,447.90 from PFRS, and these monies could be used for immediate distribution to plaintiff as an offset against her expected pension benefit. Moreover, to provide some limited protection for plaintiff, the trial court could explore some of the insurance options that are available.

An active employee is entitled to death benefits for his beneficiaries in the amount of 250% of salary. N.J.S.A. 43:16A-9. Here, defendant's active coverage is $345,000. The trial court could order that defendant designate plaintiff as his beneficiary. This would provide some protection for plaintiff should defendant die before retiring.

Upon defendant's retirement, the amount of his death benefit from PFRS is reduced to approximately $49,000. Defendant has, however, the right to convert the difference, $296,000, into private insurance. The conversion of insurance is automatic upon the payment of a premium, regardless of the health or age of the applicant. N.J.S.A. 43:16A-58. Thus, this could provide some measure of protection for plaintiff should defendant die during his retirement, whether or not defendant has remarried.

PFRS also argued in its appeal that the financial integrity of the pension fund would be jeopardized by the trial court's order. Because we find the trial court's order to be unlawful for the reasons explained above, we need not decide whether the trial court's distribution threatens the fund's financial integrity.

We reverse *LaSala v. LaSala,* 324 N.J. Super. 264 (Ch. Div. 1999), and remand the matter to the trial court for further proceedings in accordance with this decision.

Reversed and remanded.

Exhibits 5.2, 5.3, 5.4, and 5.5 detail the types of information that may be required to value various types of retirement plans.

EXHIBIT 5.2 Pension Valuation

Information/Documents Request

Please provide the following information:

Valuation Date:

Employer Name:

Plan Name:

Employee Information (If military, see additional request enclosed):

Name:

Social Security Number:

Sex:

Date of Birth:

Date of Marriage:

Date of Employment:

Employment Status: Active   Retired   Terminated   w/Vesting

Date of Termination or Retirement (if applicable):
        Is the employee disabled?
        If disabled, is the employee receiving Social Security Benefits?

Spouse Information

Name:

Date of Birth:

Please provide the following documents:

   A copy of the plan or summary plan description (this will not be returned; please send a copy).

   Employee's annual benefits statements as of a date within 12 months of the valuation date (this will not be returned, please send a copy).

   If possible, the employee should request a current estimate of retirement benefits.

   If the employee began participation in the plan prior to the date of marriage, please provide a contribution history.

   A copy of the most current pay stub.

EXHIBIT 5.3   Pension Authorization (Private)

AUTHORIZATION AND RELEASE

I, _____, authorize and direct the Plan Administrator of each pension, profit sharing, 401(k), or other retirement or deferred compensation plan or program sponsored by _____ or any such plan or program to which _____ makes contributions for the benefit of its employees or under which its employees have economic interests (the "Plans"), to release and provide to the financial adviser, upon request, any and all information relating to the Plans or my interests in or rights under any of the Plans including, without limitation, (a) all information relating to any of the Plans, (b) all documents reflecting the terms of the Plans, (c) the amount of any benefits in which I have a vested or non-vested interest under any of the Plans, (d) any account balances that may be held in my name or for my benefit in any of the Plans, (e) the actuarial equivalent or present value amounts of any optional forms of benefit payment to which I am currently entitled or to which I may be entitled at any future time, and (f) copies of any releases, waivers, beneficiary designations or other forms on file with the Plans or the Plan Administrator. The purpose of this Authorization and Release is to provide the financial adviser access to all information necessary to determine my rights, interests, and options in or under the Plans.

_____
Participant's Signature
_____
Participant's Social Security Number

Date: _____

Address: _____
_____

EXHIBIT 5.4   General Release for State Retirement Plan Member File

    I, _____, Social Security number _____, hereby authorize the state retirement plan, and all its officers and employees, to release any and all records and information that the state retirement plan (or its officers or employees) has or maintains as a result of, or pertaining to, my state retirement plan membership and state retirement plan benefits to:

or the duly authorized agents of _____.
    I also authorize all copies of all documents obtained pursuant to this authorization to be provided to _____ by the above-named person or organization, _____.

    This Release includes all records that pertain to me and that are held by the state retirement plan, including but not limited to, records and calculations of my wage history and the state retirement plan service credit; records and calculations of my state retirement plan contributions, including employer contributions on my behalf; records and calculations of withdrawn service credit, if any; records and calculations of the time eligible for (and the cost of) any service credit buy-backs, if any; any application for employment or retirement; personal records; payroll documents; employment or personnel records; physical or medical records; beneficiary designations; records pertaining to disability, workers' compensation or unemployment claims; address and phone number; divorce and child support orders; and any other records or information whatsoever in the possession of the state retirement plan (or its officers or employees) that relates to me, including computerized records.

    I hereby expressly waive any state or federal laws or regulations, and rules of ethics, that might prevent the state retirement plan from releasing such records. A photostatic copy of this Release, which contains my signature, shall be considered as effective and valid as the original and shall be honored by those to whom it is sent or provided.

_____
           [Member's Name]

STATE OF _____)
                              ss.
COUNTY OF _____)

    The above Release for THE STATE RETIREMENT PLAN Member File was sworn and subscribed to before me this _____ day of _____, 2002__.

_____
    Notary Public

My commission expires:
_____

EXHIBIT 5.5   Military Pension Valuation—Additional
Documents/Information Request

Current Active Duty Military Personnel:

If possible, obtain an estimate of retirement benefits and a retirement point summary statement from the last duty station.

Reserve Members:

If possible, obtain estimate of retired pay and retirement point summary statement from one of the following Military Personnel Centers:

US Air Force Retirement
HQ ARPC/DPK
Air Force Reserve Personnel Center
6760 East Irvington Place #2100
Denver, Colorado 80280-2100
800-525-0102, Ext 403 for Points, Ext 402 for Retired Pay
for Points, 303-676-6369 for Retired Pay
Fax: 303-676-6793

United States Naval Reserve Retirement
HQ NRPC/N211 or N212
Navy Reserve Personnel Center
4400 Dauphine Street
New Orleans, LA 70149
800-535-2699
504-678-1812
Fax 504-678-5470

US Army Reserve Retirement
HQ ARPC/PAC
US Army Reserve Personnel Center
9700 Page Boulevard
St Louis, MO 63132-5200
800-325-8311
314-538-5071
Fax 314-538-3567

All Members provide the following information:

DIEMS date—Date Initially Entered Military Service.

Rank (current or final, if retired).

Effective Date of Rank.

Pay Date—This is a computed date shown on Leave and Earnings Statement (LES).

EXHIBIT 5.5 *(Continued)*

TAFMS Date—Total Active Federal Military Service Date. Computed date showing all active duty time.

TAFCS Date (officers only)—Total Active Federal Commissioned Service Date.

1405 Date—This date should include all active service and a certain amount of in-active reserve service. Request the DIN SAI date.

INDIVIDUAL RETIREMENT ACCOUNTS, SIMPLIFIED EMPLOYEE PENSIONS, AND SIMPLE PLANS

Individual Retirement Accounts (IRAs), Simplified Employee Pensions, and SIMPLE plans are all retirement accounts that are controlled by the individual, as opposed to the employer. These plans are defined contribution plans and are typically maintained at banks, brokerage firms, insurance companies, and other institutions that qualify to trustee these types of accounts. The individual beneficiary controls the investment of the funds and makes a positive election of the funds' disbursement at death. The gross value of these plans can be determined on the face of the statements provided by the trustee. They are, however, tax-deferred accounts that have a deferred tax liability associated with the assets. As a result, there will be possible disputes on whether to use the gross value or the estimated after-tax value in dividing the marital estate.

Our government provides Social Security benefits to individuals on the death of a minor child's parent and in the event of the disability or death of the beneficiary. The amount of the benefit is based on the beneficiary's Social Security earnings base. Annual statements are available from the Social Security Administration, which estimates what those benefits will be for each person. These benefits are, by federal law, the individual's separate property and are not subject to division upon divorce. There is a provision in the law that allows a divorced individual to collect benefits based on the ex-spouse's earnings. If the person was married for ten years and has not remarried, they may collect benefits equal to the higher of one half their ex-spouse's benefit or their own benefit. This potential increased benefit can be helpful in meeting the retirement needs of a financial adviser's client.

Tax-sheltered annuities are available to employees of nonprofit and governmental organizations. These retirement vehicles allow the employee participant to defer a portion of their salary into an annuity investment vehicle. These investments can then be withdrawn for retirement purposes when the employee reaches age 59 years and 6 months. These investments can be valued by observing the investment statement. There is typically an investment-vehicle-imposed penalty if there is a withdrawal from the fund in the early years it is held.

TRANSFER OF RETIREMENT ASSETS

Most employer retirement plans encountered in domestic relations cases are qualified under Section 401 of the Internal Revenue Code. Qualified plan assets are transferable between the parties to a divorce pursuant to a Qualified Domestic Relations Order. You may hear these documents termed QDROs. Qualified Domestic Relations Orders are issued by the court and approved by the plan administrator. The order divides the benefits in a qualified plan between the employee and the nonemployee spouse. An order becomes qualified only when the plan administrator approves it. If the plan is qualified, the plan assets can be transferred without immediate tax consequence to either the plan participant or the participant's ex-spouse. A *domestic relations order* is any judgment, decree, or order, including approval of a property settlement agreement, that:

- Relates to the provision of child support, alimony payments, or marital property rights to a spouse, former spouse, child, or other dependent of a participant; and
- Is made under state domestic relations law, including a community property law.

An *alternate payee* is any spouse, former spouse, child, or other dependent of a participant whom a domestic relations order recognizes as having a right to receive all, or a portion of, the benefits payable under the plan with respect to the participant.

In order to be qualified, the order must clearly and specifically contain:

- The name and last known mailing address of the participant and the name and mailing address of each alternate payee covered by the order.
- The amount or percentage of the participant's benefits to be paid by the plan to each alternate payee, or the manner of determining the amount or percentage.
- The number of payments or period the order applies to.
- Each plan to which the order applies.

The order cannot require the plan to provide any type of benefit, or any option not otherwise provided under the plan. In addition, the order cannot require the plan to provide increased benefits, determined on the basis of actuarial value. The order also cannot require the payment of benefits to an alternate payee that are required to be paid to another alternate payee under another QDRO.

There is an additional problem that may be encountered when using a QDRO to fund the payment of alimony or child support obligations. The plans are required to withhold federal income tax on payments made from the plan, if the payment is not directly rolled into another qualified plan or individual retirement account. If the amount of the withholding is not properly anticipated in the order, this withholding can reduce the nonparticipant's payment from the plan to the benefit of the participant. Therefore, the financial adviser must anticipate the amount of withholding to properly determine the amount of withdrawal from the plan required to meet the obligation being funded.

Many large employers have drafted and will provide their employees with forms of orders that their plan administrators will accept. There are also attorneys who specialize in preparing these orders. The use of these attorneys and form orders will save domestic relations litigants both money and time in getting plan assets divided.

When assets are divided pursuant to a qualified domestic relations order, the non-employee spouse has several options regarding what to do with the proceeds. The proceeds can be rolled over into an

Individual Retirement Account. When this occurs, the proceeds are subject to all the rules applicable to Individual Retirement Accounts. The spouse can take the proceeds and keep them outside any retirement vehicle. In this case, the spouse will pay income tax on the balance received, but can avoid the ten percent early withdrawal penalty that would normally be applied. This is pursuant to Section 72(t) of the Internal Revenue Code. The spouse will also have the option of mixing these results. The administrator of the plan will forward documents to the nonemployee spouse that will detail these options and provide information regarding the timing of the disbursement.

Many plans allow participants to borrow from qualified plans. The rules allow a participant to borrow up to 50 percent of the participant's account balance or $50,000, whichever is less. These loans normally have to be repaid within five years. When the parties to a divorce have one of these loans, there are a number of issues created. If the plan participant does not keep sufficient assets, after the division, in the account to support the loan, the plan will demand repayment to bring the account into compliance. If the participant is unable to repay the loan, it will be treated as a distribution to the participant subject to both income tax and potentially the 10 percent early withdrawal penalty. The only way to keep the loan in compliance is to keep assets in the plan that are twice the amount of the current balance of the loan. Failure to do so will cause tax consequences that may not be anticipated.

It is possible to use QDROs to pay debts and divorce expenses using either pretax or low-tax dollars. There are times when a high-income plan participant and the low- or no-income spouse may wish to transfer plan assets to the nonemployee spouse to retire debts or the divorce expenses. If the high-income individual is in a high-income tax bracket (e.g., 50 percent), the spouse is in a low bracket, and there is a sufficient balance in the plan, plan assets can be transferred and leveraged to pay the debts and divorce expenses at a large savings to the high-income individual. This occurs by transferring sufficient assets to the nonemployee spouse to pay any income tax due on the distribution and then to use the balance to retire the debt and divorce expenses. When it works properly, this technique can save the high-income individual 30 to 50 percent of the debts and expenses paid. The financial adviser should be aware of this method of saving money.

On September 24, 1999, the U.S. Third Circuit Court of Appeals filed a decision providing an illustration of potential problems awaiting the financial adviser attempting to distribute retirement benefits in a marital settlement agreement. The case arose in the District of New Jersey and was docketed as No. 98–5245 in the Third Circuit. The case is entitled *Louise Robichaud Samaroo v. Winston R. Samaroo, AT&T Management Pension Plan v. Louise M. Robichaud.*

Louise Robichaud divorced Winston Samaroo on October 25, 1984. The divorce decree incorporated a property settlement that calculated the present value of Mr. Samaroo's vested monthly retirement income from a defined benefit retirement plan provided by his employer, AT&T Technologies. The settlement agreement stated that, "At the time of husband's retirement and receipt of his pension he agrees to pay to wife one half of said monthly amount."

The pension plan also provided a preretirement survivor annuity available to the surviving spouse of any participant who died after vesting, but before retiring. If there were no surviving spouse, there would be no annuity. The divorce settlement agreement did not mention the annuity. Ms. Robichaud and the attorneys for both parties in the divorce proceeding later testified that nobody involved thought about or discussed the survivor annuity. Mr. Samaroo died in 1987, while still actively employed by AT&T.

Ms. Robichaud then obtained a *nunc pro tunc* order from the New Jersey state court to amend the divorce decree, as of the date of the divorce, to entitle her to the annuity. The AT&T Management Pension Plan refused to honor this amended decree and filed a declaratory action in the United States District Court for the District of New Jersey to determine the relative rights of the parties. The district court granted AT&T's motion for summary judgment, holding that the amended decree was not a qualified domestic relations order capable of conferring the annuity benefits on Ms. Robichaud.

In affirming this decision, the Third Circuit Court first discusses that the divorce occurred prior to the enactment of the Retirement Equity Act of 1984 and that, therefore, it was not clear at the time as to whether state court divorce decrees could even convey a share in pension benefits of one spouse to the other. Briefly citing that plan, administrators are provided discretion in the

Retirement Equity Act to treat orders entered before the date of the Act as qualified domestic relations orders. The Third Circuit Court quickly disposes of that question to discuss in great detail whether either the original divorce decree, or the amended decree, could be considered as a qualified domestic relations order.

Although Ms. Robichaud chose to amend the original decree rather than relying upon it to entitle her to the annuity, she did argue in her reply brief that the original decree could have been read to give her that right. The Third Circuit Court discussed several aspects of the original decree that would not allow it to so interpret the original decree, mostly dealing with the complete lack of specificity about, or discussion of, the death benefits.

As to the amended decree, the Circuit Court agreed with the District Court that this decree violated the provisions of 29 U.S.C. §1056(d)(3)(D)(i) and (ii), which state that a domestic relations order is not a qualified domestic relations order, if it requires the plan to provide any type of benefits not otherwise provided by the plan, or to provide increased benefits. The Court stated, "A domestic decree that would have the effect of increasing the liability of the Plan over what has been provided in the Plan (read in light of federal law) is not a qualified domestic relations order, no matter what the decree's status under state law."

The Circuit Court had previously pointed out that the New Jersey court had expressly stated, in allowing the *nunc pro tunc* amendment to its order, that "whether or not the state court order resulted in any benefits becoming payable to Robichaud under the Plan was a question of federal law."

The Circuit Court then embarked on a discussion of the effect of the retroactive amended order upon the plan in question. The Court rejected Ms. Robichaud's argument that the effect of its refusal to honor the amended decree was to cheat Samaroo out of receiving any benefit from participating in the Plan. The Court pointed out that disbursement of plan benefits is based on actuarial computations and that "the plan administrator must know the life expectancy of every person receiving the Surviving Spouse Benefits to determine the participant's monthly Pension Benefits. The plan's liabilities must be ascertainable as of particular dates."

The Court then compared the provisions of a defined benefit plan to those of an insurance policy and stated: "Some annuity participants will die without ever receiving a payment and some participants will receive payments far in excess of the value of their contributions. The fact that some participants die without a surviving spouse to qualify for benefits is not an unfair forfeiture, as Robichaud contends, but rather part of the ordinary workings of an insurance plan."

The Court pointed out that, until Samaroo died, he enjoyed the rights to remarry and bestow the death benefits on his new wife, or to enter into a qualified domestic relations order bestowing these rights on Ms. Robichaud. The Court cited the provisions of 29 U.S.C. §1056(d)(3)(F) as prohibiting a current spouse from being treated as a spouse for purposes of a plan, if the former spouse is designated as surviving spouse in a qualified domestic relations order. The Court observed: "Allowing Samaroo (or his estate) to preserve the right to confer the benefits on a new wife as long as he was alive and had the possibility of remarrying, and then to designate Robichaud as the surviving spouse after his death, is allowing him to have his cake and eat it, too."

Individual Retirement Accounts, Simplified Employee Pension, and SIMPLE plans can be transferred pursuant to a divorce decree or a marital settlement agreement. The simple presentation of the filed court document to the investment firm possessing the assets will cause the transfer of the assets. The financial adviser should take care to insure that there are no investment penalties associated with a transfer. The transfer can cause the liquidation of an existing investment and a rollover into a new investment.

When a party to a divorce receives an Individual Retirement Account in a property settlement, there are several options regarding the short-term use of the proceeds. The monies can be rolled over into another Individual Retirement Account. This option, if accomplished within sixty days, will cause no current income tax consequence. Once the funds are inside a new Individual Retirement Account, they are again subject to all of the income tax and penalty provisions that accompany regular Individual Retirement Accounts.

There is a provision in Internal Revenue Code Section 72(t) that will allow the balance in the Individual Retirement Account to be annuitized penalty free, over the remaining life expectancy of the owner of the account. The annuity is computed using the balance in the account, a reasonable interest rate, and a withdrawal that can be maintained over the owner's remaining life expectancy. If these conditions are met and the payments continue for at least five years, the withdrawals are exempt from the 10 percent early withdrawal penalty. This provision may allow the annuitant to finance education or other rehabilitation expenses from Individual Retirement Accounts funds.

NONQUALIFIED PLANS

There are significant issues that must be dealt with when nonqualified plans are transferred pursuant to a divorce or separation. Because of the position taken by the Internal Revenue Service regarding the assignment of income, it is possible to cause the taxation of distributions of nonqualified plan assets to the non-employee spouse to be taxed to the employee spouse, in the resolution of a domestic relations case. These plans are a contract between the company and employee to pay an amount at retirement. They may or may not be currently funded, are always discriminatory, and are subject to many risks of forfeiture. Even if these plans are funded, the assets of the plan are generally subject to creditor claims.

Qualified domestic relations orders do not apply to nonqualified retirement plans. In Letter Ruling 9340032, the Internal Revenue Service has held that upon payment to a taxpayer's ex-spouse of amounts due under a nonqualified deferred compensation plan, the taxpayer realized income in the amount paid to the ex-spouse.

As long as the employee's benefits are subject to a substantial risk of forfeiture, the employee does not recognize any income from the plan funding, even if the plan is currently being funded. The Internal Revenue Service's position states the creditor risk is sufficient to avoid current taxation. The employer is, however, not entitled to a deduction until the employee picks up the income.

One type of these nonqualified plans is called a *rabbi trust*. In order to provide for a long-time, trusted employee, assets of a synagogue in the Midwest were irrevocably transferred into a trust for the rabbi's benefit. The trust provided the assets were subject to the claims of creditors of the employer and that the employee had no rights greater than an unsecured general creditor to those assets. In a 1981 private ruling (Letter Ruling 8113107), the Internal Revenue Service concluded that no transfer of property to the rabbi would occur as assets were added to the trust and that the rabbi would be taxed only when amounts were paid, or made available under the terms of the trust. Employers are now commonly utilizing this type of trust. These arrangements have come to be known as *rabbi trusts*.

Phantom stock plans are another type of nonqualified plan. They are designed to give a key employee an interest in the growth in the value of a business without conferring the rights and privileges of actual equity ownership. The recipients' benefit from the plan is the right to receive a percentage of the growth in value of the firm at a date in the future. Because there is not an active market that determines the value of closely held business interests, these plans include a valuation formula that allows the computation of the compensation to be paid. This formula provides the basis for the computation of the recipient's benefit. It is typical that the right to *cash in* this increase in value is based on some type of vesting schedule, or the achievement of continued employment for some period of time. The right may lapse without benefit to the employee, if he does not meet those criteria or leaves to work for a competitor. The employee does not recognize any income on the grant of the phantom stock. Income is only recognized at the time the employee derives the benefit from the phantom stock. The employer, likewise, does not achieve a deduction until the benefit is paid.

This benefit allows the employee to enjoy the theoretical increase in value of the employer's business, as a result of the employee's efforts. It is designed to create a reason for the retention of the employee by the employer. It allows the employer to promise compensation in the future, without a current funding requirement, and keeps the employee employed.

The Internal Revenue Service has issued Revenue Ruling 2002–22, which gives advisers guidance on what circumstances will lead to the taxation of deferred compensation plans. The ruling states that a taxpayer who transfers interests in nonqualified deferred compensation plans and nonstatutory stock options to their spouse incident to a divorce is not required to include an amount in gross income on the transfer and that the former spouse is required to include an appropriate amount in income when the compensation is paid or made available. The Internal Revenue Service in limited examples is stating that certain "assignments of income" are nontaxable to the transferor under Code Section 1041. The Internal Revenue Service has stated the Ruling does not apply to transfers of nonstatutory stock options and unfunded deferred compensation rights that are unvested or subject to substantial risk of forfeiture at the time of transfer. The Ruling will therefore not apply to most nonqualified deferred compensation plans divided in divorce as there is typically risk of forfeiture built into the plan to keep the employee from being currently taxed on the amounts earned. This ruling also highlights the need to be cognizant of the valuation issues associated with the taxation of the proceeds of the plans.

All of these benefits potentially provide property that must be divided on the dissolution of the marriage. Even if the courts find that these types of plans do not create current property, the plans do potentially create income to be divided for the purposes of child support or alimony. Discovering information related to these plans can be a challenge for the nonemployee spouse, but the discovery of these assets can prove valuable to the adviser's litigant client.

CHAPTER 6

The Taxation and Determination of Support in Divorce Litigation

CHILD SUPPORT

Child support is the most common support awarded in a divorce or separation. All of the states have been required by the federal government to establish child support guidelines which detail the amount of support that a custodial parent may receive when divorcing the child's other parent. These guidelines are normally based on the respective income of the parents, the amount of time the children spend with each parent, and any extra or extraordinary expenses each parent may incur. These extraordinary expenses may be for childcare, medical expense, private school tuition, or other special needs of the children.

Income determination is a prerequisite to the computation of child support under a state's guidelines. The financial adviser may be actively involved in the determination of the appropriate income for purposes of child support. Whether certain types of income should, or should not, be included is the subject of the state's statutes and case law. Many states have adopted income, as reported on the couple's income tax return, as a base from which to begin. Questions may then arise on issues such as the appropriateness of non-cash expenses such as depreciation or the tax effecting of non-taxable income to bring it on an equal footing with taxable income. There are times when there are questions regarding whether an income stream can be sustained, or whether a parent should be required to continue to work at "superhuman" levels to sustain a pre-divorce level of income. Problems arise with income that varies, income that fluctuates from year to year, or to income streams that may only be sustainable for a limited number of years. If one or both parents are not employed at a level equal to their earnings capacity, the courts may impute income to the underemployed person for purposes of determining the level of support to be paid. Some states waive the imputation if the underemployed spouse must care for small children or that spouse is physically incapable of earning an income. Finally, it is not unusual for high-income parents to argue that the guidelines may not be appropriate to their case as the level of support determined from the guidelines so far exceeds the needs of the children that it becomes a form of support for their ex-spouse. This can occur even when that spouse would not otherwise be entitled to spousal support. Each of these issues is determined on a state-by-state basis, as interpreted from local statutes and case law.

Once initial child support payments have been determined, future child support payments may be modifiable, if there is a significant change in circumstance. A change in circumstance can be as simple as a change in income level, the time a child spends with a parent, or as complicated as a change in the special needs of a child. Many states have income change or timeshare change thresholds that must be met before a change in circumstance will be considered.

Child support payments paid by a parent to the other parent are not deductible from the payer's income, or includible in the payee's income under Internal Revenue Code Section 71(c)(1). Payments are child support for tax purposes, if they are either so designated in the divorce or separation agreement or deemed child support under Internal Revenue Code Section 71(c).

SPOUSAL SUPPORT

Two terms most feared by many individuals going through a divorce or separation are alimony and spousal support. This fear originates from a negative perception of the terms and the purpose of the support. Each jurisdiction has differing rules related to the award of spousal support. There are jurisdictions that award spousal support as punishment for the wrongdoing of one of the divorcing couple. These jurisdictions are sometimes called fault jurisdictions. There are other jurisdictions that, regardless of fault, only award support in recognition of the continuing commitment the parties made to each other at the time of their marriage. These jurisdictions are called no fault jurisdictions. It is from this disparity of purpose in the various states that the negative perceptions arise.

The issue of support relates to maximizing a client's wallet dollars.

TYPES OF SPOUSAL SUPPORT

There are several types of spousal support that are awarded to a party in a divorce. There is spousal support that is permanent in nature and will continue for the remainder of the couples' lives. Most times, this type of spousal support is modifiable after the award, as a result of a change in circumstance of the parties. This change can be for any number of factors including a change of income, change in health, or other significant changes in the needs of either of the parties. The change in circumstance is defined in the local statutes and varies from state to state.

There is spousal support that is awarded for a limited period of time to provide a spouse income for the time required to be educated, trained, and to become self-supporting. This support is labeled as rehabilitative support. In some circumstances, spousal support can be utilized to reimburse a party for an expenditure of funds during a marriage, or to compensate one party for property awarded to the other. When this occurs, the amount to be paid may be nonmodifiable. Sometimes this type of support is called lump sum support because the total amount to be paid is fixed.

There are a number of factors utilized by the courts in determining spousal support awards. In addition to the possibility of support being awarded for punishment, there are any numbers of reasons for awards and factors used to determine the amount of spousal support that may be paid. There is evidence presented based on the need of the recipient, ability to pay by the payer, and the lifestyle of the parties during the period of the marriage. There are other factors such as the age of the individuals, their health, and the level of potential income of the potential recipient. There are also intangible factors such as the duration of the marriage, the amount of property awarded, and plans a party may have for rehabilitation. In *Moreno v. Moreno,* the Virginia Court of Appeals examines some of the legal issues regarding whether a retirement plan is considered property or income.

Exhibit 6.1　The Virginia Court of Appeals, *Moreno v. Moreno*

VA Court of Appeals

MORENO v. MORENO

FEBRUARY 11, 1997

Record No. 0972–96–4

RICHARD F. MORENO

v.

PATRICIA E. MORENO

Dennis J. Smith, Judge
Present: Chief Judge Moon, Judges Fitzpatrick and Annunziata
Argued at Alexandria, Virginia

OPINION BY JUDGE JOHANNA L. FITZPATRICK
FROM THE CIRCUIT COURT OF FAIRFAX COUNTY

Alan M. Winterhalter (Alan M. Winterhalter & Associates, P.C., on brief), for appellant.

(Carl P. Horton, on brief), for appellee. Appellee submitting on brief.

　　Richard F. Moreno (husband) appeals the decision of the trial court denying a request to terminate his spousal support obligation to Patricia E. Moreno (wife). He contends that the trial court erred in using income from his previously divided government pension as a source of funds to pay spousal support. Finding no error, we affirm the judgment of the trial court.

　　I. BACKGROUND

　　The facts of this case are not in dispute. The parties were married in 1970, separated in 1990, and divorced in 1992. The final decree of divorce, entered June 15, 1992, incorporated the parties' property settlement agreement (Agreement). Included in the Agreement were provisions requiring husband to pay spousal support and provisions distributing the marital portions of husband's pensions. [1]

　　Eighteen months prior to husband's mandatory retirement age of sixty years, husband voluntarily retired and received a $25,000 buy-out from his employer. At the time of his retirement, husband was living in Thailand and was a career employee of the United States government. He has since remarried, become a permanent resident of Thailand, but is prohibited by law from working in that country. Upon his retirement, husband's employer began making the pension payments as required by the Agreement.

　　On October 13, 1995, more than a year after his retirement, husband filed a motion to terminate spousal support. The trial court heard the motion on March 20, 1996. Husband argued that the only income source for making his spousal support payments since his retirement was his pension income

Exhibit 6.1   *(Continued)*

and interest earned from savings. Additionally, he argued that because he could not lawfully work in Thailand, he was unable to earn any supplemental income and none could be imputed to him. He admitted that when he reached age sixty shortly after trial, he would begin to receive an additional pension from the U.S. Army, which also would be divided pursuant to the provisions of the Agreement.

Wife testified that her need for spousal support had not diminished. Her income was limited to her salary, the spousal support paid by the husband of $2,600 per month, and her share of the husband's pension. Wife further testified that her expenses included the mortgage payments she paid on the parties' former marital home, upkeep of the home, medical care for herself and her daughter, as well as financial support for her daughter. The court denied wife's motion to require husband to pay a portion of the mortgage payment if it terminated spousal support, finding that it "had no power to modify this provision of the PSA."

At the conclusion of the hearing, the court found as follows:

[B]oth parties' testimony was credible[,] . . . the [husband] did not retire earlier than his mandatory retirement age for an improper purpose. . . . [T]he [husband's] retirement from government service did not preclude his earning income from other sources. . . . [T]he [husband] . . . chose[] to settle abroad in a country where the cost of living is substantially lower.

The court additionally found that husband "voluntarily chose to stay in Thailand and, accordingly, retired in a place which did not allow him to work[,] . . . thus preclud[ing] the [c]ourt from imputing income to him." The court denied husband's motion to terminate spousal support, but found that "there had been a change in circumstances to warrant a reduction in the spousal support from $2,600 per month to [$800] per month, beginning April 1, 1996. The [c]ourt determined the amount of the award based on the testimony as to the approximate split of the [husband's] Army pension and the other evidence."[2]

II. STANDARD OF REVIEW

"Whether spousal support should be paid is largely a matter committed to the sound discretion of the trial court, subject to the provisions of Code § 20–107.1." *McGuire v. McGuire,* 10 Va. App. 248, 251, 391 S.E.2d 344, 346 (1990). Although the decision to award spousal support rests within the trial court's discretion, "'such discretion is not absolute and is subject to review for abuse.'" *L.C.S. v. S.A.S.,* 19 Va. App. 709, 714, 453 S.E.2d 580, 583 (1995) (quoting *Via v. Via,* 14 Va. App. 868, 870, 419 S.E.2d 431, 433 (1992)).

In fixing the amount of the spousal support award, . . . the court's ruling will not be disturbed on appeal unless there has been a clear abuse of

(continues)

Exhibit 6.1   *(Continued)*

discretion. We will reverse the trial court only when its decision is plainly wrong or without evidence to support it. *Gamble v. Gamble,* 14 Va. App. 558, 574, 421 S.E.2d 635, 644 (1992) (citations omitted).

"Upon petition of either party, a court may . . . [modify] . . . spousal support . . . as the circumstances may make proper." *See* Code § 20-109. "The moving party in a petition for modification of support is required to prove both a material change in circumstances and that this change warrants a modification of support." *Schoenwetter v. Schoenwetter,* 8 Va. App. 601, 605, 383 S.E.2d 28, 30 (1989); *Furr v. Furr,* 13 Va. App. 479, 481, 413 S.E.2d 72, 73 (1992); see *also Blank v. Blank,* 10 Va. App. 1, 4, 389 S.E.2d 723, 724 (1990) (holding that spousal support must be redetermined if necessary in light of new circumstances). The material change in circumstances must have occurred after the most recent judicial review of the award, see *Hiner v. Hadeed,* 15 Va. App. 575, 577, 425 S.E.2d 811, 812 (1993), and "must bear upon the financial needs of the dependent spouse or the ability of the supporting spouse to pay." *Hollowell v. Hollowell,* 6 Va. App. 417, 419, 369 S.E.2d 451, 452 (1988). "The 'circumstances' which make 'proper' an increase, reduction or cessation of spousal support under Code § 20-109 are financial and economic ones." *Id.* at 419, 369 S.E.2d at 452-53. On appeal, the trial court's findings must be accorded great deference. See *Bandas v. Bandas,* 16 Va. App. 427, 432, 430 S.E.2d 706, 708 (1993). "In determining whether credible evidence exists, the appellate court does not retry the facts, reweigh the preponderance of the evidence, or make its own determination of the credibility of witnesses." *Wagner Enters., Inc. v. Brooks,* 12 Va. App. 890, 894, 407 S.E.2d 32, 35 (1991). "We will not disturb the trial court's decision where it is based on an *ore tenus* hearing, unless it is 'plainly wrong or without evidence in the record to support it.'" *Furr,* 13 Va. App. at 481, 413 S.E.2d at 73 (quoting *Schoenwetter,* 8 Va. App. at 605, 383 S.E.2d at 30).

III. PENSION AS INCOME

On appeal, husband posits an alleged internal inconsistency between the language of Code § 20-107.1 and that of Code § 20-107.3(G). [3] Husband argues that the language of Code § 20-107.1 requiring the trial court when setting spousal support to consider all financial resources of a party, including income from "all pension, profit sharing or retirement plans, of whatever nature" conflicts with the language of Code § 20-107.3(G), limiting division of a party's pension to fifty percent of the marital share of cash benefits actually received. Thus, husband contends that the trial court's failure to terminate his spousal support obligation resulted in "double-dipping," because wife already received her maximum marital share of his pension pursuant to the equitable distribution provisions of the parties' agreement. [4] Under the trial court's order, husband would be required to use his pension benefits to pay spousal support because he has no other income. Although

Exhibit 6.1 *(Continued)*

conceding that these code sections are "part of one legislative scheme dealing with divorce," he argues that they remain in conflict, and the dollars reflected in his disbursed marital share of pension monies cannot be used to recalculate his spousal support obligation.

A. THE RELATIONSHIP BETWEEN CODE §§ 20–107.1 AND 20–107.3

"A primary rule of statutory construction is that courts must look first to the language of the statute. If a statute is clear and unambiguous, a court will give the statute its plain meaning." *Loudoun County Dep't of Social Services v. Etzold,* 245 Va. 80, 85, 425 S.E.2d 800, 802 (1993). "As we do not believe the General Assembly intended to enact irreconcilable provisions in the Act, we construe the provisions in a way that gives full effect to all the statutory language." *Marchand v. Division of Crime Victims' Comp.,* 230 Va. 460, 463, 339 S.E.2d 175, 177 (1986).

"When the General Assembly uses different terms in the same act, it is presumed to mean different things. . . . 'In construing a statute the court should seek to discover the intention of the legislature as ascertained from the act itself when read in the light of other statutes relating to the same subject matter.'" *Campbell v. Commonwealth,* 13 Va. App. 33, 38, 409 S.E.2d 21, 24 (1991) (quoting *Robert Bunts Eng'g & Equip. Co. v. Palmer,* 169 Va. 206, 209-10, 192 S.E. 789, 790-91 (1937)) (citation omitted). "[S]tatutes addressing the same subject are to be read *in pari materia. In pari materia* is the rule of statutory construction that 'statutes which relate to the same subject matter should be read, construed and applied together so that the legislature's intention can be gathered from the whole of the enactments.'" *Alger v. Commonwealth,* 19 Va. App. 252, 256, 450 S.E.2d 765, 767 (1994) (quoting *Black's Law Dictionary* 791 (6th ed. 1990)). "Under the rule of statutory construction of statutes in pari materia, statutes are not to be considered as isolated fragments of law, but as a whole, or as parts of a great, connected homogeneous system, or a single and complete statutory arrangement." *Lillard v. Fairfax County Airport Auth.,* 208 Va. 8, 13, 155 S.E.2d 338, 342 (1967).

While Code § 20-107.3(G) precludes the non-employee spouse from receiving in the *equitable distribution* proceeding an amount *exceeding* "fifty percent of the marital share of cash benefits actually received by the party against whom such award is made," Code § 20–107.1(1) expressly requires that when setting *spousal support,* the trial court *shall* consider a party's financial resources, *including* income from "*all pension,* profit sharing or retirement plans, of whatever nature." (Emphasis added). Each of these sections concerns decidedly different aspects of the resolution of marital rights. The one-time equitable distribution of property completed by Code § 20–107.3 is based on the accrued rights of the parties in the distributed property. This

(continues)

Exhibit 6.1   *(Continued)*

is a separate consideration from that necessary to measure the current financial positions of the parties in determining spousal support under Code § 20–107.1. Different statutory considerations are mandated for each. **[5]**

Code § 20–107.1(1) evinces the General Assembly's clear intent for income from "*all* pension[s]" to be included in a trial court's calculation of spousal support. (Emphasis added). Although Code § 20–107.3(G) limits the award a spouse can receive pursuant to the equitable distribution of marital property, no language precludes that property from being considered at a later time as income for purposes of calculation of spousal support. The General Assembly could have specifically directed, as did the New Jersey legislature, that a trial court could not consider the pension share awarded in the equitable distribution proceeding in determining spousal support. **[6]** It did not do so. To the contrary, the plain language of the statute mandates consideration of "all pension[s], profit sharing or retirement plans" in the trial court's determination of spousal support.

Other states have emphasized the distinction between spousal support and equitable distribution. See, e.g., *Krafick v. Krafick,* 663 A.2d 365, 373 (Conn. 1995) (where the Supreme Court of Connecticut stated that "[a]n award of property is final; the party who receives property pursuant to § 46b–81 owns it in his or her own right and controls it. Periodic alimony, on the other hand, is conditional, subject to modification or elimination"). In *Riley v. Riley,* 571 A.2d 1261, 1264 (Md. 1990), the Court of Special Appeals of Maryland held:

Although there is an interrelationship between the two in the sense that, as to each, the court must consider the one in deciding upon the other, . . . they have quite different purposes and focuses. . . . [A]limony is intended to provide periodic support to a financially dependent spouse following the divorce. . . . [T]he principal focus is really on the future . . . . A monetary award . . . is not intended as support, and it focuses . . . on the present and past. . . . The sole purpose . . . is to assure that the disposition of that property upon the divorce will be equitable in terms of the overall contributions that each party made to the acquisition of the property and to the marriage and its breakup.

Moreover, it is generally recognized that:

[S]pousal support and equitable distribution of property are two distinct concepts. The nonpensioned spouse is not claiming rights as a co-owner in the distributed property, but is instead simply asserting that the pension should not be ignored when gauging the financial position of the two parties for purposes of awarding alimony. (*Equitable Distribution Journal* 1, July 1990).

Additionally, in another context dealing with the interplay between these two code sections, we held that "the appropriate separation between considerations of spousal support and considerations of an equitable distribution of marital wealth prevents a 'double dip' by a spouse who seeks and receives encumbered marital property under Code § 20–107.3 and also seeks and receives spousal support under Code § 20–107.1." *Gamble,* 14

Exhibit 6.1   *(Continued)*

Va. App. at 577, 421 S.E.2d at 646. In analyzing the legislative intent behind these sections, we held that, [W]hile Code § 20–107.1 requires a chancellor to consider the provisions made with regard to marital property under Code § 20–107.3, we view that requirement as a practical means by which the chancellor may fix a proper spousal support award in light of the financial result of the monetary award. Thus, for example, income producing property conveyed pursuant to Code § 20–107.3 would alter the needs of one party and the ability of the other party to pay spousal support.

Id. at 576–77, 421 S.E.2d at 646 (holding that the chancellor may not, pursuant to Code § 20-107.1, fix a spousal support award so that the receiving spouse can satisfy outstanding debts on the marital property conveyed to that spouse pursuant to Code § 20-107.3) (citing *Williams v. Williams,* 4 Va. App. 19, 24, 354 S.E.2d 64, 66 (1987), and *Reid v. Reid,* 7 Va. App. 553, 564, 375 S.E.2d 533, 539 (1989)).

"Studied in the light of its purpose and the intent of the legislature, the meaning of [these code sections] is not so ambiguous as to leave reasonable doubt of its meaning, nor are its words equally capable of more than one construction." *Tiller v. Commonwealth,* 193 Va. 418, 423–24, 69 S.E.2d 441, 444 (1952). The husband's proposed limited construction of these two statutory provisions "would be contrary to the express language used and the manifest intent of the legislature, [and] would render the statute unreasonable, . . . which cannot be presumed to have been the intent of the legislature." *Id.* Accordingly, we find that, when considered in the overall legislative scheme for the proper resolution of both property and support issues, Code §§ 20–107.1 and 20–107.3 are compatible and must be read together.

B. DUAL CONSIDERATION OF PENSION

We have recognized a distinction between equitable distribution awards made pursuant to Code § 20–107.3 and spousal support awards made pursuant to Code § 20–107.1. For example, in *Stumbo v. Stumbo,* we held as follows:

A spousal support award under Code § 20–107.1 serves a purpose distinctly different from an equitable distribution award fashioned under Code § 20–107.3. "Spousal support involves a legal duty flowing from one spouse to the other by virtue of the marital relationship. By contrast, a monetary award does not flow from any legal duty, but involves an adjustment of the equities, rights and interests of the parties in marital property." "In determining spousal support, the trial court's consideration must include earning capacity, obligations, needs, the property interests of the parties, and the provisions if any, made with regard to marital property." "A review of all the factors contained in Code § 20–107.1 is mandatory" in making a spousal support award. *Stumbo v. Stumbo,* 20 Va. App. 685, 691, 460 S.E.2d 591, 594 (1995) (citations omitted).

(continues)

Exhibit 6.1 *(Continued)*

While we have not yet determined the precise question of whether pension benefits post equitable distribution may be considered as income in a calculation or recalculation of spousal support, [7] several of our sister states have addressed this issue.

The majority of these jurisdictions do not prohibit dual consideration of the pension award for purposes of equitable distribution and spousal support. In *Riley,* a case factually similar to the case at bar, the Maryland Court of Special Appeals decided that husband's pension benefits may properly "be considered as a resource for purposes of determining his ability to pay alimony," even though wife had already been given a share of the pension as part of the monetary award. *Riley,* 571 A.2d at 1266. In that case, the parties were divorced after thirty-two years of marriage. The decree directed husband to pay alimony, gave wife a monetary award based on marital property, and awarded her an interest in husband's pension. Husband paid the monetary award to wife. He later retired and filed a motion to reduce or terminate his alimony obligation. Husband argued, as in the instant case, that the court erred in considering his pension and disability benefits as sources of income for the purpose of determining his ability to pay alimony. He contended that "his pension benefits [could not] properly be considered as a resource for purposes of alimony because [the wife] had already been given a share of the pension as part of the monetary award and [she] therefore ha[d] no claim on the balance of the pension." *Id.* at 1264. The trial court denied his motion. On appeal, the Maryland Court of Special Appeals held as follows: "[W]e see no reason why [the trial court] cannot base such an award on assets or sources of income that have not been taken from the payor and that do remain available." *Id.* The court explained:

[The pension share] he paid to her is no longer a resource of his and was not counted as such. He therefore has been given credit for the monetary award paid to [wife]. The evidence showed that [husband] receives, or is entitled to receive . . . monthly pension benefits. That is his money, and it is therefore, in fact, a resource that he has from which to pay alimony. We see nothing unlawful or unfair in the court's considering it as such. *Id.* at 1265.

Similarly, in Pennsylvania, the Court of Common Pleas divorced the parties, distributed the marital property, and awarded alimony to wife. Husband, who was receiving his retirement benefits, argued that he would be "unjustly burdened if the pension is designated as a marital asset subject to equitable distribution and also used to calculate the alimony award" to wife. *Braderman v. Braderman,* 488 A.2d 613, 620 (Pa. Super. 1985). The appellate court disagreed.

This argument ignores the provisions of the Divorce Code providing that in determining the alimony award, the court must consider numerous factors including the sources of income and the property of both parties. In determining the husband's ability to pay support, the court must consider his

Exhibit 6.1 *(Continued)*

earning power and the nature and extent of his property. Also, in determining whether [wife] lacks sufficient property to provide for her reasonable needs, the court must consider any property distributed to the wife pursuant to the equitable distribution award.

 Id. Accord *White v. White,* 192 Cal. App. 3d 1022, 1028-29 (1987) (holding that the "income from [the husband's] separate property pension must be considered along with other appropriate factors when gauging his ability to pay just and reasonable spousal support"); *Krafick,* 663 A.2d at 365 (holding that it is not double dipping to consider vested pension benefits for purposes of equitable distribution and as a source for alimony in a marital dissolution action); *Sachs v. Sachs,* 659 A.2d 678 (Vt. 1995) ("pensions may be considered as marital assets . . . they may also be considered as a source of income upon which an award of spousal maintenance may be based").

 Further, other marital awards or benefits may be considered a source of income in different contexts. In *McGuire,* we held that the trial court did not abuse its discretion in fixing a spousal support award when it considered the monthly pension payments the wife was receiving. See *McGuire,* 10 Va. App. at 251, 391 S.E.2d at 347. We stated that "Code § 20–107.1 *required* the trial judge to consider the income from the federal pension that [wife] . . . was to receive. . . . We believe that the plain language of Code § 20–107.1 requires that monthly federal pension payments be considered as akin to monthly income from an asset and not an exhaustible asset. . . ." *Id.* at 251-52, 391 S.E.2d at 347 (emphasis added). Moreover, [M]ost states have never adopted the rule that a pension cannot be a source for both property division and alimony, and several states have rejected the rule expressly. . . . It is entirely true that a pension cannot be both presently existing property and income earned in the future; it must be one or the other. . . . [A]n award of alimony can be based not only upon the payor's income but also upon his property. Where the payor owns real property, for instance, he may under some circumstances be required to sell it in order to pay alimony to his former spouse . . . . All types of property, including pensions, should be a permissible source for future alimony payments.

 See generally Brett R. Turner, *Equitable Distribution of Property* § 6.11 p. 355 (2d ed. 1995) (footnotes omitted). We find the analysis and the cases cited above equally applicable to the instant case. Thus, we hold that the income received by husband from his share of the distribution of his pension is a fungible asset that may be considered as a resource when determining the amount of his spousal support obligation. By the same token, the wife's share of the pension is a resource of hers which must be considered in determining her need for support.

 Additionally, it is noteworthy that the parties included provisions in their Agreement for the reduction and/or elimination of husband's spousal support

(continues)

Exhibit 6.1 *(Continued)*

obligation upon the happening of enumerated events. Paragraph 3 B. (2) of the Agreement provides as follows:

The obligation of the Husband to pay spousal support to the Wife shall terminate on the first to occur of: (a) the death of the Husband; (b) the death of the Wife; (c) remarriage of the Wife; or (d) the Wife living with a man to whom she is not married for a period in excess of 6 months, as though they were husband and wife.

However, the Agreement contains no provision excluding husband's share of the pension from his income for purposes of recalculating his spousal support obligation. Neither does the Agreement contain any provision excluding husband's pension share from his income in the event it becomes his only source of income.

Lastly, we address husband's reliance on the New Jersey cases of *Innes v. Innes,* 569 A.2d 770 (N.J. 1990), and *D'Oro v. D'Oro,* 454 A.2d 915 (N.J. Super. 1982), which held that a pension once divided may never be considered again. These are easily distinguished from the instant case. The New Jersey legislature amended its statute to provide that once a retirement benefit "is treated as an asset for purposes of equitable distribution, the court shall not consider income generated thereafter by that share for purposes of determining alimony." See also *Staver v. Staver,* 526 A.2d 290 (N.J. Super 1987) (holding that, pursuant to N.J.S.A. 2A:34–23, the portion of husband's pension subject to equitable distribution cannot be considered income for purposes of alimony). The comparable provisions in Virginia, Code §§ 20–107.1(1) and 20–107.3(G), contain no such prohibition. Thus, the New Jersey statutory and case law cited by the husband is inapposite.

Accordingly, we hold that the trial court did not abuse its discretion in failing to terminate husband's spousal support obligation, and that the trial court properly reduced the husband's spousal support obligation from $2,600 to $800 based upon a change in husband's financial circumstances. For the foregoing reasons, the trial court is affirmed.

Affirmed.

FOOTNOTES:

[1] The final decree of divorce "ratified, adopted and incorporated" the parties' Agreement, and provides in pertinent part as follows:

3 B. (1) The Husband agrees to pay to the Wife, for her support and maintenance, Two Thousand Six Hundred Dollars ($2,600) per month . . . .

3 B. (2) The obligation of the Husband to pay spousal support to the Wife shall terminate on the first to occur of: (a) the death of the Husband; (b) the death of the Wife; (c) remarriage of the Wife; or (d) the Wife living with a man to whom she is not married for a period in excess of 6 months, as though they were husband and wife.

Exhibit 6.1   *(Continued)*

3 C. (1) In the event that the Husband's income shall be reduced for reasons which are not wholly within the control of the Husband, the Wife agrees to consider proposals of the Husband for modification to the foregoing spousal support provisions. The Husband agrees that any such proposals made to the Wife will be made in good faith and only when any such reduction in income has a deleterious effect on his ability to make the payments required by this Agreement and his ability to support himself in a manner consistent with his standard [of] living prior to such income reduction.

3 C. (2) The Husband agrees that if the house is not sold prior to his actual date of retirement, he will not ask a court of competent jurisdiction to reduce or eliminate spousal support if the sole basis for the reduction or elimination of the support payments is his retirement.

3 C. (3) The parties agree that they shall have the right to petition a court of competent jurisdiction to modify or eliminate the foregoing support and maintenance in accordance with any statutory provision or Rule of court then in force.

* * * * * * *

11 D. (1) The Wife shall be entitled to, and receive, fifty per cent (50%) of the marital share of the Husband's military pension, when, as and if he receives said pension, based on years married (calculated up to the date of separation), during which Husband accrued a portion of his pension, over total years in military service (including Reserves) during which Husband accrued his total pension benefit.

11 D. (2) The Wife shall be entitled to, and receive, her maximum pension benefit allowable under Virginia and federal law, fifty per cent (50%) of the marital share of Husband's civil (U.S. Government) pension, when, as and if he receives said pension.

[2] The record in this case included a "statement of facts, testimony and other incidents of the case."

[3] Code § 20–107.1 provides in pertinent part:

[T]he court may make such further decree as it shall deem expedient *concerning the maintenance and support* of the spouses.

* * * * * * *

The court, in determining whether to award support and maintenance for a spouse, shall consider the circumstances and factors which contributed to the dissolution of the marriage, ... If the court determines that an award should be made, it shall, in determining the amount, consider the following:

(1) The earning capacity, obligations, needs and financial resources of the parties, including but not limited to income *from all pension, profit sharing or retirement plans, of whatever nature* . . . .

(Emphasis added). Code § 20–107.3 provides in pertinent part:

(continues)

Exhibit 6.1   *(Continued)*

(A) Upon decreeing the dissolution of a marriage, and also upon decreeing a divorce . . . the court, upon request of either party, *shall* determine the legal title as between the parties, and the ownership and value of *all property,* real or personal, tangible or intangible, of the parties and *shall* consider which of such property is separate property, which is marital property, and which is part separate and part marital . . . .

* * * * * * *

(G) [U]pon consideration of the factors set forth in subsection E: (1) The court may direct payment of a percentage of the *marital share of any pension,* profit-sharing or deferred compensation plan or retirement benefits, whether vested or nonvested, *which constitutes marital property.* . . . However, the court shall only direct that payment be made as such benefits are payable. No such payment *shall exceed fifty percent* of the marital share of the *cash benefits actually received* by the party against whom such award is made.
(Emphasis added).

[4] "Double dipping" is the term used to describe [that which] . . . occurs when property is awarded to a spouse in equitable distribution but is then also treated as a source of income for purposes of calculating alimony obligations. Double dipping disputes usually center on pensions. (*Equitable Distribution Journal,* July 1990).

[5] The spousal support award, unlike the equitable distribution award, is subject to modification as circumstances change. The equitable distribution award, once made, is final and is not dependent on future events.

[6] See N.J.S.A. 2A:34–23, which provides in significant part that "[w]hen a share of a retirement benefit is treated as an asset for purposes of equitable distribution, the court *shall not* consider income generated thereafter by that share for purposes of determining alimony." See also *Flach v. Flach,* 606 A.2d 1153, 1154 (N.J.Super. 1992) ("It is clear that the Legislature, by enacting the 'pension' amendment to N.J.S.A. 2A:34-23, eliminated 'double-dipping' for retirement benefits. . . . [O]n alimony modification application, all previously equitably distributed assets and all assets acquired with, by or through equitably distributed assets, when repaid, are not to be deemed to be income for the purpose of determining alimony.").

[7] See *Stubblebine v. Stubblebine,* 22 Va. App. 703, 709, 473 S.E.2d 72, 74-75 (1996), where we "express[ed] no opinion on the relationship between Code " 20–107.1 and 20–107.3.

When spousal support is requested, it is not unusual for the court to require the requesting party to prepare a plan that details the amount of support required, other sources of income, the uses of the support requested, and the taxes that may be paid. This analysis of cash flow may include a corresponding balance sheet detailing the changes that may occur over the period the support is to be paid. The financial adviser of the individual requesting the spousal support typically prepares documentation of this plan.

If the spousal support is awarded for rehabilitation, a rehabilitation plan may supplement the spousal support plan. This rehabilitation plan would include all of the components of a spousal support plan, but should be supplemented by an educational plan that details the cost of the rehabilitative education, the extra expenses that may be incurred to complete the education, and a justification of the cost showing the economic recovery of the rehabilitative expenditure as a result of increased earnings of the rehabilitated party.

These plans, prepared by the financial adviser, are evidence that is presented to the opposing party to justify the requested level of support. If a settlement of the issue cannot be negotiated, the documented plan and the financial adviser's testimony may be required in court to justify the level of support requested.

TAX TREATMENT OF SPOUSAL SUPPORT

The income tax deduction for spousal support is often an important factor in determining the amount that will be paid, and the amount of support that will be received. It is common for the payer to be in a higher income tax bracket than the payee. When this occurs, the couple receives a subsidy to their income from the tax benefit achieved from the payment of spousal support because of the difference in the income tax brackets. This happens when a high-income taxpayer pays support and, for example, is in a 36 percent income tax bracket. If the high-income taxpayer pays $1,000 in deductible support, it costs that individual $640. This is computed by taking the $1,000 paid, less the $360 of income tax savings achieved by the payer. The recipient receives the $1,000 in support. If the recipient were in a 15 percent income tax bracket, they would net $850 after income taxes were paid. When it costs the payer $640 and the recipient receives $850, the family has received a support supplement of $210 from the government. The financial adviser can assist in planning and maximizing this subsidy and can assist the divorcing couple in maximizing their cash flow.

The requirements for a payment to be includible in a former spouse's income and deductible from the other's income are: the payment must be made pursuant to a written divorce or separation instrument, the payer and recipient may not file a joint income tax return, the payment must be in cash or its equivalent, and the payment must be paid to the recipient of the spousal support or to a third party on behalf of the recipient. In addition, the written agreement must not state that the support, or any part of it, is not includible in the income of the recipient and not deductible by the payer. To be deductible, there can be no liability to pay support after the death of the recipient spouse. Finally, after the decree of dissolution of marriage or legal separation has been entered, the spouses or former spouses may no longer be members of the same household.

One of the important factors that financial advisers must consider is that meeting these factual conditions causes support to be tax-deductible by the payer and to be income to the recipient. This occurs whether or not the payments are treated as support for any other purpose. This concept is important for the financial adviser to comprehend. Spousal support, for purposes of income tax deductions, differs from spousal support as defined in state domestic relations spousal support statutes, and spousal support as defined under the bankruptcy law.

RECAPTURE OF SPOUSAL SUPPORT

At the time the law was enacted allowing tax-deductible spousal support to be determined by a set of factual tests, Congress was concerned that individuals involved in divorces would use tax-deductible spousal support payments to effectuate transfers of property. These transfers between the parties would be motivated by the potential tax subsidy that is described above.

Congress addressed its concern over property buyouts by creating a rule that creates a potential tax penalty that is triggered by paying accelerated spousal support. This penalty is described in Internal Revenue Code Section 71(f). The penalty does not apply if the initial spousal support payments are not reduced by more than $15,000 in any of the first three postseparation calendar years. Recapture penalties are also not a problem if the payments are not going to exceed $15,000 in any of the first three calendar years, or if the payments do not change more than $15,000 from year to year.

The amount of the recaptured income to the payer and the amount of the deduction granted to the payee is determined by a mathematical formula. The first step in determining the amount of recapture is to determine the amount of the payments made in each of the first three postseparation/divorce calendar years. The next step is to subtract from the second year payments, the amount of the third year payments and the sum of $15,000. This amount cannot be less than zero for purposes of the recapture calculation. Any positive sum from this computation is the first amount considered recaptured. The next computation first takes the second year payments, net of the amount considered recaptured above, plus the third year payments. This amount is then divided in half. The sum of the amount determined plus $15,000 is then subtracted from the payments made in year one. This sum is added to the amount determined in the first step. The sum of these two computations is the amount recaptured.

Recaptured spousal support is always reported in the third postseparation calendar year return. The amount of the recapture is added to the income of the payer and deducted from the income of the payee in the third calendar year of support. This is the reversal of the income and deduction that Congress intended to discourage front loading of spousal support payments.

Recapture rules do not apply if the payments stop because either spouse dies, or the recipient spouse remarries before the end of the third postseparation calendar year; to payments made under temporary support orders; or to payments that are a fixed portion or percentage of income that last for at least three years. Failure to pay spousal support pursuant to the marital settlement agreement can trigger a recapture.

Financial advisers must be aware of the recapture rules and the costs and opportunities they can present. It is possible to use these rules to plan transfers of income between former spouses. There may be circumstances where this third year recapture may be financially beneficial to the divorcing couple.

SPOUSAL SUPPORT TREATED AS CHILD SUPPORT

Prior to changes being enacted in the Internal Revenue Code, periodic payments between former spouses, which were not specifically designated as child support, could be treated by the as tax-deductible spousal support. This result was reached under the United States Supreme Court Case of *The Commissioner v. Lester,* 366 U.S. 299 (1961). Because high percentage marginal income tax rates exist, transfers from a high-rate individual to a low-rate individual can achieve substantial income tax savings. The law subsidizes these transfers through the savings that accrued to high-income taxpayers, while costing the lower bracket person an amount substantially less than the savings achieved.

The current Internal Revenue Code contains provisions designed to make these savings more difficult to achieve. The law is stated in Internal Revenue Code Section 71(c)(2) and in Temporary Treasury Regulation 1.71–1T. Internal Revenue Code Section 71(c) provides that where child support or payments for children are concerned, the divorce or separation instrument must require that the payments meet specific conditions before they can be treated as deductible spousal support. Amounts are considered as child support, instead of deductible spousal support, if they are to be reduced on the occurrence of an event or contingency related to a child. This can be the result of landmark events such as the child attaining a specified age, marrying, dying, leaving school, or at a time that can clearly be associated with a contingency related to a child.

An event associated with a contingency related to a child is assumed to have occurred if spousal support payments are to be reduced within six months before or after the date (a one-year period) the child reaches a landmark event. Or, if more than one child is involved, payments are to be reduced on two or more occasions which occur not more than one year before or after (a two-year period) a different child of the payer passes a landmark event. Proving that the timing of the reduced payments was determined independently of the child-related contingencies could rebut this presumption. This could be the spousal support being terminated or reduced with the prescribed time surrounding a landmark event associated with the children, if the reduction at that date is not associated with the child. If the amount by which the support will be reduced can be linked to a landmark event, the amount of the reduction will not be treated as deductible by the payer or income to the payee.

SPOUSAL SUPPORT SUBSTITUTED FOR PROPERTY AWARDS

When a court orders an individual to pay support, and that support is compensation for property, the recipient will be concerned if the stream of support payments does not survive their death. If instead of support, the individual had been awarded property, the individual would have the ability on death to pass the property to their chosen beneficiary. Because support must terminate on the recipient's death in order to qualify for tax deductibility, payments of support cannot extend past the recipient's death.

Under normal circumstances, this situation could be remedied with life insurance. It would make sense for the payer, who is receiving the income tax benefit, to provide life insurance on the life of the payee to replace the potential property lost on death. There is a problem that occurs if the payer owns the life insurance on the payee's life with the payee's estate as the beneficiary. With this arrangement, the spousal support payments deductibility will be disallowed. The temporary regulations promulgated under Internal Revenue Code Section 71, Temporary Treasury Regulation Section 1.71–1T details the circumstances in which payments occurring after the death of the payee will be treated as being disqualified. To avoid the problem, the same results are achieved by the payer increasing the amount of the spousal support payments by the insurance premium, grossed up for the tax consequences to the payee, with the payee owning and paying for their own life insurance. Because there are no required support payments after the death of the payee, the support becomes deductible.

In order to protect the payee, many decrees require life insurance on the payer's life, with the payee as the beneficiary of the benefit to insure the former spouse's support obligation. In this case, the owner may be either the payer or the payee. The beneficiary of the life insurance policy does not pay income tax on the proceeds of the policy. If the owner of the policy is the payee of the spousal support, the payee controls the named beneficiary. Court orders can cause the owner to maintain a specific beneficiary (e.g. the former spouse).

If the payer of the spousal support is obligated to pay the premiums and the obligation to pay the premiums terminates on the death of the payee, the payments will be taxable spousal support to the payee and deductible to the payer. This is pursuant to Internal Revenue Code Temporary Treasury Regulation Section 1.81–1T(b), Question and Answer 6; and Revenue Ruling 70–218, 1970–1 CB 19. If a marital settlement agreement requires the payer transfer to the payee a whole life policy, with the cash surrender value being transferred, the cash surrender value is not considered deductible support because it is not a "cash" payment but a transfer of property. This is pursuant to Internal Revenue Code Section 71(b)(1). If the policy is not transferred to the payee, but the payer retains the right to borrow against the policy, substitute beneficiaries during the payee's lifetime, or to cash in the policy, the premium payments are not deductible spousal support pursuant to *Stevens v. Commissioner.*

ALLOCATION BETWEEN CHILD SUPPORT AND SPOUSAL SUPPORT

The taxability of support ordered by the court to be paid prior to a divorce will vary between jurisdictions. In some cases, the division will be dividing funds to which each spouse was already entitled, while in other cases, the division will be treated as qualifying spousal support. In certain cases, imprecise wording of divorce or separation documents has been used by the Internal Revenue Service to circumvent the intentions of the divorcing parties

The Tax Court, in *Judith D. Lawton v. Commissioner of Internal Revenue Service,* TC Memo 1999–243, and *Renee B. Simpson v. Commissioner,* TC Memo 1999–251, has upheld the Internal Revenue Service in forcing these two Pennsylvania taxpayers to include spousal support amounts that they had characterized as child support in their gross income. These opinions were issued on July 27, 1999 and July 29, 1999, respectively.

The facts and analysis in these two cases are very similar. Mr. Lawton was ordered in several temporary (predivorce) orders to pay amounts "for support of spouse and one child." Mr. Simpson was likewise ordered in a predivorce instrument to pay monthly amounts towards the support of his spouse and two children. No specific allocation to either spousal or child support was in any of the orders. Both recipients treated these amounts as child support and did not report them as income. It can be assumed, although the opinions do not so state, that the payers deducted the payments as spousal support. This type of inconsistency attracts the attention of the Internal Revenue Service.

Section 71(a) of the Internal Revenue Code states, "Gross income includes amounts received as spousal support or separate maintenance payments." Section 71(c)(1) removes the application of that section as "to that part of any payment which the terms of the divorce or separation instrument fix (in terms of an amount of money or a part of the payment) as a sum which is payable for the support of children of the payer spouse".

In these cases, neither taxpayer tried to argue that the court orders fixed an amount as child support. Instead, both cited the fact that Pennsylvania, in compliance with federal law requiring each state to do so, had enacted child support guideline "grids." Pennsylvania law allows the court to make either an allocated or unallocated award of support. There is also a rebuttable presumption under Pennsylvania law, that if there is an obligation to pay child support, the amount determined from the guidelines is the correct amount. Thus, while the amount of child support was not fixed by the orders, the amount was "easily determinable" by reference to the "grids." In *Lawton*, the monthly amounts exceeded the guideline amounts, so the excess of the payments over the guideline amounts were, on their face, spousal support. In *Simpson*, the payment amounts were slightly less than the guideline amount, so the taxpayer position was that the payments were totally child support.

The Internal Revenue Service argued simply that "To the extent that petitioner goes outside the language of the court order of support to prove amounts for child support . . . she is improperly relying on 'evidence extrinsic to the divorce or separation instrument'." The Tax Court agreed.

The Tax Court relied upon the strict language of Section 71(c)(1) in requiring that the amounts be fixed in the instrument itself. The court cited the fact that the Pennsylvania child support "grids" assume that the order will be unallocated and "already take into account the Federal tax consequences of support payments." When an order is allocated, a special formula must be applied to adjust for tax consequences. Thus, the court reasoned, the

Pennsylvania courts must have intended that the payments would be deductible to the payers and taxable to the recipients because the payments were not allocated orders.

The Tax Court also pointed out in both opinions that, in the Tax Reform Act of 1986, Congress amended Internal Revenue Code §71(b)(1)(D) to provide that state laws terminating a payment at the death of the recipient spouse would be sufficient to characterize a payment as spousal support, even if the instrument did not provide for termination at death. Formerly, that section required that the instrument must state that liability terminates upon the death of the recipient spouse. Thus, reasoned the court, Congress made a specific effort to change that language. Had Congress intended that extrinsic state law also be utilized to characterize a payment as child support, it could have just as easily changed the provisions of §71(c)(1).

As a result, both taxpayers were required to pay tax on the entire amounts received, even though some of these amounts were unquestionably for the support of children. This result is especially puzzling in light of the provisions of Section 71(c)(2). In Section 71(c)(2) the Code states that if there will be any reduction in an unallocated support amount that relates to or "can clearly be associated" with a child-related contingency, the amount of the reduction will be considered as child support.

Ignoring for a moment that the awards in Lawton and Simpson were interim awards, if one considers that both awards would certainly have been modified or modifiable upon a change in custody or some child-related contingency, it seems that the divorce court is specifically required by the Tax Court to compute the amount of the future reduction and to, thereby, do the allocation. At that point, the divorce court would presumably be forced to look to the child support guidelines as the best source to ascertain the amount attributable to child support.

The Tax Court has now further confused the issue as to the potential tax treatment of interim support payments pursuant to a court order that does not specify the nature of the payments. While this case arises in New Jersey and the other cases in Pennsylvania, the principles discussed in these cases should be understood in order to avoid unexpected consequences. To what extent these cases are inconsistent is beyond the scope of this text and would require a detailed analysis of Pennsylvania and New Jersey laws as to the modification of interim orders. The Pennsylvania cases did not discuss the Internal Revenue Code Section 71 requirement that the payments not extend beyond the death of the recipient, or any Pennsylvania law relevant to that issue. Even given such an analysis, maybe the right answer is that the wrong argument was made in the Pennsylvania cases and that the Tax Court was not going to decide issues not put before it.

In *Marie A. Gonzalez v. Commissioner,* TC Memo 1999-332, the New Jersey court issued a *pendente lite* support order by which Dr. Gonzalez was to pay $7,500 per month to Mrs. Gonzalez for her support and for the support of the minor children of the marriage. No allocation between child and spousal support was made; nor did the order dictate how the payments would be treated for tax purposes, or when the payments might terminate.

After entry of the final decree, the Internal Revenue Service, by notice of deficiency, determined that Ms. Gonzalez should have treated her interim receipts as spousal support since no part of them was "treated as child support."

In this case, rather than attempting to support an allocation from parole sources, the taxpayer argued that the support payments would have survived her death and, therefore, were not spousal support. Internal Revenue Code Section 71(b)(1)(D) states as one of the factors in identifying any spousal support payment that there be no obligation to make the payment after the death of the recipient. In this case, the Tax Court completely adopted this argument.

Turning to New Jersey law to determine whether the payments would continue at death, the Tax Court found the case of *Farmilette v. Farmilette,* 566 A.2d 835 (N.J. Super. Ct. Ch. Div. 1989). Although a New Jersey statute specifically prohibited retroactive modifications of child support, the New Jersey court in *Farmilette* interpreted the statute as not applying to an unallocated support order (in this case a final order). The New Jersey court retroactively modified the unallocated order on the basis of a change of residence and emancipation of one of the children.

The Tax Court found the New Jersey court's willingness to modify the order as "significant." It stated:

The State court's willingness to do so leads to our affirmative response to the question posed here: Is there good reason to believe that Dr. Gonzales' family support obligation would continue after petitioner's death? We think so. Had petitioner died before the superior court entered the divorce decree, Dr. Gonzalez, as the non-custodial parent of three children, could have remained liable to pay family support, whether in full or diminished amounts.

Given the temporary, *pendente lite* nature of the order and the fact that it was retroactively modifiable at any change in circumstances and upon entry of the final order, the Tax Court concluded that the payments would terminate when the divorce became final, not when petitioner died, and "not at the happening of any other event." The court held that ". . . all payments received by petitioner under the temporary order are not spousal support."

The analysis is even more complicated in community property states. Unallocated support orders have the additional possibilities of merely being an interim division of community income or an "advance" on the distribution of community property. The Internal Revenue Service has long taken the position that "payments that otherwise qualify as spousal support are not deductible by the payer if they are the recipient spouse's part of community income." Payments are community income only if they are received before the community is ended. See Internal Revenue Service Publication 504—Divorced or Separated Individuals.

The courts in New Jersey and most states apparently have wide powers to modify interim orders and to retroactively adjust them at the time of the final order.

It now appears even more advisable where agreement can be reached to specifically state the parties' intent as to the nature of and tax treatment of all payments between married and divorced spouses. However, where no agreement can be reached and/or the court makes no specific allocation of such payments, the potential tax treatment must be analyzed with careful consideration of the characteristics of the payment, as well as the mathematical means or legal justifications for doing the allocation after the fact. Obviously, Internal Revenue Code Section 71 can be the source of diverse conclusions and a thorough analysis by a tax professional familiar with its provisions can be of significant economic benefit to divorcing parties.

The determination of the amounts, allocation, and awards of support can produce dramatically different financial results to individuals involved in divorce litigation. The financial adviser must be aware of the consequences of the various awards in order to maximize the economic return to the adviser's client.

CHAPTER 7

The Differences of Property and Income in Divorce Litigation and Issues of the Marital Residences

PROPERTY OR INCOME

A dilemma arises for the financial adviser, if property is valued on the accrual basis of accounting when courts divide property in a divorce, and income is determined for child or spousal support on the cash basis of accounting. The person earning the asset can suffer a double reduction in its value. This occurs when the item of property that has been divided in the property settlement is later received and reported as income. When this income is reported on the tax return, the reported income can be considered in the determination of child and spousal support payments. This can be further complicated when the income is subjected to payroll taxes imposed by the government.

If an individual transfers the right to receive income to another person prior to its recognition for taxes, upon its receipt, the Internal Revenue Service taxes the individual that earned the income instead of the person receiving the income. This is under the assignment of income doctrine. The Internal Revenue Service taxes the individual earning the income regardless of its assignment or receipt. This occurs even if the accrued income is divided as property for purposes of a divorce. This arises when parties to a divorce report income on the cash basis of accounting, then divide accounts receivable, work in process for a completed contract contractor, or contingent fee cases for plaintiff's attorneys. In each of these instances, the asset on the balance sheet is treated as income for taxes when received.

There is no question of the manner in which the Internal Revenue Service will construct the assignment of income in divorce litigation. When there are property transfers to third parties on behalf of a spouse or former spouse, the transfers are treated first as a transfer to the receiving spouse (under Internal Revenue Code Section 1041), followed by a transfer from the receiving spouse to the third party (not covered by Internal Revenue Code Section 1041). The second transfer is the event to which taxable income is associated [Temp. Reg. 1.1041–1T(c), Q&A–9]. This concept applies when a transfer to the third party is required by a divorce, separation agreement or decree, or the transfer to the third party is pursuant to the other spouse's written request, or the non-transferring spouse consents to the transfer in writing. The consent must state that the spouses intend the transfer to be treated as a transfer subject to Code Section 1042, and it must be attached to the transferring spouse's tax return for the year of transfer.

Transfers of Accounts Receivable

If an individual cash basis taxpayer transfers accounts receivable to a spouse, the following can occur. If $100,000 in receivables is divided in half with each party receiving $50,000; and the individual earning the receivables is taxed at a 40 percent tax rate, or $40,000; and child support is assessed for the party's two children at a 20 percent rate, or $20,000; the individual earning the receivables receives the $50,000 property division; pays a $40,000 tax; and incurs a $20,000 child support obligation. The net result to the earner is a net $10,000 outlay for the privilege of *receiving* the $100,000 receivable.

The consequence of this issue is manifested when local jurisdictions do not recognize the tax consequences associated with assets being divided and continue to use taxable income as a basis for the determination of support. Financial advisers must use diligence to recognize when this construction may affect their client.

Stock Options

Stock options are another example of property to which this principle can apply. Options are classified as qualified or nonqualified for tax purposes. Qualified options are defined in Section 422 of the Internal Revenue Code. In order to be a qualified option, the option must be issued pursuant to a plan that meets all of the requirements of Internal Revenue Code Section 422(b). One of these requirements is that the option, by its terms, cannot be transferable, except by death, and can only be exercisable by the employee during the employee's lifetime (Internal Revenue Code Section 422(b)(5)). It appears that a divorce-related transfer of a qualified option to a nonemployee spouse will disqualify that option from being qualified. The favorable tax treatment available to qualified options is lost and the option is taxed as a nonqualified option.

To be a qualified option, the underlying stock must be shares of the employer corporation, its parent, or a subsidiary. The option must be issued under a written plan, subject to specific requirements, and must be exercisable within ten years at a price no less than the fair market value of the stock at the time of the grant of the option. The option may be transferred only at death and may be exercised only by the employee or a Personal Representative. In addition, there are limitations on how much stock the employee may own, and the requirement that the employee must remain an employee of the issuing company for certain periods surrounding the date of exercise. Finally, in order for the gain on the sale of the stock to qualify for capital gains treatment, the optioned stock must be held for at least two years beyond the date of the grant of the option and one year beyond the date of exercise of the option.

There is no regular income tax due when a qualified option is issued or exercised. There is, however, a gain computed under the alternative minimum tax system at the time the option is exercised. This may result in a tax on the difference between the fair market value of the stock received, in excess of the amount paid under the alternative minimum tax system. This is despite the fact that there is no current income realized or regular income tax due. The income tax is ultimately determined and payable in the year when the optioned stock is sold for a profit. At that time, there may be a credit against the income tax on the gain from the sale of the stock based on the alternative minimum tax paid at the time the option was exercised. Income from the sale of the stock acquired from a qualified option that is held in excess of two years is taxed at capital gains rates.

Internal Revenue Code Section 422(d) does place a limitation on the number of qualified options that may be granted, based on the value of shares of employer stock that can be exercised by a taxpayer in any one year. To the extent that the aggregate fair market value for which the qualified options are exercisable for the first time in a calendar year, as determined at the time the options are granted, exceeds $100,000, the stock acquired from the options exercised is no longer treated as qualified.

Options that are not qualified are not defined in the Internal Revenue Code and may have never been qualified, or may have been qualified and then disqualified. There is no statutory definition of a nonqualified option, but it can be defined as an option that does not or no longer meets the qualifications for a qualified option. Internal Revenue Code Section 83 governs the taxation nonqualified stock options. These options are taxed when granted if the option has a *readily ascertainable fair market value* at the time the option is granted. Most nonpublicly traded stock does not have *readily ascertainable value* at the time of grant under the standard established under this Section. The taxation of a nonqualified option where the value is readily ascertainable occurs when the option is granted, and the income realized is the difference between the price paid for the optioned shares compared to the value of the stock acquired. If the ascertainable value cannot be determined at the time of grant, then income is recognized at the time the option is exercised. The income determined, at that time, is computed by deducting the amount paid for the optioned shares compared to the fair market value of the shares received. Even in a community property state, a compensatory nonqualified option received by the nonemployee spouse in a divorce proceeding may result in taxation to the recipient spouse to the extent that the fair market value of the stock exceeds the exercise price. As detailed in Chapter 5, the Internal Revenue Service has issued Revenue Ruling 2002-22 that states that vested options transferred to an ex-spouse in a divorce are taxable to the ex-spouse and not the employee. To the extent unvested options are transferred, the assignment of income principles still apply.

As a result of these factors, qualified options may be significantly more favorable to their owner than nonqualified options because the qualified options will only be taxed upon the sale of the underlying stock, and not at the time the options are exercised.

The Internal Revenue Service has issued several Private Letter Rulings on the subject. These Private Letter Rulings are statements issued by the Internal Revenue Services' National Office upon the request of a taxpayer. These rulings interpret and apply the tax laws to specific and distinct factual patterns. Although the Internal Revenue Code provides that Private Letter Rulings may not be cited as precedent, they are informative of the Internal Revenue Services' position on specific issues.

Private Letter Rulings 8451031, 8751029, and 9433010 all state that the nonemployee spouse, by virtue of the laws of a community property jurisdiction that has a beneficial interest in an unqualified option, is responsible for the tax associated with the exercise of the option when transferred. In the case of Private Letter Ruling 8451031, the nonemployee spouse is responsible even if the transfer is restricted by the issuing corporation.

Private Letter Ruling 8451031 further states that either spouse, upon the exercise of a qualified option, recognizes no income. It states that the husband or wife, as a result of the community property division of the stock options pursuant to the judgment of the court, recognizes no income.

The Internal Revenue Service does impose a requirement that payroll and income taxes be withheld from the employee, when the circumstances surrounding the option causes taxable income, and that the amount of income recognized be reported on the employee's W–2 form. The construction is consistent with the Internal Revenue Services' assignment of income doctrine. When the transfer falls under Revenue Ruling 2002–22, it requires income tax withholding on the nonemployee spouse and FICA and Medicare withholding on the employee. This creates a circumstance where the person receiving the benefit of the income may or may not be reporting the income. This is not different from a circumstance that occurs when an individual receives accrued income that has been previously divided by a divorce court.

One of the most difficult issues related to stock options that may have been transferred to a nonemployee spouse in a divorce is how the options should be valued. The tax issue further complicates this valuation. In addition, at the time of the divorce, there is no way to predict if, and when, the stock option being divided may be exercised. There is also no way to predict the price of the stock at the time of the exercise and therefore the value of the option at the time of exercise. These uncertainties may cause the parties to a divorce to choose to continue to jointly hold the right to exercise an option after a divorce. This circumstance is further administratively complicated by the fact that the parties are then tied together in the ability to exercise the options. In most cases, the employers require the employee to exercise the option. Many companies will not recognize the court's marital settlement agreement or a power of attorney that would allow the nonemployee spouse to trigger the exercise of the options.

A possible way to resolve this dilemma has been described by the Internal Revenue Service. The earliest information we have related to the Internal Revenue Services' position is in DOC 9433010. This fact pattern involves a community property state and a methodology whereby the employee can avoid taxation related to the options.

E and E's spouse married before E began to work for Y. During the marriage, Y granted E three options on Y common stock, pursuant to Y's option plans. These plans prohibited the transfer of the options except by will or the laws of descent, and distribution. The plans also required that the exercise price of an option be no less than the fair market value of Y's stock on the date when the option was granted. None of these options are qualified stock options within the meaning of Internal Revenue Code Section 422.

After E received the three options from Y, E and E's spouse were divorced in a community property state. A property settlement agreement incident to the divorce acknowledges and provides that the three options are community property. Under the property settlement agreement, each of the three original options was divided into two new options, each of which could be acquired by the original option from which it derived. E and E's spouse each received one new option from each pair of the newly created options. At the time of the review, one of the spouses had already partially exercised one of the new options.

Citing *Poe v. Seaborn*, 282 U.S. 101 (1930), the Internal Revenue Service explains that, in a community property state, property owned by one spouse during the marriage is considered owned by the community from the time of its acquisition. For this purpose, the service of the spouse who earns the property is treated as rendered by the community. This position from the Internal Revenue Service is from *Graham v. Commissioner,* 95 F.2d 174(CA 9 1938). Revenue Rulings 59–159 and 55–246 hold that the character of income earned by one spouse in a community property state retains its character when it is owned by both spouses as community property.

Thus, E and his spouse owned the original options granted to E equally from the dates when they were granted. Since the restrictions on transfer prevented the options from having a readily ascertainable fair market value at the time of their grant, the options did not result in current income to E or his spouse on their grant and will produce income only on their exercise, pursuant to Regulation Section 1.83–7(b). The Internal Revenue Service concluded that E did not have to include any amount in income due to the division of the options under the property settlement agreement incident to divorce.

Due to the division of property under the property settlement agreement, E does not realize income on the spouse's exercise of an option, but the spouse realizes income due to the exercise. As previously mentioned, the Federal Insurance Contributions Act, the Federal Unemployment Tax Act, federal income tax withholding, and state income tax withholding apply to the amount the spouse must include in income on exercise of the option, as if E received the compensation.

Y is entitled to a deduction for the amount that the spouse must include in income, as the result of a partial exercise of a new option. The amount the spouse is required to include in income is the difference between the fair market value of the Y stock on the date of exercise and the amount paid for the stock.

With this basic understanding of the tax treatment of options, consider Field Service Advice 200005006 published by the Internal Revenue Service. Field Service Advice 200005006 deals with the question of the tax effect of the transfer of compensatory options between spouses incident to a divorce. The options begin as qualified. This transfer is considered by the Internal Revenue Service as consideration at an arm's length that determines fair market value of the option. This is because the transfer is made in exchange for marital rights. Because the transfer disqualifies the options, the husband receives compensation income when the divorce transfer occurred, the wife's basis becomes an amount equal to the income taxed to the husband, and the wife is taxed on any capital gain only when the stock is sold.

The Internal Revenue Service reasoned that any qualified option becomes unqualified upon the divorce transfer since qualified options require only that the employee can cause the exercise. Thus, on transfer, the husband is considered to have sold the option in exchange for whatever the value of the offsetting marital rights may be, and any difference between the two is treated as income. Because the husband has recognized the income, the wife defers most taxation on exercise and is taxed only on any gain realized upon ultimate sale of the stock. The provision of Internal Revenue Code Section1041 (preventing recognition of gain or loss on transfers between former spouses incident to divorce) does not apply since the husband (who received the option as compensation from his employer) received compensation income, not gain or loss from a transfer. The Internal Revenue Service relies upon *U.S. vs. Davis,* 370 U.S. 65 (1962) for the proposition that the transfer of stock under a divorce decree was a disposition for tax purposes and was therefore *arm's length.*

When considering the transfer of stock options between spouses, be aware that the tax obligation of the employee spouse may be accelerated and may not be calculated based upon the value of the underlying stock. Likewise, the basis of the stock in the hands of the recipient spouse may not be related to the value of the stock.

As an alternative, financial advisers should consider the immediate exercise of such options and then transfer the optioned stock in the divorce decree or Marital Settlement Agreement. Internal Revenue Code Section 424(c)(4) says that a transfer of qualified stock option to a spouse or former spouse incident to divorce is not a disposition for those purposes and does not trigger taxation. As a result of the predivorce transfer, the employee spouse would not be taxed, and the transferee spouse presumably would owe the tax on the later sale of the qualified stock. In most cases, this strategy would create a desirable result. It allows the transfer of the asset while keeping the underlying stock qualified. Income division occurs when the income has been valued and divided.

There is a third type of property that is divided in divorce cases that many financial advisers would suggest is the subject of potential double-dipping. This asset is the divorcing couple's closely held business.

Having explored the methods available for the valuation of these businesses, it is apparent that both the income and market techniques of valuation can include the income of the business as a determining factor in the conclusion of value. When this occurs, and that same income is utilized to determine child or spousal support, the double-dipping takes place. A multiple of the income determines the value of the business, and the same income is included in the support computation.

The potential result of this set of facts is illustrated as follows. Assume an income stream of $100,000. That income is capitalized at a 40 percent rate to determine the value of the income generating business. That would generate an asset valued at $250,000, which would be divided on the dissolution of the marriage. Each party to the divorce would receive $125,000. If that same income is included in the computation of child support, it may create a child support obligation of $20,000 per year that will continue until the child reaches majority as defined under state law.

Each of the circumstances detailed is the result of an item of income being treated and divided as property. The financial adviser must be diligent to ensure clients are treated as fairly as possible under local law. Many jurisdictions have not recognized the potential inequities that can occur under these circumstances. Where it is possible, advisers may wish to become politically active, petitioning local legislators to implement laws to change the local result.

MARITAL RESIDENCE

When couples divorce, the marital residence usually becomes an object of contention. The most common issue is the valuation of the asset. There are three different options that the court can exercise when valuing a residence. A credentialed real estate appraiser can appraise the property, a local realtor can perform a market analysis, or the court can order the property sold. Courts are increasingly appointing their own experts to perform these valuations or sales.

If the residence is to be sold at a gain, the tax on the gain can become a valuation issue. In addition, the expenses to sell the property may become an issue. Many courts will not consider expenses of sale or the tax consequences of a hypothetical transaction, if it will not occur in the immediate future. The legal theory that may be applied considers these expenses to be speculative, unless they can be determined in a timely manner. Expenses and taxes that will be paid in the distant future may be considered to be too speculative to be considered in a property division.

Expenses of sale may include a realtor's commission, legal fees, expenses for closing the transaction, title insurance, inspections, prorations, and other sale-related costs. Over time, the amount and timing of these types of expense can change.

The gain on the sale of a principal residence is computed by deducting the property's income tax basis from the net sales price. This computation is independent of the amount of cash realized from the transaction. The property's tax basis may be affected by the sale of prior residences on which taxation of the gain has been deferred. The taxation of the gain is subject to a number of special rules.

Several years ago, legislation was passed that impacted the taxation of the gain on the sale of an individual's principal residence. This legislation modified the amounts of gain that are subject to tax to such an extent that most residence sales are now consummated without an income tax being paid. The old law still impacts the current sale of a residence, as its income tax basis may be determined under that law. For this reason, it is important for the financial adviser to understand the old law and how it impacts current sales.

The old law provided that the tax on the gain from the sale of a primary personal residence could be deferred if the sale price, net of selling expenses, was reinvested into a new primary principal residence within a two-year period beginning on the date of the sale of the old residence. It is important to note that this comparison was made without regard to the use or disposition of the cash proceeds from the sale. If the entire sale price were not reinvested, the gain was partially deferred. The amount taxed currently was the lesser of the gain on the sale, or the difference between the purchase price of the new residence and the net sale price of the old residence.

The gain was determined by computing the basis of the old residence sold under these rules, adding any improvements made to the property while held, less any depreciation that may have been allowed, and comparing the result to the net sale price of the property. To the extent the taxation of the gain was deferred, the amount of the deferred gain reduced the taxpayer's income tax basis in the new residence. This is important because under the new law this rule may impact a party's current income tax basis in the residence.

If the primary residence is community property or marital property and the sale occurred before the divorce, the couple may have been deemed to have each received one-half of the net sale price and, because of reinvestment, avoided taxation on their share of the gain. If the primary residence was community property or marital property owned by the couple as tenants in common, and the sale occurs after the divorce, then each party could have avoided the tax on the gain by reinvesting their respective percentage of the net sales price.

Taxpayers over the age of 55 could have elected, on a once in a lifetime basis, to exclude up to $125,000 of gain on the sale of a principal residence. The residence must have been used as the taxpayer's principal residence for at least three out of the past five years as of the date of the sale. If a taxpayer's spouse, at the time of the sale, had ever claimed this election, the taxpayer was prevented from claiming the deferral. However, a couple over the age of 55 who have never claimed the deferral could have first divorce, and then both could claim the election on their individual returns.

The importance of these rules to the financial adviser is to promote the understanding and enhance the computation of the current basis in a couple's residence.

Under the new law, each individual has the ability to exclude from taxation up to $250,000 of gain on the sale of his or her principal residence, or up to $500,000 by a married couple filing a joint return. The residence must have been used as the individuals' principal residence for an aggregate of two of the prior five years before the sale. The exclusion can only be used once per individual in each two-year period. If the individual's spouse has taken the exclusion within the past two years, the individual can still utilize his or her own exclusion. An individual who fails to meet the two of the past five years' ownership and use test, by reason of a change of place of employment, health, or other unforeseen circumstances, can exclude a fraction of the $250,000 equal to the fraction of the two years that the tests are met.

There are a number of ways to meet the two-year test. If an individual has deferred the gain under the prior law on a principal residence, that residence's use and ownership tacks onto the current residence. If an individual receives a residence in a divorce under Section 1041, the ex-spouse's holding period and use period is added to that individual's use and holding period. If a taxpayer continues to own, but not occupy, a residence after a divorce, and that individual's ex-spouse occupies the residence under a *divorce or separation instrument,* the ex-spouse's use is treated as the taxpayer's use for purposes of the holding period and use tests.

Real estate sales are reported to the Internal Revenue Service by the institution closing the transaction. If the parties are splitting the sale in one of the manners described above, it is important to request that two 1099 forms be issued. These forms would report each party's portion of the gross sale proceeds. Failure by an institution to properly report the sale can create correspondence with the Internal Revenue Service years after the transaction occurs.

Divorcing couples are also concerned about the deductibility of the interest on the mortgage, as well as the property tax payments on their principal residence. Mortgage interest is deductible under Internal Revenue Code Section 163. The deduction is limited to interest paid on a mortgage attributable to a taxpayer's primary and second residence. Normally, to take the deduction, the individual must be both liable on the indebtedness and make the payments. Interest on the payments is otherwise not deductible. Further, interest specified in a judgment or agreement for deferred payout on the equalization of distribution between ex-spouses that is properly allocable to an equity interest in a qualified residence may be deductible if properly structured. In order to comply with the Internal Revenue Service rules, the interest paid must be pursuant to a mortgage and must be allocable to the residence. The financial adviser can assist in the allocation of this interest and can suggest to legal counsel that the allocation would be most helpful if detailed in the Marital Settlement Agreement.

It is important to note that interest does not have to be paid on notes executed between divorcing parties. Notes executed following a divorce or separation are excluded from the Internal Revenue Service's interest imputation rules. As a result, the financial adviser has an economic tool in a divorce that does not exist in other financial transactions.

Mortgage Interest and Property Taxes

The Internal Revenue Code provides limitations as to the amount of a mortgage on which the home mortgage interest deduction can be taken. Qualified residence interest is interest that is paid during the tax year on acquisition or home equity indebtedness with respect to a qualified residence. A qualified residence includes the principal residence of the taxpayer and one other residence. A qualified residence also includes a residence in which the taxpayer's children reside with the taxpayer's ex-spouse. Married taxpayers who file separate tax returns are treated as one taxpayer, with each entitled to take into account one residence, unless both consent in writing to having only one taxpayer take into account both residences. Acquisition indebtedness is debt incurred in acquiring, constructing, or substantially improving a qualified residence and is secured by such residence. Any debt that is refinanced is treated as acquisition indebtedness to the extent it does not exceed the principal amount of the acquisition debt immediately before refinancing. Home equity indebtedness is all debt (other than acquisition debt) that is secured by a qualified residence to the extent it does not exceed the fair market value of the property reduced by any acquisition indebtedness. The use of the proceeds of home equity debt does not affect its deductibility. The aggregate amount of acquisition indebtedness on which interest may be deducted may not exceed $1 million. The aggregate amount of home equity debt may not exceed $100,000. These amounts are halved for married individuals filing separate tax returns. Indebtedness incurred on or before October 13, 1987 is not subject to the $1 million limitation; however, it does reduce the amount of the limitation available for new acquisition indebtedness. While the $1 million limitation may seldom create a problem, the $100,000 limitation on home equity debt can be a significant issue. This is especially true if the limitation is halved because the couple is filing separate tax returns.

Real property taxes are generally deductible only by the person upon whom they are imposed and in the year they are paid. These taxes are imposed on interests in real property and are levied for the general public welfare of the community.

While residences are one of the assets over which parties to a divorce are most concerned, the recent changes in the law related to the taxation of gain on a sale and the deductibility of mortgage interest have made it one of the issues more easy to deal with from a financial perspective.

CHAPTER 8

Tax Issues in Divorce Litigation

INCOME TAX

One of the ongoing issues that must be resolved in divorce litigation is the allocation of past and current income tax liabilities. Taxes may be due for the current and past years. Those years, not yet closed by the statute of limitations, are subject to audit by the Internal Revenue Service. The result of those audits can be taxes due for periods in which the couple was married that must be paid after they are divorced. Sometimes the parties to the litigation are aware of prior unpaid income tax balances, or of potential possible adjustments to their returns that may cause balances to become due. The Internal Revenue Code holds that any balance due on a jointly filed income tax return is the joint and several liability of both parties. Even though this is the law, the parties to the divorce can agree to allocate the known and unknown liabilities between themselves. While this allocation is not binding on the Internal Revenue Service, the agreement can allow possible recourse for an individual forced to pay income taxes payable by their ex-spouse pursuant to the marital settlement agreement.

There are also any number of income tax attributes that accompany the time and duration of the custody of the children, the resulting allocation of the dependency exemptions, and numerous tax attributes that accompany the property being divided by the parties. There are other attributes that may be divided by the parties or the court in the final marital settlement document.

It is important for the financial adviser to understand the client's concerns related to these matters and to advise the client on minimizing any future tax exposure that can unexpectedly appear in the future.

INNOCENT SPOUSE RELIEF

Another area of potential income tax-related conflict arises in domestic relations litigation when one party is not aware of unreported income or improper deductions claimed by the other. In order to remedy the liability for the unknown taxes being imposed, Congress has passed legislation to protect the innocent spouse. The latest round of legislation came when the House and Senate passed the Internal Revenue Service Restructuring & Reform Act of 1998. President Clinton signed the bill on July 22, 1998, which became the effective date for many of its provisions.

This legislation has been characterized as "six acts in one" due to its impact on innocent spouse relief. In addition to provisions affecting capital gains rules, technical corrections to the Taxpayer Relief Act of 1997, and electronic filing provisions, the Act also contains the "Taxpayer Bill of Rights 3," creating an array of new rights and protections and creating many planning opportunities and pitfalls for financial advisers.

Innocent spouse provisions have provided a method whereby a divorced or separated taxpayer can be relieved from the liability for understatements of income on joint returns when the taxpayer did not know, or had no reason to know, that the income was understated.

Under law prior to this legislation, to qualify for relief from the joint and several liability provisions, the taxpayer had the burden of proving:

- A joint return was filed for the taxable year.
- The joint return contains a substantial understatement of tax attributable to a grossly erroneous item of the other spouse ("substantial" was defined as in excess of the greater of $500, or a specified percentage of the innocent spouse's adjusted gross income for the most recent year).
- The taxpayer did not know, and had no reason to know, of the substantial understatement when he or she signed the joint return.
- It would be inequitable to hold the taxpayer liable for the deficiency in income tax attributable to such substantial understatement.

Under the new legislation, innocent spouse relief is easier to obtain. There are now three ways to obtain relief: Expanded Innocent Spouse Relief, Separate Liability Election, and Equitable Relief.

EXPANDED INNOCENT SPOUSE RELIEF

"Expanded innocent spouse relief" eliminates the requirements that the understatement be substantial and that the income items be grossly erroneous. The understatement must now be only erroneous and need not be substantial. Also, even if taxpayers knew of an understatement, but not its extent, they may be relieved from liability for the portion of the understatement they did not know about and had no reason to know about.

SEPARATE LIABILITY ELECTION

In addition to seeking relief as described in the preceding paragraph, a qualified taxpayer may elect to limit liability for any deficiency on the basis of allocations made as if the couple had filed separate returns. To qualify, the taxpayer must be either no longer married to, legally separated from, or living apart for at least 12 months from the person with whom the joint return was filed. The taxpayer has the burden of establishing the allocation. This election is not available if the Internal Revenue Service can show that assets were transferred between the couple as part of a fraudulent scheme.

EQUITABLE RELIEF

Equitable relief is available when tax is shown on a joint return, but not paid with the joint return, when the taxpayer did not know, or have reason to know, that funds intended for the payment of the tax were taken by the other spouse for the other spouse's benefit. This relief is available when there is an understatement of tax for which relief as described above is not available. This relief was not available until the Internal Revenue Service issued guidance. Equitable relief is also available to an individual filing a separate return in a community property state.

A taxpayer must elect to receive these types of relief, except for equitable relief, within two years from the commencement of Internal Revenue Service collection action. It can be expected that large numbers of taxpayers will now seek relief. The system may also become burdened by taxpayers already in the collection process since the new rules apply, not only to liabilities arising after the date of enactment, but also to liabilities that are unpaid on that date.

In Revenue Procedure 2000–15, effective on January 18, 2000, the Internal Revenue Service issued its final guidance on conditions for equitable relief. The guidance sets forth conditions for relief when one spouse did not know, and had no reason to know, that the other spouse had taken funds intended for tax payment for his or her own benefit. The guidance also establishes conditions for equitable relief for taxpayers in other situations, where it would be inequitable to hold an individual liable for all, or part of, an unpaid tax deficiency.

The guidance established that all of the following conditions must be met to obtain equitable relief:

- A joint return must have been made for the tax year for which relief is sought.
- Relief must not be available under the innocent spouse or separate liability election provisions.
- Relief must be applied for no later than two years after the Internal Revenue Service's first collection activity after July 22, 1998, with respect to the individual.
- The liability must remain unpaid at the time relief is requested (emphasis added). However, a refund can be obtained for amounts paid after July 21, 1998 and before April 16, 1999 (prior to any interim guidance) or for installment payments made after July 22, 1998, under an agreement not in default and made after the claim for relief was made.
- No assets were transferred between the individuals filing the joint return as part of a fraudulent scheme by them.
- There were no disqualified assets transferred to the individual by the non-requesting spouse (property transferred for the principal purpose of avoidance of tax or payment of tax). Relief can be obtained to the extent the liability exceeds the value of disqualified assets.
- The individual did not file a joint return with fraudulent intent.

Individuals meeting these criteria can be relieved of liability if, taking into account all of the facts and circumstances, it is inequitable to hold that individual liable for all, or part, of the tax liability. Obviously, given that statement, the list is not an exclusive one since other "facts and circumstances" could presumably exist which would justify denial of equitable relief, even where the express criteria are met. Thus, the Internal Revenue Service offers guidance by stating that equitable relief will "ordinarily" be granted to individuals meeting the above-listed requirements where relief is available:

- Only to the extent of the liability shown on the tax return.
- Only if the unpaid liability is attributable to the spouse who is not requesting relief.

The guidance gives other examples in which relief may be granted. In an effort to provide relief from the community income concept of the taxation of income one-half to each spouse, Congress provided Internal Revenue Code Section 66. This code section deals with the application of the taxability of community income when certain criteria are met.

Code Section 66(a) provides relief from the community sharing of income when five tests are met:

- The couple is married at some time during the calendar year.
- The couple live apart an entire year.
- The couple does not file a joint return.
- One or both have earned income under local law that is treated as community property.
- None of that earned income is transferred between the spouses during that year.

Some call this section abandoned spouse relief. It was enacted by Congress at a time when the Internal Revenue Service was pursuing individuals still married, but physically and financially living apart on their share of the tax on the community portion of the taxpayer's and spouse's income. The result was inequitable, as taxpayers were being required to pay the tax on income from which they never benefited.

According to IRC Section 66(b), the Internal Revenue Service can ignore local community property laws if the recipient spouse fails to notify the nonrecipient spouse of income, deductions, payments, and credits prior to the income tax filing due date.

Internal Revenue Code Section 66(c) provides similar equitable relief to married individuals who have community property income. If the innocent spouse did not know, or have any reason to know about the income, it is not treated as community property for purpose of computing income taxes.

The Internal Revenue Service also details a nonexhaustive list of factors favoring and weighing against relief. Some of the factors include favoring relief when the individual requesting relief was abused by his or her spouse, and where the payment of the tax was the legal obligation of the other spouse by divorce decree or marital settlement agreement. Factors weighing against relief include attribution, where the unpaid liability is attributable to the spouse requesting relief; significant benefit, where the spouse requesting relief has significantly benefited from the unpaid liability of items giving rise to it; and previous tax noncompliance, where the requesting spouse has not made a good faith effort to comply with federal income tax laws after the year for which relief is sought.

Procedurally, a requesting spouse must file a Form 8857, Request for Innocent Spouse Relief, "or other similar statement signed under penalties of perjury," within two years of the first collection activity against them. Those who had already filed prior to the guidance will "automatically" be considered for equitable relief.

In Information Release–2001–23, the Internal Revenue Service has taken steps to protect victims of domestic violence. An individual that has been a victim of domestic violence and fears retaliation for filing for relief should write "Potential Domestic Abuse Case" on the top of Form 8857. This is intended to alert the Internal Revenue Service to the taxpayer's situation. Concerns should be explained in a statement attached to the claim, in addition to why they should qualify for innocent spouse status. The need for this notification arises from the requirement that the Internal Revenue Service notify the taxpayer's spouse or former spouse that relief has been requested. This notification allows the spouse or former spouse to provide information to the Internal Revenue Service and to receive limited information from the Internal Revenue Service about the request.

The Internal Revenue Service's adherence to provisions requiring confidentiality means that they will not release to the taxpayer's spouse or former spouse, a new name, address, employer information, phone or fax number, or other information not related to the innocent spouse claim. All correspondence is centralized to one location so the postmark of Internal Revenue Service correspondence does not provide clues to the ex-spouse's location. The mere designation as "Potential Domestic Abuse Case" does not lead to special Internal Revenue Service consideration, but abuse is listed as one of the factors the Internal Revenue Service may consider under innocent spouse relief.

The Internal Revenue Service recently issued a Legal Memorandum (ILM 200006013) stating that a bankruptcy court, as well as the Tax Court, has jurisdiction over a debtor's request for innocent spouse relief, but that no court has jurisdiction to consider equitable relief. Thus, the Internal Revenue Service proclaimed that the granting or denial of equitable innocent spouse relief was in its sole discretion. The Tax Court has express jurisdiction over §6015(b) and (c) requests. IRC §6015 does not give the Tax Court express jurisdiction over equitable relief request under §6015(f). The Internal Revenue Service reasoned that Congress intended that the Internal Revenue Service's determination as to equitable relief be within its sole discretion and not revisable by any Court.

This position was addressed quickly by the Tax Court in *Michael B. Butler, et ux. v. Commissioner,* 114 T.C. No. 19 (2000), by declaring that it does indeed have the authority to review the Internal Revenue Service's denial of equitable relief to Ms. Green under an "abuse of discretion" standard. This authority arises, "As a part of our traditional authority in deficiency proceedings." Given the "strong presumption that the actions of an administrative agency are subject to judicial review," the court rejected any implied limitation on its jurisdiction arising from the failure of Congress to expressly grant such.

The court upheld the denial of Ms. Green's request for equitable relief. She and her husband were still married and living together, and she did not fit the statutory requirements for innocent spouse relief. The tax deficiency action arose from Mr. Green's failure to report S Corporation income in their joint return. The denial was based upon the following:

- Ms. Green's education and the experience of operating her own S corporation.
- Ms. Green's substantial involvement in family finances.
- Mr. Green was never evasive about his finances and Ms. Green had actual knowledge of the transaction, which generated the income flowing from the S Corporation.

These facts led the Internal Revenue Service to conclude, and the court to agree, that Ms. Green should have known about the unreported income, or at least should have inquired regarding its existence.

In a strong reversal of precedent under the prior innocent spouse rules, the Tax Court has ruled in *Culver*, (2001) 116TC No. 15 that the Internal Revenue Service must show actual knowledge of the underreported income, by preponderance of evidence, to deny innocent spouse relief under the separate liability election of Code Sec. 6015(c). The Culvers were married from 1978 until their divorce in 2000. In 1984, Ms. Culver was terminated from her job for embezzlement and pleaded guilty to felony theft. In 1991, she began work as a city clerk in a small town and, by 1994, had been promoted to financial director.

Ms. Culver always handled the party's finances, writing out the bills, making deposits, and balancing the bank accounts. Mr. Culver seldom even wrote checks. While Ms. Culver was a compulsive shopper, large purchases made by the couple were financed. During an audit in 1996, it was discovered that Ms. Culver had embezzled about $225,000 from the city. She was terminated from employment, convicted, and ordered to pay restitution.

Ms. Culver prepared the couple's 1994 and 1995 joint federal income tax returns, correctly reporting all income except the embezzlement income. Mr. Culver claimed relief from joint liability under the traditional Code Sec. 6015 (b) innocent spouse relief and under the separate liability election of Code Sec. 6015(c).

The Tax Court held that the Internal Revenue Service did not meet its burden under Code Sec. 6015(c)(3)(C) by demonstrating that Mr. Culver had actual knowledge of the embezzlement at the time the joint return was signed. The Court also ruled the Internal Revenue Service must meet its burden by the preponderance of the evidence.

MISCELLANEOUS TAX ISSUES

The Internal Revenue Service uses its "matching programs" as an audit tool. These programs match the consistency of tax return filings between parties with common entries reported on their returns. Using social security numbers, the Internal Revenue Service is "matching" the following items that may be reported on an individual's return:

- *Filing Status*—Persons filing as "Married Filing Separately" must list the social security number of their spouses.
- *Dependency Exemptions*—To claim a dependency exemption for an individual over age one, the taxpayer must list that individual's social security number.
- *Alimony*—To claim a deduction for alimony, the payer must list the recipient's social security number.
- *Interest and Dividends Received*—The payer must file a 1099 form with the Internal Revenue Service, listing the recipient's social security number and the amount paid.
- *Mortgage Interest*—The recipient must file a form with the Internal Revenue Service listing the amount of interest received and the social security number of the payer.
- *Proceeds of Real Estate Sales*—The institution closing the sale must provide the seller's social security number and the amount of sale proceeds received.
- *Proceeds of Security Sales*—The institution closing the sale must provide the seller's social security number and the amount of sale proceeds received.

If the reporting of these, or other entries on the return are inconsistent, the Internal Revenue Service will issue a bill to the appropriate party for the amount of income tax on the item mismatched. This bill (issued two to three years after the return is filed) will be for additional tax, penalties, and interest. The states have a cooperative agreement wherein the Internal Revenue Service notifies the appropriate states of the difference in taxable income.

If the identification numbers on accounts are not changed and/or the parties report items inconsistently, the year of a divorce can create problems.

In the year of divorce, the Internal Revenue Service generally requires the application of community income concept with respect to earned and other community income, deductions, payments, and credits earned by both parties during the part of the year prior to the entry of the divorce decree. Such income is reportable half by each spouse on his or her separate returns (or joint return with a new spouse) filed for the year of divorce. This allocation is determined by the application of appropriate state law. That law is usually the law of the state with jurisdiction in the divorce. The exceptions relate to Social Security benefits and taxes, and Individual Retirement Account deductions, which are considered by federal law to be the owner's separate property without regard to local law.

If the parties are in a common law state, the income, deductions, payments, or credits are treated as belonging to the party that earned the income or owned the property from which it was generated. This is again determined by the application of state law. There are few exceptions to these rules.

Upon divorce, there are a number of factors that will impact the couple's income tax liabilities in future years. The basis of property follows the property awarded to each spouse. Generally, the other attributes associated with that property also follow the property award. These would include investment interest, passive loss, and alternative minimum tax carryovers. Net operating losses, capital losses, and credit carryovers generally follow the individual whose property created the tax attribute. If the property was jointly owned, the attribute is split between the parties in proportion to the ownership. There are practitioners who believe these attributes can be divided in whatever manner agreed by the divorcing couple. At this time, there is little or no Internal Revenue Service guidance on these matters.

The Internal Revenue Service allows two different methods to allocate income from Subchapter S Corporations and Partnerships in the year the taxpayer's ownership of the entity terminates. Depending on the nature of the ownership, this can impact the income taxes payable in the year of the divorce. One method takes that year's tax attributes and allocates the attributes based on the ratio of the time of ownership of each individual allocated to the whole year. The second method determines the actual income, or loss, and other tax attributes through the date ownership terminates and allocates those according to the computation of the pre-divorce versus the postdivorce amounts. Particularly where one spouse controls the entity after the divorce and/or there are seasonal fluctuations in the business, large differences in tax liability can occur to the nonparticipating spouse. It is important to determine which method is in your client's best interest and to specify the method in the marital settlement agreement or decree.

TAX ATTRIBUTES IN DIVORCE

The filing status of a taxpayer is generally determined by the individual's marital status on the last day of the year:

- *Married Filing Jointly*—The individual must be married on the last day of the tax year to qualify for this status.
- *Head of Household*—Generally, the individual must be unmarried on the last day of the tax year and must pay over one-half the cost of the household that is the principal residence of the taxpayer and a dependent. Married persons living apart for the last six months of the year may qualify for this filing status if they are entitled to the dependency exemption for a child.
- *Single*—The taxpayer must be unmarried on the last day of the tax year to claim this status.
- *Married Filing Separate*—This status is used by taxpayers married on the last day of the tax year that wish to file separately from their spouse. In general, community property/common law principles still apply to the income, deductions, and credits to be claimed on the return. Exceptions to this rule are possible for community property filers. See Internal Revenue Code Section 66(a).

There are many aspects of the Internal Revenue Code that financially penalize married individuals, compared to single individuals with identical income, deductions, and credits. The largest of these penalties relate to the income tax brackets and standard deductions of married couples compared to single individuals. This is the result of the amount of the brackets and the standard deductions for married individuals not being twice the amount of a single person. There are many additional examples of the "marriage penalty" in the tax law. When advising divorcing couples, the financial adviser needs to consider the financial impact of all of the income tax consequences to individuals married through the end of the year.

Medical expenses are only deductible if the taxpayer can itemize and if they exceed 7.5 percent of the taxpayer's gross income. They are allowed when paid for children, whether or not the child can be claimed as the taxpayer's dependent. In order to qualify, the expense must be paid directly to the provider of the medical services (Internal Revenue Code Section 213).

For deductibility, the Internal Revenue Code categorizes interest paid to third parties in the following manner:

- *Mortgage interest* (Internal Revenue Code Section 163) is deductible to a taxpayer if the payments are directly made to the lender, the residence is a first or second home as defined, and the taxpayer is liable on the mortgage. A taxpayer not residing in the home can deduct mortgage interest, if the home is the residence of the taxpayer's child, under the second home provisions of the Internal Revenue Code. See Chapter 7 for additional information related to the deductibility of home mortgage interest.
- *Investment interest* is interest incurred on the proceeds of borrowings traceable to an investment and is only deductible to the extent of investment income. To the extent the interest exceeds the current investment income and cannot be currently deducted, it can be carried into future years. Upon a divorce, the carryover is allocated to the party awarded the underlying investments. If the investments are split between the couple, the carryover is prorated between the couple.

- *Business interest* is interest on borrowings used for business purposes. Business interest is fully deductible. It also includes interest paid on income-producing property such as properties producing rents and royalties. Because business interest is currently deductible, there are no carryovers to be considered in a divorce.
- *Personal interest* is interest not otherwise deductible under one of the provisions of the Internal Revenue Code. This is an issue where the financial adviser can add value for his or her services by assisting the client in minimizing the interest that falls in this classification.

The nature of interest is generally determined by tracing the proceeds of the loan to the use of those proceeds. The Tax Court in 1997 held in *Seymour v. Commissioner* that interest paid on a deferred payout for the equalization of the distribution of assets between former spouses is not classified as personal interest. To qualify interest as deductible, the interest must be properly allocated among the various assets that are distributed. The characterization of the allocated interest then follows the fair market value proportion of the underlying assets distributed. The portion of interest attributable to the distribution of investment property can be characterized as investment interest, to passive activities as passive activity interest, to business properties as business interest, or to a qualified residence as qualified residence.

In *Armacost v. Commissioner,* T.C. Memo 1998–150, the Tax Court ruled that notwithstanding, the separation agreement was silent as to which properties received by the husband were attributable to a promissory note. "Interest on indebtedness must be allocated in the same manner as its underlying debt."

Attorney's fee and expenses incurred in connection with obtaining a divorce are nondeductible personal expenses. However, tax advice is deductible, as are fees paid to obtain taxable alimony or spousal support. These fees fall under a category under Section 212(1) that are deductible as ordinary and necessary expenses for the production or collection of income which, when realized, is required to be included in taxable income. Fees paid for the defense of these items are a nondeductible personal expense. The professional fees paid to obtain assets are added to the basis of the assets obtained. The attorney to whom the fees are paid can determine, based on the attorney's records, the amounts allocable to each asset, deductible expense, and nondeductible expense category. The Internal Revenue Service regularly accepts attorney's billings as appropriate documentation on these items.

Internal Revenue Code Section 152 (e) provides the "support test" for children of divorced or legally separated parents. This section states that the parent having custody of the child during the greater portion of the year is deemed as having contributed more than half of the support for the child and, as custodial parent, gets the exemption. In general, to claim a dependency exemption (for 2002–$3,000), it is required that taxpayers provide more than one-half of the support of the dependent. With divorced parents, the exemption is assumed to be allowed to the parent with physical custody of the child for over one-half the year provided that parent along with the noncustodial parent provides over one-half of the support for the child in that year. Exceptions are then set out for cases in which the custodial parent voluntarily releases the exemption for the year, for "certain pre-1985 instruments," and in the case of "multiple support" agreements.

The custodial parent filing Form 8332 to allow the noncustodial parent to claim the exemption can modify the residency requirement of the child. Form 8332 can be executed for a single year, or for the duration of time until the child reaches a majority age. Financial advisers seldom see this form executed for more than a single year at a time. Attorneys view the execution of the form on an annual basis as insurance that child support and other actions required by the marital settlement document are timely and up-to-date.

Internal Revenue Code Section 152 (c) also deals with "multiple support" agreements, declaring that when no one person contributes more than half of the support of a child, and when all persons collectively contributing more than half of the support are otherwise entitled to the exemption, any person contributing more than 10 percent of the support may claim the exemption. Any other persons contributing over 10 percent, who would have otherwise been entitled to the exemption, must also file a written statement with the Internal Revenue Service stating that they will not claim the child as a dependent in any tax year commencing within the relevant calendar year.

Practices of state courts with respect to these allocations have been long-standing and virtually uniform. The states view themselves as having the power under state court order to order the allocation of dependency exemptions. The Internal Revenue Service and the Tax Court have taken a literal reading of the law as their approach to claiming the exemptions. The Internal Revenue Service's position is that if the custodial parent refuses to sign a Form 8332 despite a state court order to do so, the custodial parent is allowed the exemption. In spite of these rules and tests promulgated by Congress, in recent years courts in a vast majority of the states have continued to rule that these federal laws do not preempt allocation of the dependency exemption by the state courts, exercising their traditional roles in promoting the well-being of the child by allowing for greater tax savings through allocation of the exemptions. Such allocations, according to state courts, may be made despite the Internal Revenue Code provisions discussed above. This conflict appears to be continuing and unresolved. State courts have gone as far as executing a Form 8332 in lieu of the custodial parent, when the custodial parent has refused to execute the documents. The state's position was clearly stated when, in October, 1998, the New Mexico Court of Appeals "joined the bandwagon" by formal adoption of this position. In *Macias vs. Macias,* 126 N.M. 303 (Ct. App. 1998), the Court followed the reasoning of many decisions in other states when it declared, "We are not disposed to presume that Congress intended to tie the hands of our state judiciary, especially when the law on its face does not preclude the state from acting." The Court went on to say, "As other courts have done, we read the federal law not as a deliberate choice in favor of the custodial parent, but more as a method of facilitating tax preparation by invoking a presumption in favor of the custodial parent that is easy to administer and yet which provides flexibility for parents and state courts to decide differently."

High income taxpayers begin to lose the benefit of exemptions under Internal Revenue Code Section 1(g) if 2002 income (amounts are adjusted each year for inflation) exceeds:

- Married Filing Jointly $206,000
- Unmarried Head of Household $171,650
- Single $137,300
- Married Filing Separately $103,000

The amount is reduced by 2 percent of each $2,500 (or fraction thereof) over the threshold amounts, except for married individuals filing separate returns. The amount is reduced by 2 percent of each $1,250 (or fraction thereof) over $103,000. The amount of the dependency exemption is adjusted each year for inflation.

The Taxpayer Relief Act of 1997 created a Child Tax Credit based solely on the number of a taxpayer's dependent children. The credit is generally nonrefundable, except when there are three or more qualifying dependents, and the credit is limited by the alternative minimum tax. This situation usually occurs when the taxpayer qualifies for the earned income credit and does not have sufficient taxable income to utilize the child credit. A qualifying dependent is a child, descendant, stepchild, or foster child who is a U.S. citizen, for whom the taxpayer may claim the dependency exemption, and who is less than 17 years old as of the close of the tax year. The child credit phases out for taxpayers with gross incomes in excess of $110,000, if the taxpayer is married, and $75,000 if the taxpayer is single. The credit phases out at the rate of $50 per $1,000 of income in excess of the threshold amount. The ability to take the child credit is tied to the ability of the taxpayer to claim the exemption for the child. The credit is computed at $600 times the number of qualifying children. If there are two or more children, a portion of the credit may be treated as a supplemental child credit amount and allowed as refundable, in addition to the regular earned income credit. This supplemental credit equals $600 times the number of qualifying children, but no more than the amount by which the income tax liability (net of applicable credits other than the earned income credit) exceeds the taxpayer's tentative minimum tax liability (determined without regard to the alternative minimum foreign tax credit), minus the sum of the taxpayer's income tax liability (net of applicable credits other than the earned income credit) and the employee share of FICA (and one-half of the taxpayer's self-employment tax liability, if applicable), reduced by any earned income credit amount. In no case will the total amount of the allowable child credit exceed the amount that would result from its calculation as a nonrefundable personal credit.

If there are three or more children, the maximum child credit for the taxpayer's tentative minimum tax liability each year cannot exceed the greater of the following:

- The taxpayer's regular tax liability (net of applicable credits other than the earned income credit) minus the taxpayer's tentative minimum tax liability (determined without regard to the alternative minimum foreign tax credit).
- The sum of the taxpayer's regular income tax liability (net of applicable credits other than the earned income credit) and the employee share of FICA (and one-half of the taxpayer's self-employment tax liability) reduced by the earned income credit.

To the extent that the amount determined under the first method is greater than the amount determined under the second method, the difference is treated as supplemental child credit. This calculation serves an additional purpose. For the taxpayer with three or more qualifying children, if the amount of the allowable supplemental child credit exceeds the taxpayer's regular tax liability before the computation, the excess is a refundable tax credit.

The Child Care Credit under Internal Revenue Code Section 21 varies between 20 percent and 30 percent of the amount of qualified childcare expenses paid, depending on the taxpayer's level of income. The child being cared for must be under 13 years of age and, in general, be claimed as a dependent on the taxpayer's return. The dependency requirement can be waived if the following tests are met:

- Taxpayer had custody of the child for a longer time in 1998 than the other parent.
- One or both of the parents provided over half of the child's support.
- One or both of the parents had custody of the child for more than half of the tax year.
- The child was under age 13, or was disabled and could not care for himself/herself.
- The other parent claims the child as a dependent because the custodial parent signed Form 8332, or a similar statement, agreeing not to claim the child's exemption for the tax year.

It is important to note that under these rules only the parent with custody of the child for over one-half of the tax year can claim the childcare credit. It is important for the financial adviser to structure the payment and allocation of the childcare expenses in a manner to take full advantage of any credits available. If the parent that does not have primary physical responsibility for the child is to be responsible for the payment of childcare expenses, those payments can be structured as reimbursements to the parent with primary physical custody. This will insure that the maximum credit allowable can be received.

A taxpayer can establish Educational Individual Retirement Accounts for the benefit of a child or children. The amount deductible for the tax year 2002 is limited to a maximum of $2,000 per child. There is no taxation on the withdrawal if the proceeds are used for qualified education expenses, including room and board. These expenses include qualified elementary, secondary, and higher education school expenses incurred at public, private, or religious schools. Deductions phase out for married couples with adjusted gross income between $190,000 and $220,000, and for single individuals with adjusted gross income between $95,000 and $110,000. The beneficiary can be changed from one child to another without taxation. Contributions cannot be made when contributions are made to a Qualified State Tuition Program for the same beneficiary in the same year.

Withdrawals can be made from a taxpayer's Individual Retirement Accounts without the 10 percent penalty applying to distributions utilized to pay higher education costs or to pay up to $10,000 of first-time home buyer expense for the taxpayer, their spouses, and their children or grandchildren.

Up to $2,500 in interest is deductible on a dependent's student loans by an eligible taxpayer. In addition to the requirement that the student qualify as the taxpayer's dependent, the deduction is allowable for loans paying the cost of attendance, room and board for higher education, including graduate school. The full deduction is limited to married taxpayers with adjusted gross incomes less than $100,000, and single taxpayers with adjusted gross incomes less than $50,000. The deduction phases out to zero for married taxpayers with incomes in excess of $130,000, and single taxpayers with incomes in excess of $65,000.

A Hope education credit against a taxpayer's income tax has been established. In order to claim the credit, the student must qualify as a dependent of the taxpayer. The credit is limited to a lifetime amount not to exceed $1,500. The credit is computed based on 100 percent of the first $1,000 and 50 percent of the next $1,000 of qualified tuition and related expenses, not including room and board or books, for the first two years of the student's postsecondary education in a degree or certificate program. The amount of the credit will be indexed for inflation in the future, but cannot be taken in addition to the Lifetime Learning credit within a single year. The credit is calculated per student, and a family with more than one student can claim a different credit for each. The credit cannot be claimed in a tax year in which there has been a tax-free withdrawal from an Educational Individual Retirement Account. However, a taxpayer can waive the tax-free treatment in order to claim the credit. The credit can be claimed in a year in which the taxpayer has made a withdrawal from a Qualified State Tuition Program. The ability to take the credit phases out for married taxpayers with adjusted gross incomes of $82,000 to $102,000, and for single taxpayers with adjusted gross incomes of $41,000 to $51,000.

An additional credit enacted is called the Lifetime Learning Credit. It can be claimed by taxpayers able to claim the student as a dependent. The $1,000 credit is computed as 20 percent of the first $5,000 of qualified expenses paid by a taxpayer on the student's behalf. "Qualified tuition and related expenses" includes tuition and books for undergraduate and graduate school, but does not include room and board. In the future, the amount of the credit will be indexed for inflation. The credit cannot be claimed in the same year for the same student as the Hope credit. However, a family with two or more students can claim different credits for each. The Lifetime Learning credit is calculated per family.

The credit cannot be claimed in the same year a tax-free withdrawal from an Educational IRA is made. However, the tax-free treatment can be waived in order to benefit from the credit. The credit can be claimed in the same year as a withdrawal is made from a Qualified State Tuition Program if the funds qualifying for the credit come from a source other than the withdrawal. The ability of married taxpayers to claim the credit phases out between $82,000 and $102,000, and between $41,000 and $51,000 for single taxpayers.

There are any number of other income, deduction, and credits associated with individuals' income tax returns. The items listed above are those that can be impacted by the allocation of exemptions, or other factors related to a divorce or separation. The financial adviser needs to be aware of these items when advising a client of the financial impact of a divorce.

CHAPTER 9

The Financial Adviser's Testimony

TESTIMONY

When all is said and done, the financial adviser must communicate his analysis to the trier of fact. In almost all cases, this will be a judge in domestic relations litigation. When acting as a witness, the financial adviser needs to consider every component and aspect of the testimony given to properly teach the results of the work performed. Do not treat the opposing side and attorney as enemies, but as students that may not understand the positions you are taking.

During opening statements or at other times during the trial, the attorneys may invoke "the rule". This refers to the exclusion of fact witnesses from the courtroom prior to their testimony. "The rule" does not apply to the parties to the case and generally does not apply to experts. It is not unusual for the expert to be requested to listen to all, or parts of, the factual testimony. This occurs when the attorney wants you to rely on specific information given in the testimony, in forming the opinions on which you will be testifying.

Your personal appearance when testifying is very important. If you are to be considered the expert, you must look the role. Power suits are the rule of the day. Some authorities say that individuals in gray or blue suits appear to be more credible than those wearing other colors. Polished shoes, neatly trimmed hair, and neat files are a requirement. Your demeanor and attitude are also very important. Be respectful to everyone in the courtroom, including the opposing party and their attorney. Exhibit confidence and high energy levels.

221

Remember to give the answers first, and then give details. Always answer loudly. An individual that is difficult to hear is not communicating. Communication and teaching are the keys to testimony. Avoid jokes. Jokes can backfire and offend someone in the courtroom. It is an easy problem to avoid. Sit up on the front of your chair to appear ready and willing to answer questions rendered by either side. Maintain eye contact with the judge throughout your testimony. If you do not know the answer to a question, readily admit you do not know.

There are times when you and the opposing expert may come from different geographical locations. When this occurs, realize there are advantages each of you possess. It is not unusual for a greater level of expertise to be imputed to the out-of-town expert. Remember this when going through your qualifications. It is also not unusual for the in-town expert to be imputed more knowledge of local issues that may impact the testimony. When working as the out-of-town expert, insure the opposing expert is thoroughly deposed on any uniquely local issues that impact his opinion. By doing so, you can be prepared to address those issues.

There are a number of problems with testimony that can be avoided. Leading the list is the expert's demeanor in the courtroom. Arrogance and cockiness should be avoided. When individuals are offended by the expert's behavior, they are not learning. Communication is a two-way process. Advocacy and defensiveness also have a negative impact on the judge. It becomes obvious to the judge when the expert takes extreme positions. When this occurs, all of the expert's conclusions are questioned, regardless of how conservative the conclusions may be. The expert should also avoid appearing listless, evasive, or long-winded.

It is important to keep explanations in testimony simple. Concepts must be reduced to their simplest form. Financial advisers must assume that if any concept takes over 30 seconds to explain, the principle will be lost on the judge. This is not a reflection of the judge's intelligence, but is a reflection of how we now receive information from the media. Television and radio news are now reduced to "sound bites." Society, as a whole, anticipates similar brevity from other sources of information. When they do not get that brevity, they "tune out."

As we work in our professional lives, we begin to develop a jargon of technical terms and acronyms. This jargon becomes a shorthand that is used to communicate with other professionals. When the financial adviser enters the courtroom, it is important that the professional jargon is left at the door. The financial adviser must not only simplify the concepts to be presented but must also present the concepts in simple and understandable language. The presentation should be free of jargon. Remember that jargon is a foreign language to the judge.

PREPARATION FOR TRIAL

As the time for trial approaches, it is important for the financial adviser to begin to prepare for participation. The first part of the preparation will probably be the preparation of exhibits that will be introduced at trial in support of the adviser's opinions. These exhibits should link the facts in the case to the analysis performed, the assumptions made, and the conclusions reached. This does not have to be done on a single sheet of paper. Exhibits can summarize factual information, or detail computations made to reach conclusions. They should provide the judge with a visual replica of the expert's verbal testimony. Because most of the financial adviser's testimony will relate to financial matters, exhibits become a compilation of numbers. Exhibits should be kept simple and should limit the quantity of numbers presented to a single sheet of paper. Again, simple is better. Some would say that financial advisers are numbers people. It is important to remember judges are lawyers, and lawyers are trained to be word people. By presenting the same data in verbal form as well as in a summarized written form, the financial adviser gives the judge two different ways to learn the same information.

When it is possible, it is useful to utilize graphics and charts as exhibits and to summarize information and testimony. The process of taking numbers and converting them into graphics makes the information presented much easier to understand. This use of pictures as part of the exhibits gives the judge another way to learn the information being presented in the courtroom.

Another method used in the courtroom is to produce the exhibits on flipcharts as the testimony progresses. This provides the judge with a direct connection to the explanation of a concept and its entry on the chart. There are times the attorney will ask the financial adviser to complete the chart, and other times where the attorney will complete the chart as testimony progresses. This technique gives the attorney the ability to have his most important concept be in the forefront of the courtroom the entire time the flipchart is left in place. Many times, the charts are not moved for the entire trial.

Another method of presenting concepts graphically, as the testimony progresses, is through the use of computerized electronic presentation programs. This concept involves giving the judge a hardcopy of the slides to be presented and projecting the slides in the courtroom as the testimony progresses. When this method of presentation is used, the computer, electronic projector, and screen that are required can complicate the trial. When computer problems arise, the attorney and financial adviser must be prepared to proceed with an alternative presentation. Judges are very impatient when waiting for a problem to be solved, and many times will direct the trial proceed without the benefit of the equipment. There also may be difficulty in getting the hard copy of the slides admitted as an exhibit. This depends on the jurisdiction and the local rules in effect.

The next step in the preparation process is to review all of the material that is relevant to the opinions that will be presented at trial. This includes responses to interrogatories, documents produced, and depositions given. This information should be very familiar to the financial adviser, as it may be the subject of cross-examination questions at trial. It is important to determine if any of the information contained in the discovery results is contrary to any testimony to be given by the financial adviser. If this is the case, the financial adviser must be prepared to offer an explanation of why the information was ignored or not used. Particular attention should be given to reading both your own and the opposing expert's depositions. Your deposition will be the subject of cross-examination questions. The opposing expert's deposition will provide you with a roadmap to assisting your counsel in preparing for the opposing experts cross-examination.

After this work has been completed, it is time to meet with the attorney who will be presenting the financial adviser's testimony.

This meeting will insure that any questions that the financial adviser may have are answered. The attorney will review how the expert will be qualified and the presentation of the testimony. Some attorneys will have prepared a detailed list of questions for the expert. Others will not, but will rely on an understanding of the concepts to be presented. In some instances, the attorney may ask the expert to prepare questions for the attorney to ask the financial adviser, as well as the opposing expert. The financial adviser may also be asked to rehearse the testimony with the attorney.

DIRECT EXAMINATION

Direct examination is where the financial adviser has the opportunity to testify regarding opinions formed and conclusions reached. It is the portion of the trial in which the financial adviser's influence may impact the judge's findings and conclusions. It is important for the expert to allow the attorney to control the direct examination. In many respects, the financial advisers are like puppets as they can only answer questions asked and cannot offer explanations without an appropriate cue from the attorney. It is for this reason that preparation is so important.

The first question posed to financial advisers will be to state their name. After that formality, which is for the court reporter to insert in the record of the proceedings, the qualification of the financial adviser to testify as an expert begins. It is not unusual, at this time, to have the financial adviser's resume introduced as an exhibit. It is the information contained in one's resume that is presented to the court to detail an individual's qualification as an expert. An example of an expert's resume is attached as Exhibit 9.1. Questions will include the individual's education and work background, memberships in professional organizations, articles and books written or edited, courses taken, courses taught, and experience in the matters before the court. It is not unusual for the expert to be asked if, and how many times, they have been qualified as an expert in these matters in other courts. Upon completion of this part of the exam, the individual will be offered to the court as an expert. At this time, the opposing attorney has the opportunity to cross-examine the financial adviser on qualifications in a process called "voir dire". Upon completion of this process, the opposing attorney has the opportunity to object to the designation of the financial adviser as an expert. With or without the objection, the judge either confirms or denies the financial adviser's status as an expert.

Exhibit 9.1   Example of an Expert's Resume

Thomas F. Burrage, CPA/ABV, CVA, DABFA
Principal
Meyners + Company, LLC
500 Marquette NW, Suite 400
Albuquerque, NM 87102

BORN:	January 24, 1947–Ft. Collins, Colorado
EDUCATION:	Sandia High School—May 1965 Albuquerque, New Mexico
	University of New Mexico Bachelor of Business Administration—May 1973
PROFESSIONAL DESIGNATIONS:	Certified Public Accountant — August 1973 New Mexico
	Certified Valuation Analyst—November 1998
	Accredited in Business Valuation—January 1999
PROFESSIONAL EMPLOYMENT:	Meyners + Company, LLC Principal—Litigation and Valuation Services Albuquerque, New Mexico
PROFESSIONAL ASSOCIATIONS:	American Institute of Certified Public Accountants • Management Advisory Division • Family Law Tax Force • Tax Division
	Editorial Advisor, *Journal of Accountancy*

	National Association of Certified Valuation Analysts (NACVA)
	    2001/2002 NACVA's Speakers Bureau
	    2001/2002 NACVA's Mentor Support Group

	New Mexico Society of Certified Public Accountants
	American College of Forensic Examiners

Exhibit 9.1 *(Continued)*

PROFESSIONAL
  APPOINTMENTS: New Mexico District Court Rule 11–706 Expert
                       Witness

                       New Mexico District Court Special Master

                       New Mexico Second Judicial District Settlement
                       Week Facilitator

                       Member 2nd Judicial District Alimony Guideline
                       Committee

PARTICIPATION IN
  PUBLISHED CASES: *Roberts v. Wright,* 117 N.M. 294, 871 P.2d 390 (Ct.
                       App.1994)
                       Ruggles v. Ruggles, 116 N.M. 52, 860 P.2d 182
                       (1993)
                       Zemke v. Zemke, 116 N.M. 114, 860 P.2d 756 (Ct.
                       App. 1993), cert. denied, 116 N.M. 71, 860 P.2d
                       201 (1993)
                       Mattox v. Mattox, 105 N.M. 479, 734 P.2d 259 (Ct.
                       App. 1987)
                       Allied Products Corp. v. Arrow Freightways, 104
                       N.M. 544, 724 P.2d 752 (1986)
                       Mitchell v. Mitchell, 104 N.M. 205, 719 P.2d 432
                       (Ct. App. 1986)
                       Schwartzman v. Schwartzman Packing Co., 99
                       N.M. 436, 659 P.2d 888 (1983)
                       Boutz v. Donaldson, 38 N.M., St. B. Bull. 45 (Ct.
                       App. 1999)
                       *Mary E. Walta v. Gallegos Law Firm & J.E. "Gene"
                       Gallegos,* 41 N.M. St. B. Bull. 24 (Ct. App. 2002)
                       The Bank of Santa Fe v. Marcy Plaza Associates,
                       41 N.M., St. B. Bull. 25 (Ct. App. 2002)

PUBLICATIONS: *C.P.A.'s Role in Divorce,* New Mexico Society of
                       Certified Public Accountants, Continuing
                       Professional Education Course.
                       *Understanding Financial, Accounting and Tax
                       Issues in Divorce Cases,* New Mexico Society of
                       Certified Public Accountants, Continuing
                       Professional Education Course.
                       Lining Up an Expert, *The Family Advocate,* Vol.
                       17, No. 4, Spring 1995

                                                        (continues)

Exhibit 9.1 (*Continued*)

PROFESSIONAL
SPEAKING:

Contributing Editor: *Guide to Divorce Taxation,* Biebl Ranweiler Portfolio Series, Practitioner's Publishing Company, 2000 and 2001
Contributing Editor: *Guide to Tax Planning for High Income Individuals,* Practitioner's Publishing Company, 2001.

- **Date:** September 1980
  Group: New Mexico Society of Certified Public Accountants
  Topic: Management of an Accounting Practice
  Location: Albuquerque, New Mexico

- **Date:** November 1981
  Group: New Mexico Society of Certified Public Accountants
  Topic: Management of an Accounting Practice—Roundtable
  Location: Albuquerque, New Mexico

- **Date:** September 1984
  Group: New Mexico State Bar—Family Law Section
  Topic: Divorce and Separation: Alimony and Separate Maintenance Payments
  Location: Albuquerque, New Mexico

- **Date:** March 1986
  Group: New Mexico State Bar—2nd Annual Family Law Institute
  Topic: Preparing and Using an Expert in Valuing a Professional Practice
  Location: Albuquerque, New Mexico

- **Date:** October 1986
  Group: New Mexico Trial Lawyers
  Topic: Overview of Goodwill
  Location: Albuquerque, New Mexico

- **Date:** June 1987
  Group: New Mexico State Bar—3rd Annual Family Law Institute
  Topic: Problems of Withholding/Taking Pension Benefits, What to Say about Taxes in a Settlement or Decree
  Location: Albuquerque, New Mexico

Exhibit 9.1   (*Continued*)

- **Date:**   May 1987
  Group: Professional Education Systems
  Topic: Valuation Strategies in Divorce
  Location: Albuquerque, New Mexico

- **Date:**   June 1988
  Group: New Mexico State Bar—4th Annual Family Law Institute
  Topic: Use of Tax Returns and Financial Statements for Discovery
  Location: Albuquerque, New Mexico

- **Date:**   December 1988
  Group: New Mexico State Bar—Corporation, Banking and Business Section
  Topic: Financial Analysis for Attorneys, Business Valuation
  Location: Albuquerque, New Mexico

- **Date:**   June 1989
  Group: New Mexico State Bar—5th Annual Family Law Institute
  Topic: Effective Use of Experts in Domestic Relations Cases
  Location: Albuquerque, New Mexico

- **Date:**   February 1991
  Group: New Mexico Trial Lawyers
  Topic: Family Law—The Hard Stuff: Tax Consequences in Divorce
  Location: Albuquerque, New Mexico

- **Date:**   July 1991
  Group: National Business Institute
  Topic: Drafting and Litigating Prenuptial Agreements in New Mexico and Tax Considerations: The IRS Wants to Benefit from the Agreement
  Location: Albuquerque, New Mexico

- **Date:**   October 1991
  Group: New Mexico Society of Certified Public Accountants
  Topic: The CPA's Role in Divorce
  Location: Albuquerque, New Mexico

(*continues*)

Exhibit 9.1   *(Continued)*

- **Date:**   October 1991
  Group: New Mexico Society of Certified
                Public Accountants
  Topic: Financial Expert: CPA
  Location: Albuquerque, New Mexico

- **Date:**   April 1992
  Group: University of New Mexico School of
                Law
  Topic: The Tax Consequences of Divorce
  Location: Albuquerque, New Mexico

- **Date:**   June 1992
  Group: New Mexico Society of Certified
                Public Accountants and New Mexico
                State Bar
  Topic: Accounting Issues in Divorce
  Location: Albuquerque, New Mexico

- **Date:**   December 1992
  Group: National Business Institute
  Topic: Tax Aspects of Divorce in New
                Mexico: Miscellaneous Domestic Tax
                Provisions and Tax Issues of the
                Marital Residence, Valuation of a
                Closely Held Business Asset, and
                Using Tax Returns in Domestic
                Relations Cases
  Location: Albuquerque, New Mexico

- **Date:**   January 1993
  Group: New Mexico Trial Lawyers
  Topic: Trying a Difficult Domestic Relations
                Case: Valuing Community
                Labor/Tracing Funds
  Location: Albuquerque, New Mexico

- **Date:**   October 1993
  Group: National Business Institute
  Topic: Key Issues in Family Law in New
                Mexico, Miscellaneous Domestic Tax
                Provisions and Tax Issues of the
                Marital Residence
  Location: Albuquerque, New Mexico

Exhibit 9.1 (*Continued*)

- **Date:**   January 1994
  Group: National Business Institute
  Topic: Tax Aspects of Divorce in New
  Mexico: Miscellaneous Domestic Tax
  Provisions, Valuation of a Closely
  Held Business Asset, and Tax Issues
  of the Marital Residence
  Location: Albuquerque, New Mexico

- **Date:**   April 1994
  Group: University of New Mexico School of
  Law
  Topic: Tax Consequences of Divorce
  Location: Albuquerque, New Mexico

- **Date:**   September 1994
  Group: New Mexico Society of Certified
  Public Accountants, New Mexico
  State Bar—Taxation Section, and
  R.O. Anderson School of
  Management
  Topic: 34th Annual New Mexico Tax
  Institute: The Tax Aspects of Marital
  Settlement Agreements
  Location: Albuquerque, New Mexico

- **Date:**   February 1995
  Group: New Mexico Trial Lawyers
  Topic: The Divorce Aftermath: Problems and
  Solutions and Taxes and Audits in the
  Divorce Aftermath
  Location: Albuquerque, New Mexico

- **Date:**   February 1995
  Group: University of New Mexico School of
  Law
  Topic: Retirement Plans and Qualified
  Domestic Relations Orders
  Location: Albuquerque, New Mexico

(*continues*)

Exhibit 9.1   *(Continued)*

- **Date:**   July 1995
  Group: National Business Institute
  Topic: Tax Aspects of Divorce in New Mexico:
  Tax Treatment of More Complicated
  Property Transfers, Valuation of a
  Closely Held Business Asset
  Location: Albuquerque, New Mexico

- **Date:**   January 1996
  Group: New Mexico Trial Lawyers
  Topic: The Alimony Case: Financial,
  Psychological and Legal Strategies
  Location: Albuquerque, New Mexico

- **Date:**   January 1996
  Group: University of New Mexico School of
  Law
  Topic: Valuation Concepts
  Location: Albuquerque, New Mexico

- **Date:**   May 1996
  Group: Lorman Business Center, Inc.
  Topic: Minimizing the Tax Consequences of
  Divorce
  Location: Albuquerque, New Mexico

- **Date:**   December 1996
  Group: New Mexico Society of Certified
  Public Accountants
  Topic: New Mexico Tax Conference: Divorce
  Tax Issues
  Location: Albuquerque, New Mexico

- **Date:**   December 1996
  Group: National Business Institute
  Topic: Tax Aspects of Divorce in New
  Mexico
  Location: Albuquerque, New Mexico

- **Date:**   January 1997
  Group: New Mexico Trial Lawyers
  Topic: Premarital and Cohabitation
  Agreements in New Mexico
  Location: Albuquerque, New Mexico

Exhibit 9.1   (*Continued*)

- **Date:**   June 1997
  Group: Association of Family and
  Conciliation Courts
  Topic: 2nd World Congress, Cutting Edge
  Family Law Issues: Division of
  Property and Financial Support
  Location: San Francisco, California

- **Date:**   January 1998
  Group: National Business Institute
  Topic: Tax Aspects of Divorce in New
  Mexico
  Location: Albuquerque, New Mexico

- **Date:**   January 1998
  Group: New Mexico Trial Lawyers
  Topic: Domestic Relations: Recent Complex
  Issues in Family Law
  Location: Albuquerque, New Mexico

- **Date:**   June 1998
  Group: National Business Institute
  Topic: Tax and the General Practitioner in
  New Mexico
  Location: Albuquerque, New Mexico

- **Date:**   September 1998
  Group: New Mexico State Bar
  Topic: Understanding Financial Statements
  Location: Albuquerque, New Mexico

- **Date:**   November 1998
  Group: International Association of Financial
  Planners
  Topic: Financial Impacts of Divorce
  Location: Albuquerque, New Mexico

- **Date:**   November 1998
  Group: University of New Mexico School of Law
  Topic: Basic Divorce Taxation
  Location: Albuquerque, New Mexico

- **Date:**   January 1999
  Group: State Bar of New Mexico
  Topic: Financial Forensics in Litigation
  Location: Albuquerque, New Mexico

(*continues*)

Exhibit 9.1 *(Continued)*

- **Date:** March 1999
  Group: New Mexico Trial Lawyers
  Topic: Alimony/Lifestyle
  Location: Albuquerque, New Mexico

- **Date:** May 1999
  Group: National Business Institute
  Topic: Tax Aspects of Divorce in New Mexico
  Location: Albuquerque, New Mexico

- **Date:** May 1999
  Group: National Institute for Trial Advocacy, Southwest Regional Program
  Topic: Trial Practice Seminar; Expert Witness Participant
  Location: Albuquerque, New Mexico

- **Date:** September 1999
  Group: State Bar of New Mexico
  Topic: Alternative Dispute Resolution in the Workplace
  Location: Albuquerque, New Mexico

- **Date:** March 2000
  Group: State Bar of New Mexico
  Topic: When the Business Is the Third Party to the Divorce
  Location: Albuquerque, New Mexico

- **Date:** April 2000
  Group: UNM School of Law
  Topic: Advanced Domestic Relations Taxation
  Location: Albuquerque, New Mexico

- **Date:** May 2000
  Group: The Federal Judicial Center and The American Institute of Certified Public Accountants
  Topic: Financial Statements in the Courtroom
  Location: Albuquerque, New Mexico

- **Date:** May, June, July 2000
  Group: Meyners + Company, LLC
  Topic: Tax Aspects of Divorce in New Mexico
  Location: Albuquerque, New Mexico

Exhibit 9.1   *(Continued)*

- **Date:** September 15, 2000
  Group: Court Alternatives, Division of the Second Judicial District Court and State Bar Center for Legal Education
  Topic: Settlement Facilitation Training
  Location: Albuquerque, New Mexico

- **Date:** October 7, 2000
  Group: State Bar of New Mexico
  Topic: Valuing A Business: Who You Gonna Call, What You Gonna Get?
  Location: Ruidoso, New Mexico

- **Date:** October 7, 2000
  Group: State Bar of New Mexico
  Topic: Cross-Examination of the Business Appraiser: How to Find the Target
  Location: Ruidoso, New Mexico

- **Date:** February 16, 2001
  Group: State Bar of New Mexico
  Topic: Demystifying Financial Statements in Litigation and Negotiation
  Location: Albuquerque, New Mexico

- **Date:** April 16, 2001
  Group: University of New Mexico Law School
  Topic: Advanced Domestic Relations
  Location: Albuquerque, New Mexico

- **Date:** April 20, 2001
  Group: State Bar of New Mexico
  Topic: The Art and Practice of Managing Your Law Office "Financing and Evaluating Your Practice"
  Location: Albuquerque, New Mexico

- **Date:** May 22, 2001
  Group: National Institute for Trial Advocacy, Southwest Regional Program
  Topic: Trial Practice Seminar; Expert Witness Participant
  Location: Albuquerque, New Mexico

(continues)

Exhibit 9.1   *(Continued)*

• **Date:**	June 11, 12, 13, 2001
Group:	American Institute of Certified Public Accountants
Topic:	Tax Traps in Domestic Relations Taxation; Establishing Your Business Valuation Practice; Business Valuation Update
Location:	Orlando, Florida
• **Date:**	September 13, 2001
Group:	Meyners + Company, LLC
Topic:	Tax Aspects of Divorce in New Mexico
Location:	Albuquerque, New Mexico
• **Date:**	December 12, 2001
Group:	New Mexico Society of Certified Public Accountants
Topic:	Tax Traps in Domestic Relations in New Mexico
Location:	Albuquerque, New Mexico

COMMUNITY
ACTIVITIES:

Former Treasurer, Explora Science Center and Albuquerque Children's Museum

Advisory Board, People Living Through Cancer

THOMAS F. BURRAGE, CPA
Expert Testimony
Five Prior Years

Client	Participation	Counsel	Date
Temp Associates	Deposition	Steve Schmidt	Oct. 1996
Dunigan v. Dunigan	Trial, 11–706 Expert/Divorce	E. Whitefield/ D. Kelsey/ B. Manning	Feb. 1997
Dvorak v. Dvorak	Trial, Arbitration	Mary Vermillion	May 1997
Martinez v. Martinez	Trial	Michael O'Loughlin	Sept. 1997
Olguin v. Olguin	Trial	Filosa & Filosa	Feb. 1998
Sehr v. Sehr	Trial	Anne Assink	Mar. 1998
Hess v. Hess	Deposition/Trial	Jan Gilman	Mar 1995, May 1998, Sept. 1998

Client	Participation	Counsel	Date
Woodin v. Woodin	Deposition/Trial	Michael Golden	July 1996, Sept. 1998
Boutz v. Donaldson	Trial, Divorce	William Henderson	Nov. 1998
Montano v. Montano	Trial	Robert Levy	Dec. 1998
Cho v. Cho	Deposition	Michael Golden/ Eileen Mandel	Mar. 1999
Hedges v. Hedges	Trial	Barbara Johnson	Apr. 1999
Institute of American Indian Arts v. Daymon & Associates	Deposition	Tanya Trujillo	May 1999
McMullin v. McMullin	Trial	Libby Atkins	June 1999
Huitfeldt v. Smith	Trial	Barbara Shapiro	July 1999
Huffstodt v. Huffstodt	Trial, 11–706 Expert/Divorce	Leslie Becker/ Betty Reed	July 1999
Walta v. Gallegos Law Firm	Trial	Maureen Sanders	July 1999
Bornfield v. State Farm	Deposition	Alan Torgerson	July 1999
Galante v. Whitmire	Deposition/Trial, Arbitration	Frank Herdman	Sept. 1999
Parra v. Parra	Trial	James Beam	Sept. 1999
Dozzo-Otero v. Otero	Trial, 11–706 Expert/Divorce	S. Siegel/ Hartley Wess	Oct. 1999
Schenk v. Lopez	Trial	Chris Grisham/ Alison Arias	Oct. 1999, Feb. 2000
Unser v. Unser	Deposition/Trial	Sandra Little/ Armand Carian	Oct. 1999, Jan. 2000
Winstead v. Winstead	Trial	E. Whitefield	Oct. 2000
Worrell v. Sanger	Deposition	Karen Mendenhall	Feb. 2001
Seis v. Seis	Deposition/Trial	Denise Ready	June 2001, July 2001
Jones v. Jones	Deposition/Trial	Lloyd Bates	June 2001, July 2001
Eaves v. Eaves Trust	Deposition	Tom Toevs	June 2001
Briske v. Briske	Trial	Sandra Morgan Little	July 2001
Deutsch v. Deutsch	Special Master	Janet Clow/ Randolph Felker	August 2001
HBS Partnership v. AIRCOA Hospitality Services, Inc.	Deposition	John Baugh	October 2001
Wilson v. Wilson	11–706 Expert	Tom Montoya/ Maria Geer	October 2001
Bursum v. Bursum	Trial, 11–70 Expert	Tom Montoya/ Mary Han	Nov. 2001, Dec. 2001

The next step in the process of testimony is to render the opinions that have been formed over the course of the financial adviser's work. It should be noted that many times, the opinions are rendered before any background information is explored. After the opinions are rendered, the "foundation" of those opinions is detailed. The foundation is detailing the facts, assumptions, and data relied upon in reaching the opinions rendered. During this process, it is not unusual for exhibits to be admitted. When this occurs, a foundation must be established for the contents of the exhibit before it can be admitted. The foundation is the underlying documents and information that is summarized in the exhibit, or the calculations performed by the financial adviser inside the exhibit. Once the foundation has been established, the exhibit is offered for admission, the opposing attorney has an opportunity to object, and the judge rules on its admissibility.

After all of the underlying information related to the opinions rendered is presented, it is usual for the fees paid, or to be paid, to the financial adviser to be discussed. The method by which the financial adviser has billed for services, the amounts billed, and the amounts paid on the billings are all examined. At this stage, it is important the financial adviser is comfortable and candid regarding the nature and amount of fees charged.

If there are any weaknesses in the financial adviser's testimony or opinions, it is important to get the bad news out on direct examination. By confronting these issues in an up-front manner, their negative impact on the case can be explained and minimized.

CROSS-EXAMINATION

Cross-examination is the opposing attorney's opportunity to point out problems with the opinions you have rendered. They will question the facts that you relied upon, the assumptions made, and the theories that helped reach your conclusion. They will not, however, ask questions to which they do not know the answer. It is, therefore, helpful to review prior deposition testimony and other evidence collected in the discovery process, as this will be the source for the opposing attorney's questions. Only issues raised in the direct examination can be questioned in the cross-examination. In rare cases, the opposing attorney may choose not to cross-examine the expert. This is to de-emphasize the expert's testimony in the case.

During the questioning by the opposing attorney, be polite. Do not interrupt the attorney asking questions. Always answer what is asked and only what is asked. Recognize there is an advantage associated with being the expert. When opposing counsel does not know the correct question to ask, you should not correct the mistake by expanding your answer to cover the error. Do not volunteer information. Your counsel will come back on redirect to fill in any gaps in information that were omitted on cross-examination. It is correct, however, to question the question being asked. If the question is worded awkwardly or leaves out critical information, it is proper and effective to ask the attorney to reword the question or to state in your answer that critical data was omitted from the question, which would alter your answer. This will give your counsel the signal to pick up on the subject on redirect examination. Never be drawn into an emotional exchange with the attorney.

It is not unusual for the opposing attorney to ask hypothetical questions to illustrate the impact of a change in fact or assumption on your opinion. Require the attorney to give you all the specific information required to answer the question. When the opposing attorney asks you to confirm a statement that is true, readily agree; not to do so detracts from the financial adviser's credibility. When the answer that is given is misleading, always finish answers with statements such as "I can explain."

Many attorneys develop a rhythm to the pattern of questions and answers. It is wise for the financial adviser not to get caught in the rhythm. Slow down when answering questions, and do not forget to think about the question and its appropriate answer. If a document would be helpful in answering, state so in your answer, and request the document prior to answering. Always defend positions and opinions, and do not retreat during cross-examination. Never argue with the opposing attorney because to do so will detract from the strength of the testimony. Use the cross-examination as a further opportunity to teach why the opinions rendered are correct and applicable to this case.

It is not unusual for the opposing attorney to use the financial adviser's deposition transcript in the process of cross-examination. The transcript is used to impeach the adviser's testimony. In this setting, impeach means to show that the financial adviser has given different testimony on the same subject at a different time. Attorneys use impeachment to detract from an expert's credibility. If this occurs, the attorney will follow a question with a second question such as: "Do you remember when you testified in deposition on a given day and your testimony was . . . ?" If this technique is used in the adviser's cross-examination, the adviser should answer questions truthfully, agree that the testimony given at the deposition is correct, and wait for their attorney to rehabilitate the financial adviser on the issue on redirect examination.

REDIRECT EXAMINATION

Only issues arising in the cross-examination can be raised on the redirect examination. Two areas that will always be addressed will be hypothetical questions addressed in the cross-examination, as well as any attempts to impeach the financial adviser. In addition, the attorney will address instances where the expert was not allowed to completely explain an answer.

RECROSS EXAMINATION

Again, only issues raised in the redirect examination can be raised on the recross examination. For this reason, even if it is allowed, it is always very brief.

THE DECISION

Judges seldom make decisions from the bench at the conclusion of trial. It is not unusual for them to ask the attorneys to prepare "findings of fact and conclusions of law." It is possible the attorney may ask the financial adviser to participate in the drafting of this document. Even when these documents are submitted, there can be months of delay before a decision is rendered. After the decision, there is the possibility of appealing the trial court's findings. The ultimate result of the financial adviser's testimony may be months, or years, after the conclusion of the trial.

Index

Printed and bound by CPI Group (UK) Ltd, Croydon, CR0 4YY

23/04/2025

14660922-0003